The Daily Way

365 Daily Devotions

Michael Youssef, Ph.D.

Revised 2023

Copyright © 2005 by Michael Youssef, Ph.D.
ALL RIGHTS RESERVED

No portion of this devotional may be reproduced in any form without written permission.

For information, please contact:
Leading The Way with Dr. Michael Youssef
P.O. Box 20100, Atlanta, GA 30325
877-251-8294

In Canada, call:	In the United Kingdom, call:	In Australia, call:
877 251 8294	0800 432 0419	1 300 133 589

Scripture taken from *The Holy Bible, New International Version*
Copyright © 1973, 1978, 1984 by International Bible Society

DEDICATION

to

Henry F. McCamish, Jr.

A man who was totally committed to Jesus, and blessed with a tender heart for His Gospel.

He is the reason, humanly speaking, that *Leading The Way* is broadcasting around the world.

Yet he gave God ALL of the glory.

Table of Contents

January 9
Praying So God Will Answer

February 41
God's Greatest Gifts, Part I
God's Greatest Gifts, Part II

March 73
Receiving Daily Victory Over the Enemy

April 105
Receiving Healing Through True Spirituality

May 137
Discovering the Power in Praise

June 169
Looking Up When Life Knocks You Down

July 201
Developing Your Faith Muscles

August 233
Champions Are Made, Not Born

September 265
Becoming a Hero to Others

October 297
Cultivating Relationships That Please God

November 329
The Names and Character of God

December 361
Preparing for the Coming Glory

Praying So God Will Answer

The Daily Way

January 1

Our Rock and Fortress

The prophet Isaiah wrote, "When the enemy comes in like a flood, the Spirit of the Lord will lift up a standard against him" (Isaiah 59:19, NKJV). At some point, all of us have felt the weight of the enemy surrounding us.

We experience panic or stress over work deadlines, bills to be paid, or relationship conflicts. We catch ourselves focusing on what people think or say. Then we begin to suffer discouragement and even depression.

No one wants to be scorned, ridiculed, or taken for granted. Even Jesus suffered the ridicule of others. The chief priests, mocking with the scribes and elders, said, "He trusts in God. Let God rescue him now if he wants him, for he said, 'I am the Son of God'" (Matthew 27:43).

No matter what we face or how others ridicule us, God is our rock and our fortress. He is our deliverer. We can find refuge and security in Him. Although you may not feel God's presence or help, He is near. Psalm 91:15 states, "He will call upon me, and I will answer him; I will be with him in trouble, I will deliver him and honor him."

Do you feel that God has forgotten you? The writer of Hebrews reminds us that the Lord will not forget us, as God Himself has said, "Never will I leave you; never will I forsake you" (Hebrews 13:5).

So no matter what others say or how discouraged you may feel, remember that the Lord has the answer for your anxiety and despair. All you have to do is cry out to Him. He longs for you to seek His power. Ask Him to be the source of your strength and deliverance.

Why are you downcast, O my soul? Why so disturbed within me? Put your hope in God, for I will yet praise him, my Savior and my God (Psalm 42:11).

January 2 — The Daily Way

A Cure for Depression

The writer of Psalm 42 is disheartened. Maybe he is dealing with a problem that has continued for some time. Then he hits on a truth that changes his feelings of depression into thoughts of hope. He writes, "Why are you downcast, O my soul? Why so disturbed within me? Put your hope in God, for I will yet praise him, my Savior and my God" (Psalm 42:5-6 and Psalm 42:11).

Each of us will experience feelings of rejection, fear, and hurt. For the psalmist, the heart of the problem was the need for him to feel fulfilled and not oppressed, for his feelings to be improved, and for his questions to be answered.

Emotional depression can result from anger, disappointment, or discouragement. If we dwell on these feelings, then they will consume us. If we fail to look to God in the midst of our difficulty, then we will be overwhelmed and defeated.

When you are tired and discouraged, do you find yourself thirsty for God's wisdom, guidance, and protection? If so, pray: "Lord, show me Your face. Help me to understand what I need to know about this situation and how to handle it."

If we seek God, then we will find Him (Matthew 7:8). Despair, hatred, malice, envy, and feelings of bitterness will fade. Is there something in your life that fills you with misery? Ask for God's light to come upon you and for His truth to guide you.

Prayer: Lord, help me to understand my feelings of anxiety and concern. Help me to focus on You and not on my anger, disappointment, and distress. Shine Your light on my life as I thirst for You.

Send forth your light and your truth, let them guide me; let them bring me to your holy mountain, to the place where you dwell (Psalm 43:3).

The Daily Way

January 3

He Is Our Joy!

No matter how frustrated or anxious we become, we do not have to lose hope. Our hope should never be in ourselves or in our abilities, nor should it be in other people. At some point, others will let us down. Rather, our hope should be in the living Christ, who has kept every one of His promises to us!

We can have hope because Christ Jesus is our Savior. He is our joy. He is our peace. He is our fulfillment. If we try to get our joy from our feelings or from our possessions, then we will be constantly disappointed. However, if we find our joy in the Lord and in trusting in His Word, then we will experience hope—regardless of our circumstances.

Have you ever experienced the joy of the Lord? There comes a time when we must stop dwelling on our despair. We must stop giving in to the moaning and groaning that keeps us from experiencing the hope and the joy that God freely gives. He does not cast us away.

As His children, we have a hope in Christ that never fails. We can know a life filled with contentment, peace, joy, praise, and love when we commit our way to God. Moreover, as long as we are consumed with fear, envy, pride, selfish ambition, and greed, we cannot be filled with God's Spirit. The choice is ours—contentment in Christ or discontentment in ourselves.

Christ is waiting with open arms. Begin by thirsting for Him. Come before Him in humility. Recognize that He has the answers for your feelings of fear and despair. Don't give up. God is always with you.

My soul thirsts for God, for the living God. When can I go and meet with God? (Psalm 42:2).

January 4

The Daily Way

Guiding Our Prayer Lives

Have you ever noticed that when you are ready to pray, the phone rings or somebody knocks on your door? How often is your prayer time distracted with things on your to-do list, with daydreams, or with sleepiness?

Prayer is the most important thing we can do as believers. Through prayer, we communicate with our heavenly Father. We also learn more about Him when we pray. We grow in our faith through prayer. When we pray, we find the encouragement, the strength, and the power we need to face life.

Satan, however, seeks to interfere with the sacred intimacy of prayer. He did not want Adam and Eve to communicate with God in the Garden, nor does Satan want us to communicate with God. Rather, he seeks to find ways of making us spiritually weak. He knows that prayer is our vital source of power and strength.

When you receive good news or something wonderful happens in your life, do you immediately thank the Lord? Many of us pray only when we are facing a problem. We cry out to the Lord in our pain, but we often fail to praise Him in times of joy. This is when we realize that we have not made prayer part of our daily lives.

Prayer is not to inform, to persuade, to manipulate, or to cajole God. It is the evidence of our surrender before God, of our obedience to God, and of our sincerity before God. He wants to commune with us. When you understand that prayer is joyous, intimate fellowship with the Lord, you will want to make prayer a consistent part of your life.

What does it mean to pray? To pray is to talk intimately with God. To pray is to open continuously the floodgates of heaven's blessings. To pray is to breathe spiritually and, thus, to be spiritually alive.

Be joyful in hope, patient in affliction, faithful in prayer (Romans 12:12).

The Daily Way

January 5

Prayer Is a Way of Life

There are numerous books and seminars designed to teach us how to communicate better in the workplace and at home. But how is our communication with the Lord?

We have many examples in the Bible of praying men and women. When Abraham's servant Eliezer prayed, Rebekah appeared. When Moses prayed, powerful Amalek was defeated. When Hannah prayed for a child, Samuel was born. In the midst of battle, Joshua prayed and the sun stood still. When Elijah prayed for the rain to stop, there was a three-year drought.

Each of these individuals sought God in prayer for a specific need—and through His answer, He was honored. The purpose of prayer is for God to be glorified. While prayer is a blessing to us, it also is an opportunity to see God's goodness and power at work in the lives of others.

When children are small, they ask their parents for all kinds of things. Does that mean that a parent gives everything a child asks for? Of course not! Neither does our heavenly Father give us all that we ask of Him. However, He knows our every need, and He is committed to meeting those needs—but not always in our timing or in the way we think is best.

God is sovereign, and in His sovereignty He responds to the prayers of His people. As a result, we are blessed when we trust His purpose and plan.

Jesus does not dictate when we should pray. Rather, for Him, prayer is a way of life—and it should be for us, too. We can learn to pattern our lives to match His by beginning to pray on a consistent basis. Adoration, praise, and petition of our Lord and Savior will change our lives.

I will do whatever you ask in my name, so that the Son may bring glory to the Father (John 14:13).

January 6

The Daily Way

He Is Our Father

Many of us have memories of our fathers. Some memories may be good, but others may be sad or painful. Whatever our feelings are toward our earthly fathers, there is no comparison to our heavenly Father. He is greater than any earthly father could possibly be. He loves us with an unconditional love and never ceases to demonstrate His mercy and grace toward us. He spends time with us and has promised never to leave us. We are always the center of His concern, attention, time, and planning.

That is why Jesus taught His disciples to pray by saying, "Our Father." The phrase "Our Father" reduces all of the complications of life to a very simple relationship. Through faith in the shed blood of Christ, we have been redeemed from sin and have been adopted into God's family. As a child of God, have you exercised your right to say "Our Father"?

When we come to our heavenly Father in prayer, He removes our fear. He gives us hope and confidence. He banishes our uncertainty. The apostle Paul said, "You did not receive a spirit that makes you a slave again to fear, but you received the Spirit of sonship. And by him we cry, 'Abba, Father'" (Romans 8:15).

Your heavenly Father is interested in every area of your life. In Him you have protection, safety, security, serenity, peace, and salvation. Friends may disappoint you and family may let you down, but your heavenly Father will never leave you nor forsake you (Hebrews 13:5). He is eager to hear your prayers to Him.

Therefore, call upon Him. Place your trust in Him. Share your hopes, problems, dreams, and concerns with the One who knows you better than you know yourself. As your Father, He will give you joy for today and hope for tomorrow.

I will be a Father to you, and you will be my sons and daughters, says the Lord Almighty (2 Corinthians 6:18).

The Daily Way — January 7

The Honor of Prayer

Do you think of God as your loving, heavenly Father? Many people find this hard to do. The notion of calling God—who is holy and righteous—your Father can be overwhelming. We can call Him Father because of the shed blood of Christ.

The Bible tells us that without the sacrificial death of Jesus, there can be no forgiveness. Because of Christ's death and resurrection, we are redeemed and restored into right fellowship with God. When we place our faith in Christ, we can call God our Father.

Biblical repentance means accepting Christ's free gift of salvation. When we repent, we have the power to overcome. He gives us new life—freedom from our past, strength to change our ways, and the right to come to God in prayer.

Charles Spurgeon explains the honor of prayer this way: "What a privilege is intimate communion is with the Father of our spirits! It is a secret hidden from the world, a joy with which even the nearest friend intermeddleth not."

Have you been crying out to God, feeling that He is not responding? Don't give up. He hears you and will answer. Spurgeon reminds us of Psalm 103:13:

> "As a father has compassion on his children, so the Lord has compassion on those who fear Him" (Psalm 103:13). Your sigh is able to move the heart of Jehovah; your whisper can incline His ear to you; your prayer can stay His hand; your faith can move His arm. Do not think that God sits on high taking no account of you. Remember that however poor and needy you are, yet the Lord thinks upon you.

For us there is but one God, the Father, from whom all things came and for whom we live; and there is but one Lord, Jesus Christ, through whom all things came and through whom we live (1 Corinthians 8:6).

January 8

The Daily Way

You Can Go Home

Jesus told the parable of a father who showed his son unconditional love (Luke 15:11-24). This father was patient, slow to anger, and quick to forgive. When the son asked for his inheritance, the father gave it to him. When the son left, the father let him go, knowing that he could not keep his son against his will.

Even though the father's heart was breaking over his son's rebellion, he never gave up loving him. While he longed for his son's return, he did not change his convictions to suit his son's behavior.

Eventually, the son's sinful actions caught up with him. He lost all of his inheritance and out of desperation had to do the only work available—feeding pigs! Suddenly, a thought came to the son: He could go home. He knew his father had an abiding love for him. Still, he would have to make a decision to repent.

Even from a distance, the father saw his son returning and ran to meet him. Instead of belittling the son, the father threw open his arms, welcoming him home with love and forgiveness.

God is our heavenly Father. We all have sinned against Him. However, when we come to Him with a repentant heart, He welcomes us. If the prodigal son had sent someone to speak to his father on his behalf, he may not have been forgiven. He had to ask for his father's forgiveness himself.

The father of the wayward son was caring, compassionate, patient, long-suffering, slow to anger, and quick to forgive. How much more does our heavenly Father demonstrate these characteristics toward us!

If you have wandered away from God and find yourself alone, "feeding the pigs," remember that you can go home. Don't delay; God is waiting for your return.

How great is the love the Father has lavished on us, that we should be called children of God! (1 John 3:1).

The Daily Way

January 9

Hallowed Is His Name

Imagine that you have been granted an audience with the king. This is the moment you've been waiting for—the chance to bring your requests before his majesty. The great doors open, and you are standing before the throne. In awe and reverence, you first address the king. It would be improper to just begin asking for your needs.

Jesus instructed His disciples, "This, then, is how you should pray: 'Our Father in heaven, hallowed be your name'" (Matthew 6:9).

The dictionary defines hallow as "to make or set apart as holy." God is holy. He is sovereign and omniscient. He is the King of kings, the Creator of the universe. When we place our faith in His Son, Jesus Christ, He becomes our heavenly Father. As such, we have the honor and the privilege of being able to come to Him in prayer.

It is important that we know the character of God, and honor and revere Him in our prayers, actions, and thoughts. God's character is pure, holy, flawless, loving, compassionate, righteous, just, merciful, kind, long-suffering, honest, true, dependable, faithful, and understanding.

The more we know about God, the more we grow in fellowship with Him. This carries over into our prayers. Placing Him first and foremost in our minds keeps our focus on Him instead of on our needs and desires.

However, Jesus did not intend for our prayers to become ritualistic. Nor does He tell us how to pray. But by beginning with God's name, we are reminded that we are coming before almighty God. As children of God, we have been given free access to the throne room of the King of kings. We can address the King as our Father. There is no greater honor!

O Lord God Almighty, who is like you? You are mighty, O Lord, and your faithfulness surrounds you (Psalm 89:8).

January 10

The Daily Way

How to Pray

The key to knowing how to pray the prayer that God answers is to cultivate our relationship with God. The more we know Him, the more we will be attuned to His will and desires.

An important part of prayer is our attitude. First, we should have an attitude of gratefulness. How often do you tell God how thankful you are? Instead of complaining, sulking, or grumbling, try expressing your gratitude to the Lord. Begin by thanking Him for His saving grace, His forgiveness, and His unfailing love.

Second, we should have an attitude of giving. God does not need anything that we could possibly give Him. However, the Bible makes it clear that we are to give to the Lord out of the blessings that He gives to us. The discipline of giving reminds us that all we have is from God. When you give, think about His blessings—never doubt His provision for you.

Finally, we should have an attitude of obedience. When we accept Christ as our Savior, we are making a commitment to live in obedience to God and to His Word. This is never easy. However, we have the power of Christ to strengthen and to help us overcome. Obedience means we must submit our will to God's. We bring glory and honor to the Lord when we resist temptation and obey His commandments.

Maybe it is easier for you to express your gratitude than for you to give. Or perhaps it is easier for you to obey God's Word than to tell Him thanks. Whatever the case, to pray as Jesus directed, we need to give, to be obedient, and to express our thankfulness. After all, we are children of almighty God—whose name is above all other names. He is holy, just, and attentive to our prayers.

Do not be anxious about anything, but in everything ... present your requests to God (Philippians 4:6).

A Life Filled with Praise

We all have a choice—either we put God first or we put ourselves first. If we choose the latter, then we will not have successful prayer lives. To live successful Christian lives, we need to learn to praise God no matter how we feel. It is a life filled with praise that establishes the foundation of prayer. The key to hallowing the name of God is praise.

The apostle Paul knew the value of praise. In the book of Acts, Paul and Silas were arrested in Philippi for preaching the Gospel. Beaten and bleeding, they were still singing praises to the Lord. The result of their praise was an earthquake that shook the city and opened the prison gate. Even the prison warden wanted to know Christ.

Do you feel that God is not responding to you? Try praising Him. Praise is powerful and can change your outlook. Ask yourself if you are a person of praise or whether you have yielded to thoughts of doubt and negative thinking. You certainly can learn to praise God! How you act and talk is a reflection of the character of Christ within you. Regardless of your situation, praise comes as an overflow of His joy.

Practice praising the Lord by telling Him that you surrender to His power and authority, that you desire to place Him first in your life, and that you want to obey His Word. To honor and to uplift the name of the Lord brings delight to our heavenly Father.

Do you feel as if you are in a spiritual desert? Develop a life of praise by praising the Lord each day, regardless of how you feel or what you are experiencing. Can you praise God in the midst of pain and despair like Paul and Silas did? When you praise the name of God, you will feel the joy of the Lord!

Praise be to God, who has not rejected my prayer or withheld his love from me! (Psalm 66:20).

January 12   The Daily Way

God's Kingdom

There are two kingdoms—the kingdom of God and the kingdom of this world. When we accept Christ as our Lord and Savior, we are adopted into the kingdom of God.

Being a citizen of a country means that you have special privileges. These vary from country to country. However, as a citizen of God's kingdom, we become members of the royal family. We are joint heirs with Christ. We have access to the throne of God. We have personal fellowship with the King of kings. We are His beloved children.

In order to become a citizen of a country other than the one in which you are born, you must meet certain requirements. The kingdom of God requires its citizens to accept the reign of a wise and loving King. It means acknowledging Christ as our Lord and Savior. It means being obedient to the Word of God. It requires our saying, "Lord, not my will, but Yours be done."

Human nature is selfish. What we think we need is foremost in our actions and prayers. Prayer that revolves around our own plans, desires, and needs, however, can be contrary to God's Word.

When we surrender our lives to Christ and submit ourselves to Him, we are placing our will in submission to the Lord's. Thus we begin to pray, "Lord, reign in my life, dominate my thoughts, show me Your will."

Within each of us rages the war between the kingdom of God and the kingdom of this world. With Christ we have the victory. Knowing this, press on, armed with the confidence that God hears us and will answer our prayers.

The eyes of the Lord are on the righteous and his ears are attentive to their prayer, but the face of the Lord is against those who do evil (1 Peter 3:12).

The Daily Way
January 13

Thy Kingdom Come

After Jesus was arrested and questioned by the high priest, he was brought before Pilate, the Roman governor. But Jesus refused to be intimidated and told Pilate, "My kingdom is not of this world" (John 18:36).

The kingdom of God is all-encompassing. It is present in the lives of those who willingly submit to His rule. It is a future kingdom where Jesus will rule supreme—not only in our lives, but also over the new heaven and earth.

When we pray the prayer that Jesus taught us to pray, "Thy kingdom come," we are asking for His rule to extend to every area of our lives. However, if we pick and choose those areas to submit to Him, we limit His power.

Through this prayer, we also are asking for God to work in the lives of others. There are those who never have made a commitment to the Savior—family members, friends, and co-workers who never have experienced God's saving grace.

By praying this prayer, we express our longing for His second coming. As believers, we should have a natural desire to be in God's presence. Our citizenship is in heaven, not on this earth (Philippians 3:20).

You may know Christ as Savior, but perhaps you have never made a serious commitment to Him as your living Lord. Maybe you have blocked off areas of your life from His rule. If this is the case, then you are not fully experiencing His love and power.

No matter what your situation may be, you can come to Christ today and ask Him to be the Lord of your life. When you draw near to God, He draws near to you. Take the opportunity to experience a glimpse of heaven while you are still here on earth.

Your kingdom come, your will be done on earth as it is in heaven (Matthew 6:10).

January 14

The Daily Way

Thy Will Be Done

One of the most common questions asked by believers is: "How can I know the will of God?"

We all struggle at times with knowing how to discern God's will. It seems so complicated that we allow ourselves to get bogged down with making decisions. "Should I go on this trip?" "Do I take this promotion?" "Should I get married, and if so, whom should I marry?" "Is this the right career for me?" "Is this ministry where God wants me to be?"

So how do we discern the will of God for our lives? By studying and obeying His Word. The Bible has the answers we need to live godly lives. While we may not find the specific answer to what we are asking, we will find godly principles that will guide every area of our lives. When we study the Bible, we learn more of God—who He is and what He desires of those who walk with Him.

We may endeavor to live in obedience to the Word of God and still not know which way to go or what to decide. The next time you are faced with a decision, ask yourself, "Is my choice consistent with the Word of God?" To answer this question correctly, you must spend quality time in prayer and study of God's Word each day.

From this day forward, ask the Holy Spirit to guide you in every decision you face. Don't hesitate to request the wisdom of prayerful counsel from mature and godly people. Expect and wait for God's answer with patience. You may even doubt His answer. Just remember: His delay does not mean His denial.

We should seek to know God's will because we find joy in doing the will of our Father, not because we are afraid of displeasing Him or doing the wrong thing. Our lives belong to the Lord, and our destinies are in His hands. Trust Him. Obey His commands. He will guide you in His will.

I know, O Lord, that a man's life is not his own; it is not for man to direct his steps (Jeremiah 10:23).

The Daily Way — January 15

Doing What He Asks

The psalmist said, "I desire to do your will, O my God; your law is within my heart" (Psalm 40:8). Like the psalmist, we can be content to pray "Thy will be done on earth as it is in heaven" until what God desires of us clashes with what we want.

How often do we know what God is calling us to do, but we want to do something else? Maybe we don't want to give up something important to us. Maybe we are afraid that we won't succeed.

Maybe we are too busy focusing on what we want that we lose sight of what God desires for us. Oswald Chambers says, "When God draws me, the issue of my will comes in at once—will I react on the revelation which God gives—will I come to Him?"

As followers of Christ, we are called to a life of obedience to God's Word. However, we often find that there are areas in our lives in which we struggle against His plan. The Christian walk is all about knowing Christ and becoming like Him through the surrender of our selfish ways and desires.

When we make God the priority of our lives, we will want to obey Him—not just because He tells us to, but because we love Him. It is then that we gain a transcending peace (Philippians 4:7).

We should enjoy the journey of obedience. It is only when we make a commitment to follow the principles in God's Word that we find true joy and contentment. Have you discovered the pleasure that comes from doing what God asks you to do?

Begin this journey today. Remember, it is not through your own strength that you will succeed. Only through the power of Christ can you do whatever He asks of you.

If you obey my commands, you will remain in my love, just as I have obeyed my Father's commands and remain in his love (John 15:10).

January 16

The Daily Way

Categorizing Sins

Typically, when we hear the word sin, our minds rush to thoughts of transgressions that to us seem huge: murder, adultery, stealing, homosexuality, and more. While some of these sins do have far-reaching consequences, none are beyond the reach of God, and none are beyond His ability to forgive and to restore.

The truth is that many Christians have different categories for varying sins. They have a category for "really big" sins and one for "not so big" sins. They believe the "really big" sins are the ones that receive the most punishment, while the "not so big" sins are the ones everyone commits. These also are the ones we mistakenly believe that God overlooks.

But this is not how God operates. There are sins that are horrendous and that can impact our lives with great force and sorrow. However, the sins we view as being "smaller" and easily dismissed can also have devastating effects on our lives.

Few people view worry and anxiety as sin, but they are. The reason this is true is because they symbolize a lack of faith in God and His ability. Worry and doubt are the results of an even greater problem—fear—which is a favorite tool of the enemy and a key factor in setting up strongholds in the life of the believer.

Therefore, instead of becoming anxious or fearful, we need to turn to the Lord and seek His provision for our lives on a daily basis. Be determined to trust Him to lead you through every difficulty, knowing that wherever He guides you, you will find blessing and hope. Put your faith in God and you will know the joy of a victorious life.

Hear my cry, O God; listen to my prayer. From the ends of the earth I call to you, I call as my heart grows faint; lead me to the rock that is higher than I (Psalm 61:1-2).

The Daily Way — January 17

Catch the Foxes

God wants you to be wise and surefooted in your daily walk with Him, not allowing anything to come into your life that would cause you to doubt His goodness. He also knows that there will be times when the enemy will tempt you to feel fearful and out of control. When this happens, you need to remember that you serve a sovereign God who has good things in mind for your life.

Even when troubles come, we may begin to wonder if we will ever realize the hopes and dreams that God has given us. Joseph, Daniel, Moses, David, and Peter and the other disciples probably faced the same temptation to doubt God's blessing and goodness. However, these men of faith remained steadfast in their belief in the Lord's ability. They had to come to a point of faith where they boldly confronted their fears—and we do, too.

The English word worry comes from a German word meaning "to strangle or choke." This is exactly what worry does. It chokes and prevents us from living victorious lives by stifling our godly potential.

Solomon, however, admonishes us to "catch ... the foxes, the little foxes that ruin the vineyards, our vineyards that are in bloom" (Song of Songs 2:15). The "little foxes" of sin have the ability to derail our Christian faith and sense of virtue.

On the surface, few of us would think that a little worry, doubt, or fear is enough to harm our devotion to God. However, they can steal our joy and create within our hearts and minds a sense of distrust for the things of God.

God is merciful. He has the power to conquer doubt, fear, and worry. When our lives are surrendered to Him, we don't have to be anxious about tomorrow. He provides all that we need perfectly and on time.

Blessed are you who hunger now, for you will be satisfied (Luke 6:21).

January 18 — The Daily Way

Give Us This Day Our Daily Bread

There are people living in some of the most influential countries in the world who do not have enough to eat. They don't know where they will get enough money to buy their next meals. Maybe they have been laid off from their jobs, or due to some serious illness, they cannot work.

Perhaps you know the sinking feeling that comes from hearing the news that you will no longer be employed. When setbacks occur, we must immediately turn to God to renew our hearts with His hope and encouragement. Never be ashamed of crying out to God through prayer. He knows what you are facing even before you drop to your knees to pray.

Being laid-off from our jobs does not mean that we are without hope. God provides for us each day. We may not know how His provision will come, but if our lives are submitted to Him, then we can be sure that we will receive His blessings.

In Luke 11, Jesus taught His disciples to pray, "Father, hallowed be your name, your kingdom come. Give us each day our daily bread" (Luke 11:2-3). During the Exodus, God did just that. Daily He provided a fresh stock of manna, a grain-like substance that also was called the bread or "grain of heaven" (Psalm 78:24).

Through Jesus Christ, God has provided all that we need for this life. We do, however, have a responsibility to fulfill. We must sincerely seek Him each day and be willing to let go of past hurts.

Let go; trust God to provide daily bread—His manna—for you. When you do, you will see Him at work on your behalf.

They asked, and he ... satisfied them with the bread of heaven (Psalm 105:40).

The Daily Way — January 19

Hope for the Future

The world is filled with people who are struggling. Many feel as though they never will realize their full potential. Some believe that they have no potential. Others are deeply entangled in sin. Millions of lives are bound by Satan's lies and deception. At the root of their distress is a deep need to experience the eternal forgiveness of God.

Most of us have heard someone say, "I just feel empty, restless, and unhappy. I have tried to motivate myself, but it seems as though there is no hope for the future." However, there is hope because there is eternal life through Jesus Christ.

The power to overcome sin and feelings of hopelessness is ours when we turn to Christ through prayer. He meets us at the point of our greatest need. He does not come to us as a scolding parent, but as a loving heavenly Father who hears our prayers.

Sin prevents us from experiencing the fullness of God's blessing. Unconfessed sin will leave us feeling spiritually out of balance and, many times, frightened. This is because our spiritual armor has been penetrated and we are vulnerable to attack. People who have not placed their trust in Jesus Christ as Savior and Lord will feel empty and void of joy and eternal hope.

Once a person turns to Christ and seeks His forgiveness, this all changes. He or she receives eternal life and victorious hope for each new day. If you have never prayed and asked God to forgive your sins, you can do that right now.

If you have drifted in your devotion to the Lord, turn to Him, be willing to confess any sin, and recommit your life to the Savior.

If we confess our sins, he is faithful and just and will forgive us our sins and purify us from all unrighteousness (1 John 1:9).

January 20

Forgive Us Our Sin

Many times, we try to cope with the feelings of emptiness that result from sin by burying ourselves in work, relationships, or even church activities. However, until we confess our sin to the Lord, there is no relief.

This is because sin builds a barrier between God and us. Unconfessed sin also leads to feelings of guilt and shame, which make us feel isolated from the only One who can bring lasting peace to our troubled hearts and lives.

In the Garden of Eden, Adam and Eve hid from the Lord. They had sinned and realized they could not face a holy God. When we allow sin to gain a foothold in our lives, problems quickly arise.

We must deal with the matter immediately. Running away from God is not an option. Jonah ran and ended up in the belly of a big fish. God, however, is merciful. Once Jonah realized his sin and became determined to obey God, he was delivered onto dry land.

Adam and Eve also experienced God's merciful grace. He made a covering for their sin, and He has done the same for you (Genesis 3:21). Sin demands punishment. This is why Jesus Christ died for your sins and rose from the grave so that you might have eternal life and forgiveness.

Jesus taught His disciples to pray, "Forgive us our sins, for we also forgive everyone who sins against us" (Luke 11:4). While we know God has forgiven us, we also need to remember that sin can still affect our lives. A lack of forgiveness also can prevent us from experiencing the wonder of God's joy and peace.

Make sure nothing comes between you and the Lord. The most precious gift you have been given is your relationship with Christ. Seek to grow in it and learn to worship the God who loves you with an everlasting love.

Blot out all my iniquity (Psalm 51:9).

The Daily Way — January 21

Lead Us Not into Temptation

During the construction of the Union Pacific Railroad, builders had to construct an elaborate trestle across a deep canyon. After it was built, the chief engineer wanted to test it. A train loaded with double the normal train cars and supplies was driven to the middle of the bridge, where it stayed for an entire day.

Someone asked the builder, "Are you trying to break the bridge?" The answer was no. "I am trying to prove that the bridge will not break," was his reply.

In the same way, God allows us to be tempted by the enemy. There is a spiritual hedge of protection around the life of the believer that can only be penetrated with God's approval.

In times of testing, we must remember that God wants to see how we respond. He also wants to strengthen us through the trials so that we will be made ready for His service.

Prayer is the most powerful form of communication that we have. By teaching the disciples to pray, "Lead us not into temptation," Jesus was preparing them to face life's trials and temptations correctly.

The Lord knew the disciples would face many trials and temptations. Their only source of wisdom and help was found in God—"Lead us not." But the sense of the Greek words used here also implies that there must be necessary training.

God does not allow us to face needless trials. Most of what we face comes as a result of living life in a fallen world. However, we must learn to say no to anything that would prevent us from living holy lives before a holy God.

No temptation has seized you except what is common to man. And God is faithful; he will not let you be tempted beyond what you can bear. But when you are tempted, he will also provide a way out so that you can stand up under it (1 Corinthians 10:13).

January 22 — The Daily Way

Take Down the Wall

Perhaps you have struggled with a certain sin or temptation for a long time. Each time you yield to it, you find yourself crying out to God, asking for strength to overcome it. It could be a temptation to gossip, to deceive, or to misuse your power in order to exalt yourself.

Temptation leads to sin, and sin creates within our hearts and minds an emotional and mental wall between God and us. However, sin does not change God's eternal love for us. But if we fail to make the necessary corrections needed to restore our fellowship with Him, then we will reap the consequences of our sin, which can include disappointment, stress, sorrow, defeat, and broken relationships.

In fact, in times of sin, the greatest loss is our fellowship with the Lord. Knowing that we have grieved God through our sinful actions should be enough to turn us back to Him in sincere repentance, but sometimes we stubbornly press on to sin again and again. Finally, when the circumstances of our lives are unbearable, we fall to our knees in desperation.

Though God does not promise to erase all the damage caused by our sin, He certainly promises to restore the joy of our salvation when we turn back to Him. When we practice humble confession and repentance, we can experience God's mercy and grace. Through temptation, God allows us to confront the wickedness of our hearts. If we trust God, we can turn away from the sins that prevent us from living victorious lives.

Remember, God allows you to be tested so that you will be refined and readied for use in His Kingdom. Therefore, say no to temptation and sin and yes to the Lord your God.

Look, the Lamb of God, who takes away the sin of the world! (John 1:29).

The Daily Way

January 23

The Rock

Peter's denial of Christ seemed to be a horrendous failure. Only hours before, he had confessed that Jesus was the Son of God. Then he claimed that he did not even know the Lord.

At some point, each of us has fallen into temptation. This is exactly what happened to Peter. Pridefully, he had said, "Even if all fall away, I will not" (Mark 14:29). Peter's intentions were honorable. After all, Jesus had changed Peter's name for a purpose—he became Petra, meaning "the rock."

Jesus was direct with Peter, "I tell you the truth. ... Today—yes, tonight—before the rooster crows twice you yourself will disown me three times" (Mark 14:30). Peter, however, persisted to tell Jesus that he never would leave His side. Later that evening, he ran from the Lord out of fear of arrest.

Peter was not the only one that night to make this promise. Mark writes, "And all the others said the same" (Mark 14:31). We often associate the denial of Christ only with Peter, but the truth is that each of us would have been tempted to do the same.

Later, Peter wrote a letter to other believers who were facing tremendous trials, temptations, and sorrows. He told them:

> Be self-controlled and alert. Your enemy the devil prowls around like a roaring lion looking for someone to devour. Resist him, standing firm in the faith. ... And the God of all grace, who called you to his eternal glory in Christ, after you have suffered a little while, will himself restore you and make you strong, firm and steadfast (1 Peter 5:8-10).

Set your goal to live a holy life. Ask God to protect you and to give you the strength and wisdom you need to stand against Satan's attacks.

You are a chosen people ... that you may declare the praises of him who called you out of darkness into his wonderful light (1 Peter 2:9).

January 24

The Daily Way

Deliver Us from Evil

There was an elderly woman who was known for always having something good to say about others. One day, two young men thought they would trap her. Surely, she would not have anything good to say about Satan. They walked up to her and said, "Tell us: What do you think about the devil?"

The woman paused and then said, "Well, there is only one thing that I can think of—he is always on the job!"

The woman was right. There is nothing good about Satan. However, we can say that he never becomes weary of tempting believers.

This is why Jesus taught His disciples to pray, "Deliver us from evil," which really means, "Deliver us from the evil one." Jesus did just that on the Cross. He shattered the power of sin and death. The Resurrection is evidence of His victory.

One of Satan's greatest deceptions is convincing us that it is OK for us to have a little pride in our lives. Ironically, pride was Satan's own downfall. It was his desire to become like God.

If asked, most of us would say that David's greatest sin was his adulterous relationship with Bathsheba. However, the root to David's sin goes much deeper. While other kings were off fighting in battles, David stayed at home—and the enemy made note of it. The king became lazy and self-serving—the right posture for pride to make its mark.

The enemy waited for the right opportunity, and then he tempted David by appealing to his flesh. If you have been drawn away from God through sin, stop what you are doing and turn back to the Lord. Be sure you are following Christ closely and that all you desire begins and ends with Him.

For the eyes of the Lord range throughout the earth to strengthen those whose hearts are fully committed to him (2 Chronicles 16:9).

The Daily Way

January 25

Power Talk

There is no doubt about it: Power is enticing. It also can be intoxicating. But it is the one thing people want more of today. In the 1990s, the trend was not just to have lunch with a colleague—it was to have a "power" lunch.

Even today, this trend continues at a feverish pace. Instead of asking how a person is doing and listening to him or her talk over lunch, laptop computers are opened, cell phones are turned on, and handheld devices are readied to record important data. We don't just talk; we "power" talk!

Sadly, those who get caught up in this whirlwind usually want those around them to take notice. They want others to think that they are powerful. The truth is that if they are not living lives submitted to Jesus Christ, then they are powerless.

A large number of people were drawn to the early church thinking that they would receive a certain degree of power. However, they quickly realized that if they wanted to experience God's power, then they would have to change by leaving their quest for control and personal gain behind.

God's power is something that He gives to those whose lives are submitted to Him. The power that we experience as believers is not a power that takes advantage of others, rules over individuals, or seeks to be well-known. It is a power born of humility and sacrifice.

Are you living life with the goal of gaining more power, money, or influence? Remember, the Resurrection was the single most powerful event in history. Yet, it could not have taken place apart from the Crucifixion. If you want to experience true power, begin your quest at the foot of the Cross.

Shout with joy to God, all the earth! ... So great is your power that your enemies cringe before you (Psalm 66:1, 3).

January 26

The Daily Way

His Power Is Glory!

At the turn of the 19th century, there was a lady who lived alone in a house on the west coast of Scotland. She was a traditional, frugal Scot. Therefore, when she announced her plans to have electricity installed in her home, her neighbors were stunned!

This was not yet a common practice, but she had made up her mind and called the newly formed electric company. Within a few weeks, the power lines were up and she had electric light.

However, a strange thing happened. The company began to notice that she was not using the electricity. A company representative decided to visit her in order to find out why she was not enjoying what had been made available to her.

He explained to her, "It's just that your meter shows you've had electricity for three months, and you have scarcely used it."

"Oh," she said, "You see, I don't use very much of it. Every evening when the sun sets, I turn the electric lamps on long enough to see to light my candle, and then I turn them off again!"

Sadly, this is how many Christians live their lives. They attend church on Sunday, but the rest of their week is spent living apart from the principles written in God's Word. Difficulties arise, and they wonder why their lives spiral downward. The answer is simple: They are connected to the power source, but they are not using His power.

God has chosen you to be His light of hope to a sin-darkened world. However, you must choose to use His power by yielding yourself to Him. Ask God to show you the areas of your life that need the light of His love and conviction. His power through you is amazing and real.

You will receive power when the Holy Spirit comes on you; and you will be my witnesses (Acts 1:8).

The Daily Way

January 27

More Than a Wish List

Dr. R.A. Torrey, a great man of God, wrote:

> Prayer is the key that unlocks all the storehouses of God's infinite grace and power. All that God is and all that God has is at the disposal of the one who prays.

If this is true, why do we spend so little time in prayer? There are several answers. First, some people simply do not know how to pray. They struggle in prayer and wonder if the Lord hears their words.

Second, many have the wrong idea about prayer. They believe that there is a specific formula to prayer—something they can repeat in order to have their prayers answered.

For three years, the disciples were with Jesus—morning, noon, and night. It was not long before they asked Him to teach them how to pray. They saw the benefits of prayer displayed in His life, and they quickly realized that prayer was a tremendous source of power.

Prayer is also our greatest form of communication with our heavenly Father. It is meant to be a place where we can bare our souls and be refreshed by His unconditional love and grace.

In contrast, prayer is not meant to be:
- A repetition of mere words.
- The result of our pulling together a "wish list" for God to answer.
- An opportunity for us to demand a miracle.
- An opportunity for us to try to manipulate God so that our wills become His will for our lives.

Well-phrased words or eloquently stated sentences will not usher you into the throne room of God. However, a humble heart and a deep desire to worship the Savior are the very keys that will open heaven's door to God's inner chamber.

When you pray, go into your room, close the door and pray to your Father, who is unseen. Then your Father, who sees what is done in secret, will reward you (Matthew 6:6).

January 28

The Daily Way

The Power of Prayer

There is no power over temptation nor victory over sin without spending time with God in prayer. James Montgomery, who was a great man of prayer, wrote, "Prayer is the Christian's vital breath. The Christian's native air; his watchword at the gates of death; he enters heaven with prayer."

Prayer should be our first option rather than the last opportunity. When trouble approaches, we need to run to God in prayer. If you are weary and feel heavy-laden, take time to pray. When life is joyful, take time to praise God for His goodness through prayer.

Moses prayed, and water flowed from a rock. Joshua prayed, and the sun stood still. Hannah prayed, and God gave her a son, Samuel, who was one of Israel's greatest prophets.

David prayed, and Goliath fell. Elijah prayed, and fire rained down from heaven. Daniel prayed, and God closed the lions' mouths. Jesus prayed, and 5,000 people were fed and satisfied with a little boy's lunch.

When Jesus prayed in the Garden of Gethsemane, the demons shook with terror. Heaven's boundless power and strength are ours when we pray and align our will with His perfect plan.

Are you discouraged and despondent? Pray. Do you feel defeated by sin? Pray. Does it seem as if your life and personal relationships are falling apart? Your greatest needs can be met through prayer.

God is not challenged by your sin or difficult circumstances. Prayer is the avenue He uses to restore your soul and to prepare you to live the life He has given you. Therefore, pray, knowing that when you draw near to Him, He will draw near to you.

Come near to God and he will come near to you. ... Humble yourselves before the Lord, and he will lift you up (James 4:8, 10).

The Daily Way — January 29

Guidelines for Prayer

A sign posted in a Nebraska high school read: "In case of a nuclear attack, the Supreme Court's ban on school prayer will be temporarily suspended."

There is a deep sadness that comes from knowing that public prayer is forbidden in our schools. Why is it so important to pray? Prayer is the spark that ignites the heart of God. When He hears His people praying, He is moved to action. He is blessed by our prayers and glorified by our words of faith and adoration.

When we tap into the mind of God, we gain His perspective concerning our circumstances. When it comes to prayer, there are three basic considerations:

1. Give prayer adequate time. The average Christian spends only five minutes in prayer each day. Yet God continues to draw us to Himself through prayer. Make sure you take time to build a personal relationship with the God who loves you with an infinite love. Prayer is the way you accomplish this.

2. Give prayer adequate space. There are no boundaries to prayer. In His presence, our souls find rest and refreshment. Make sure that you find a place to pray where you can concentrate without being disturbed—a place where you can focus only on God and not be distracted.

3. Give prayer adequate attention. You can pray standing up or sitting down. But to pray effectively, you need to make prayer your No. 1 priority. Therefore, begin each day with prayer.

Be joyful always; pray continually; give thanks in all circumstances, for this is God's will for you in Christ Jesus (1 Thessalonians 5:16-18).

January 30 — The Daily Way

The Weapon of Victory

In Jeremiah, the Lord admonishes us to pray, saying, "Call upon me and come and pray to me, and I will listen to you. You will seek me and find me when you seek me with all your heart" (Jeremiah 29:12-13).

Each of us would like to see great and mighty things from God. However, if we fail to pray, then we will never fully experience the power of God in our lives.

Prayer is our declaration of faith in a mighty God. When we pray, we acknowledge our need of Him and our dependence on Him alone. Calling out to God also declares our desire for His wisdom, guidance, and protection.

We have the awesome privilege of entering God's presence through prayer. It is here that we discover the will of God for our lives and receive His power so we can victoriously face the enemy of our souls.

In this life, there will be times when we struggle with feelings of disappointment. In those times, we may be tempted to wonder how life ended up feeling so unfair. If we are not careful, our spiritual focus will shift, and we will wonder, "Why pray?"

Never allow this attitude to rest within your heart. Prayer is our mighty weapon of victory. It is a matter of the will rather than emotion or intellect. When the bottom drops out of life, we must become more determined than ever to pray.

In Scripture, Paul reminds us that a spiritual battle rages around us (2 Corinthians 10:4). However, we are not defenseless. Prayer is a powerful and sure weapon. Therefore, we can pray and by faith know that God hears us when we call to Him.

For though we live in the world, we do not wage war as the world does. The weapons we fight with are not the weapons of the world. On the contrary, they have divine power to demolish strongholds (2 Corinthians 10:3-4).

The Daily Way — January 31

Having Ears to Hear

Have you ever known someone who would call you on the telephone, talk what seemed like a thousand words a minute, and then, when he finished telling you what he needed to say, would hang up? Even before you had a chance to say a word, you heard a click.

Sadly, this is how many people treat God. They don't stay on the line long enough to hear from Him. They pray to Him in a flurry of words, expressing needs and desires, but they miss the most important part of prayer: worship and listening for God's still, small voice.

Prayer is a two-way form of communication. One of the reasons many avoid spending silent time in prayer is because they are afraid to hear what God has to say to them. They are sure that if they listen, He will say something that they don't want to hear.

Someone has called American Christianity "decaffeinated Christianity." If you think about it, decaffeinated Christianity won't keep you awake at night. It won't disturb you. It won't motivate you, and it certainly won't change you!

God is a gentleman. He will never force you to listen for His voice. He will never coerce you into meditating on His Word or taking time to pray. However, He will continue to draw you to Himself. Sometimes this is pleasant; other times it is not.

Allowing us to experience disappointment and frustration is one of the ways God gets our attention. If you feel as though you have been running away from God and prayer, ask yourself, "Isn't it time I stop running and avoiding the Lord?" Great things come to us when we stop rushing and begin seeking God with a humble, obedient heart.

The Lord detests the sacrifice of the wicked, but the prayer of the upright pleases him (Proverbs 15:8).

God's Greatest Gifts, Part I: The Gift of His Son

The Daily Way

February 1

The 'I Am' Sayings of Jesus

Today, more than ever, believers have a responsibility to know what they believe and why they believe it. They are being called to sort through this world's deception, which often comes under the guise of Christianity.

In this day of half-truths, it is important to know what Jesus had to say about Himself. When we focus on the truth that God provides through His Word, we will be well-equipped to discern the lies of the world.

Whatever need you have, the "I Am" sayings of Jesus will encourage your heart.

In John 6, He says, "I am the bread of life." In John 8, He says, "I am the light of the world." In John 10, He says, "I am the door." In John 11, He tells us that He is "the resurrection and the life." In John 14, He says He is the "the way and the truth and the life," and in John 15, He says He is "the true vine."

In each of these statements, Jesus reveals something that we need to know about His character. His words to us also reveal certain truths we need for personal spiritual growth.

For example, as the bread of life, Jesus is the only One who can satisfy our spiritual hunger. Just as He fed the multitude, He feeds us through His Word and the presence of the Holy Spirit.

Do you have a heart that longs to know God? Jesus is the One who will meet your need. Do you struggle with disappointment and frustration? The presence of Christ in your life will fill you up to overflowing with contentment and hope.

Whatever your need, turn it over to Jesus. You will be amazed by His ability to feed and to provide for you.

I am the bread of life. He who comes to me will never go hungry, and he who believes in me will never be thirsty (John 6:35).

February 2

The Daily Way

'I Am the Bread of Life'

Jesus offered all of us a sure way to experience peace, contentment, and complete satisfaction. In John He tells us:

> I am the bread of life. He who comes to me will never go hungry, and he who believes in me will never be thirsty. ... All that the Father gives me will come to me, and whoever comes to me I will never drive away (John 6:35, 37).

Jesus embraces us with an unconditional love—one that will never cease. Just when we think that there is no hope, no understanding, and no way out of our predicament, our loving Lord speaks words of affirmation and encouragement to our hearts.

In times of extreme difficulty, it is important to trust Him and to not faint with weariness. Remember that whatever He does concerning our lives will end up being for our good and for His praise and glory. Are you fit for the battle? Are you partaking of the true Bread of Life—the One who will sustain you through times of victory and disappointment?

If you are eating from the bowl of the world's expectations and dreams, then you will be soundly disappointed, and you probably will experience defeat in your spiritual and emotional life. You can spend your lifetime trying to gain wealth and prominence, but no amount of money is sufficient enough to purchase the gift that God offers you through the life of His Son.

If you want to be sure of your eternal salvation, then take and eat of God's beloved manna. There is not a man or a woman on earth who can satisfy your needs. Only Jesus can do this, and this is exactly what He did for those who listened and accepted His words and nourishment.

I tell you the truth, it is not Moses who has given you the bread from heaven, but it is my Father who gives you the true bread from heaven (John 6:32).

The Daily Way — February 3

Heavenly Food

After Jesus fed the multitude, a crowd gathered and greedily sought His provision. They were both curious and physically hungry. The Savior knew the intent of their hearts. He also knew they had not learned the lesson He had taught the day before as He fed the multitude of people. It was there that He first proclaimed, "I am the bread of life" (John 6:35; 6:48).

Instead of focusing on Christ and the spiritual bread He had to offer, their eyes were set on material provision. Instead of focusing on the glory of God, they were anxious to have their stomachs filled.

Many times, we have the same attitude. We tell ourselves, "As long as God meets my needs, then I will give Him a pat on the back and tell Him that He is all right." In some circles, this is the total depth of Christianity, and it is exactly why there is a lack of sincerity in many churches today.

Satan loves to water down the Gospel message so that we begin to view it as weak and not worth our commitment. However, God demands nothing less than our complete obedience.

He is the bread of life. This means that He satisfies us—He fills us with His Word so that we are no longer hungry or discontent. He wants to elevate our vision and teach us to focus on things that are far more important than food and earthly possessions.

The bread Jesus offers not only will satisfy your physical hunger, but also it will satisfy your soul hunger, your emotional hunger, and your intellectual hunger. When you give your life to Him and seek His heavenly food, you will be fed with food that does not perish—and every hunger you have will be perfectly satisfied.

Taking the five loaves and the two fish and looking up to heaven, he gave thanks and broke them. ... They all ate and were satisfied (Luke 9:16-17).

February 4 — The Daily Way

'I Am the Light of the World'

A few years ago, there were a number of scientific writings dealing with the nova experience (from the Latin word novus or "new"). The nova phenomenon occurs when a medium-sized star suddenly gets brighter and hotter for a period of about a week to two weeks. Then it becomes darker and cooler. Each year, scientists observe about 14 of these nova experiences.

Based on this research, astronomers are now concerned that the previously held theory—that our sun could maintain its present heat or energy output level for at least eight million years—is no longer true. Scientists reached this conclusion because they believed that half of the sun's hydrogen energy has been used up.

When other stars were observed to "nova out" as soon as half of their hydrogen was exhausted, it became popular to believe that the same could happen to our sun. Should a nova happen, within 40 days, the earth would freeze and disappear into the solar system like a small ball of foil.

Can the sun suddenly cease from warming us and from providing the energy we trust and seek each day? The answer is yes! In Revelation, we read that in the final days the earth will be destroyed. There will be a new earth and a new heaven. And there will be no need for a sun because we will have the Lord Jesus Christ. He will be our source of light, which will be much brighter and warmer than the sun.

Jesus is "the light of the world" (John 8:12), and we do not have to wait until the end to walk in His light. Today, He is the one who brings light to the murky areas of our lives. No darkness is powerful enough to eliminate His light. When you step into the light of His love, your pathway will be lit with heaven's hope.

I am the light of the world. Whoever follows me will never walk in darkness, but will have the light of life (John 8:12).

The Daily Way

February 5

No More Night

Throughout the Bible, we see God leading and comforting His people with the presence of His holy light. In Exodus, the ninth plague upon the Egyptians was one of darkness so great that the people could not see one another. However, the children of Israel had light in their homes (Exodus 10:23).

The Light of the World shines not only in the hearts and minds of those who follow Him, but also in the homes and dwelling places of those who know Christ as their Savior.

Once Israel was released from Egyptian bondage:

> By day the Lord went ahead of them in a pillar of cloud to guide them ... and by night in a pillar of fire to give them light. ... Neither the pillar of cloud by day nor the pillar of fire by night left its place in front of the people (Exodus 13:21-22).

However, when God's people reached the Red Sea:

> The angel of God, who had been traveling in front of Israel's army, withdrew and went behind them. The pillar of cloud also moved from in front and stood behind them, coming between the armies of Egypt and Israel. Throughout the night the cloud brought darkness to the one side and light to the other side (Exodus 14:19-20).

Jesus Christ is the light of the world. He will light your way when you can no longer see clearly. No matter how dark your world seems, God's light cannot be extinguished.

Have you taken time to share this life-changing truth that no one has to walk in darkness because Jesus is the light of the world?

There will be no more night. They will not need the light of a lamp or the light of the sun, for the Lord God will give them light (Revelation 22:5).

February 6 — The Daily Way

'I Am the Door'

At the turn of the last century, Sir George Adam Smith, a prominent British visitor to the Syrian hills, watched with fascination one evening as shepherds drove their sheep into the sheepfold.

He noticed that the fold was no more than a simple, four-wall enclosure with only one opening—no door and no gate. He asked the shepherd: "How can you ensure that the sheep will not wander off at night? And what about the wild beasts—will they not come and attack these helpless sheep?"

"No," was the shepherd's reply, "because I am the one whose body blocks the opening at night. I lie down across this opening; no sheep can get out without going over me, and no thief or wolf can get in except over my body."

In John 10, Jesus says:

> I am the gate for the sheep. ... Whoever enters through me will be saved. ... The thief comes only to steal and kill and destroy; I have come that they may have life, and have it to the full (John 10:7, 9-10).

Only Jesus can save you from sin. Muhammad cannot save you. Buddha cannot save you. Krishna cannot save you, nor can Joseph Smith, Mary Baker Eddy, or even the law of Moses.

Nothing opens heaven's door except the One who is the door, and that is Jesus Christ. The moment a person prays the following prayer, Jesus opens heaven's door: "Lord, You are the Son of God. In You and You alone, I find eternal security. To You and You alone, I surrender my life. I repent of my sins. Please forgive me."

There is no discrimination—no one is refused. Our loving heavenly Father will welcome us with words of love and acceptance: "Come right in. I have been waiting for you, and I am so glad you have come."

I am the gate; whoever enters through me will be saved. He will come in ... and find pasture (John 10:9).

The Daily Way

February 7

'I Am the Good Shepherd'

Many Americans can't forget the news that came out of Washington, D.C., after an Air Florida plane crashed into the Potomac River in 1982. Millions heard the reports of a courageous young man who was more interested in saving others than himself.

Each time the helicopter sent the lifeline his way, he would pass it to someone else. No doubt he knew that he could not hold on any longer as he passed the line to the last person. This man's death, as a result of rescuing others instead of saving himself, was the tragic outcome of an accident.

Jesus said, "I lay down my life for the sheep" (John 10:15). He came from heaven so He could die for His sheep—every person who calls upon His name. This incident was not an accident.

It was not by chance that Jesus came to earth, took on human form, and gave His life so we might be saved. He says:

> No one takes [my life] from me, but I lay it down of my own accord. I have authority to lay it down and authority to take it up again (John 10:18).

The death of a shepherd means disaster for the sheep. If a shepherd dies in defense of his sheep, it is often an accident. The shepherd plans to live for his sheep, not to die for them. However, Jesus is different from any other shepherd. He is the only door into the sheepfold; therefore, He is the only good shepherd. The hired hand runs at the first sign of trouble, but Jesus will never leave.

We can take comfort in the words of the psalmist:

> The Lord is my shepherd, I shall not be in want. He makes me lie down in green pastures, he leads me beside quiet waters, he restores my soul. He guides me in paths of righteousness for his name's sake (Psalm 23:1-3).

When the Chief Shepherd appears, you will receive the crown of glory that will never fade away (1 Peter 5:4).

February 8

The Daily Way

Listen for His Voice

In the Middle East, the relationship between the shepherd and the sheep is special. Sheep know their shepherd's voice, and they follow him when he calls. If a stranger comes along, the sheep shrink back.

It is no surprise that during World War I, when a group of Turkish soldiers decided to steal a flock of sheep from a hillside near Jerusalem, they had to face the fact that the shepherd was the only one who could control the sheep. But even he knew he could not recapture his flock single handedly against all those soldiers.

He did the only thing he could; he put his hand to his mouth and gave his own particular call that he used each day to gather his sheep. When the sheep heard the familiar sound, they stopped, turned, and came back to their shepherd.

The same is true with us—the body of Christ. Those who are children of God will hear His voice through His Word. Jesus says in John 10:27-28, "My sheep listen to my voice; I know them, and they follow me. I give them eternal life, and they shall never perish; no one can snatch them out of my hand."

The way to know whether you are one of His sheep is in how you respond to His voice and His Word. Do you recognize the voice of Jesus? He knows you better than you know yourself.

Jesus says, "I am the good shepherd; I know my sheep and my sheep know me" (John 10:14). Jesus is the good shepherd who gave His life for you. However, He longs for you to draw even nearer to Him. Can you hear His voice? Do you know His special call to you? Be still, listen, and pray, and you will be blessed by the Savior's intimate care.

Know that the Lord is God. It is he who made us, and we are his; we are his people, the sheep of his pasture (Psalm 100:3).

The Daily Way — February 9

'I Am the Living Water'

I doubt whether there is any person who would not understand the importance of water for survival. In fact, next to air, water is the most important substance for life.

The Bible teaches that while Jesus is God incarnate, He also was human and experienced the same feelings and temptations that we encounter each day. However, He never succumbed to even one temptation.

In John 4:4-8, we read how the Savior became tired and stopped to rest beside the well of Jacob. While His disciples were buying food in a nearby town, a Samaritan woman arrived at the well to draw water. Jesus, being thirsty, asked her for a drink of the well's water. Immediately, she protested and reminded him that she was a Samaritan, and He was a Jew.

Jews believed the Samaritans were unclean. Another fact to consider is that this woman was at the well alone at high noon. More than likely, she also was considered unclean and came to the well at a time when no one else would see her.

We know her story. She had been married many times and was in need of a Savior, and Jesus met her need. He told her:

> Everyone who drinks this water will be thirsty again, but whoever drinks the water I give him will never thirst. Indeed, the water I give him will become in him a spring of water welling up to eternal life (John 4:13-14).

Christ confronted the deepest need of this woman and offered her a chance to begin life anew. The more you drink from the world's water, the worse your thirst will become.

Are you restless and discontent? Just as He offered living water to the woman at the well, He offers it to you. When you drink of Him, you will thirst no more.

He will lead them to springs of living water. And God will wipe away every tear from their eyes (Revelation 7:17).

February 10

The Daily Way

Your Water Source

The River Jordan originates from the springs of Dan. Geologists have concluded that it is the largest spring system in the world. The spring is at the base of Mount Hermon, which rises 9,232 feet above sea level. In the wintertime, a large quantity of snow accumulates. When it melts, it percolates through limestone and supplies water to these magnificent springs.

From that unseen and inexhaustible source hidden in the depths of the earth springs forth life-giving water. Near the springs of Dan are some enormous fruit-bearing trees growing as a result of close access to water. If you move away from the spring a short distance, you will find fields that are dry and brown.

In the same way, when you distance yourself from Christ, who is your spring of living water, your spiritual life becomes parched and dry. However, if you remain close to the Lord in devotion and fellowship, you will accomplish many things without becoming weary. This is because you are close to your "water source," the living water, which is Jesus Christ.

The water that flows from the Dan springs is perfectly clear and pure. But as it continues downstream, it doesn't stay pure. It picks up contaminants, such as dissolved salts and minerals—becoming bitter water.

Is there bitterness in your life that is poisoning God's gift of living water? If so, you can be refreshed and purified by spending time in prayer with Jesus. Does your spiritual life seem to be parched? All you need is Jesus and His living water—the Word of God.

We cannot live more than seven days without drinking water. But we can live for an eternity if we are drinking the living water God provides through Jesus Christ.

As the deer pants for streams of water, so my soul pants for you, O God (Psalm 42:1).

The Daily Way

February 11

'I Am the Way and the Truth and the Life'

Our world is filled with empty promises; anyone can claim anything. But only Jesus Christ delivered on His claim to be the divine Son of God. The disciples had left everything to follow Jesus of Nazareth, who claimed to be the anointed Son of God. They were excited and thrilled with the miracles they witnessed. They were impressed by His exercise of spiritual authority. His teaching encouraged them. And now Jesus was telling them of His death, and that one of them would betray Him.

Jesus knew the disciples were confused and discouraged. Therefore, He comforted them with these words, "Do not let your hearts be troubled. Trust in God; trust also in me" (John 14:1).

If you feel that the frenzy of the world is consuming you, remember that you have a Savior who loves you and who will fight for you. Don't become worried and anxious. Jesus is near to you. He has promised never to leave you, no matter how dark life seems to be. Don't let sorrows and suffering take joy from you. Jesus has a place for you with your name written over it. "In my Father's house are many rooms; if it were not so, I would have told you. I am going there to prepare a place for you" (John 14:2).

No matter how many times you see the hand of God working in your life or experience His provision, it is easy to lose sight of God's love and faithfulness. If you only focus on your current difficulty or discouragement, you may lose sight of His blessings and promises.

Don't become discouraged. Despondency says things are hopeless, and life is aimless. Jesus says there is hope beyond suffering and the grave. There is a way out of all difficulties. Jesus is the way, the truth, and the life (John 14:6). He will never let you down. He will not forsake you.

The fear of the Lord leads to life: Then one rests content, untouched by trouble (Proverbs 19:23).

February 12 — The Daily Way

A Zest for Life

In this day, truth is relative. We joke that there are three sides to each story—your side, my side, and the truth.

There is a story about a great defense lawyer defending a client who was a victim of trumped-up charges. The main witness against the client took the stand and gave his testimony. Then the defense lawyer began his cross-examination.

Immediately, the defense lawyer challenged the witness's honesty. The witness protested vigorously and vehemently, saying, "But I am wedded to the truth." The defense lawyer replied, "Oh yes, I see. And how long have you been divorced?"

Even the greatest men and women of God experience times of doubt and mental conflict. Every person has a thirst for life. We want to live our lives to the fullest. Things that clog or impede our lives become objects of our hate, discomfort, and dislike. We abhor sickness, impediments, or whatever diminishes or destroys life.

God created us with a zest for life. Sin in the Garden of Eden brought about the curse of disease and death. No matter how long we may live, we all must face the prospect of lying in a cold grave.

Most people live their lives either in fear of death, or denying that they will have to face it. The truth is that physical life will fail, but it is Jesus and trust in Him that bring us the assurance of eternal life. In Him we receive a new spirit, and in Him are we daily invigorated and renewed.

The more time you spend with Christ, the more energy and vigor you will receive. The more you cling to His Word, the more vitality you will experience. The more you seek Him, the more victory you will have because your focus will be on God and on what is eternal.

I have chosen the way of truth; I have set my heart on your laws (Psalm 119:30).

The Daily Way

February 13

Set Down Your Bundle

If you are like most people, you do not board an airplane or train without knowing where it is headed. When you get in your car, you have a good idea of where you are going. Are you as aware of your eternal destination? Jesus Christ is the way, the truth, and the life (John 14:6). There is no other way to get to heaven.

You may be a person who is looking for God, yet you are looking in all the wrong places. There is an anonymous poem about a man who carried a bundle.

> He carried a bundle of false beliefs,
> Musty and heavy as lawyer's briefs;
> Prejudice, jealousy, bitterness, strife—
> These were the wares of his troubled life.
> He carried the bundle wherever he went—
> Anger, suspicion, and selfish intent;
> He saw what he sought, injustice and sin.
> Life was a tempest without and within.
> He mumbled and stumbled;
> The world was all wrong,
> His bundle grew heavy as he shuffled along.
> Worry, impatience, discord, and doubt—
> These were the things
> He dragged all about.
> Tired of his bundle, he set the load down,
> He prayed long to God; his face lost its frown.
> In his eyes dawned a light by which he could see.
> He forsook his old bundle and walked away free.

The harder you try in your own strength, the further you are from God. He doesn't move away; you do. He is waiting for you. Come to Jesus today. He will lead you to truth and to eternal life with Him.

Show me your ways, O Lord, teach me your paths (Psalm 25:4).

February 14 — The Daily Way

'I Am the True Vine'

There are two kinds of trees that contrast each other in every way. One grows in the Middle East, and the other grows in the tropics.

The tree that grows in the Middle East looks like an olive tree. It takes the same space as an olive tree. It absorbs the same vast amount of sunlight. It grows in the same soil as the olive tree. However, it does not produce fruit. This tree is called an oleaster.

There is another tree, which grows in the tropics, called the banyan tree. This particular tree's height, spread, and thickness of trunk make it a glorious tree in terms of shade and beauty. Its branches reach out and down to the ground. Whenever the tips of the branches touch the earth, it takes root and a new tree begins to grow.

Is your life spreading and multiplying itself in the lives of others—like the banyan? Are you sharing the love of God with friends, family members, and co-workers?

God has given the Great Commission to make Him known—to bring men, women, and children to a saving knowledge of Him. Jesus brings healing, forgiveness, and deliverance. His acceptance is unconditional.

Jesus told the disciples, "I am the true vine, and my Father is the gardener" (John 15:1). Without abiding in Christ, you cannot have fruitfulness. Jesus says, "No branch can bear fruit by itself; it must remain in the vine. Neither can you bear fruit unless you remain in me" (John 15:4).

You must abide in Christ. You become one with Christ when you adopt His purpose to be your purpose. You become one with Christ when His agenda becomes yours. You are one with Christ when His perspective becomes your perspective.

The fruit of the righteous is a tree of life, and he who wins souls is wise (Proverbs 11:30).

The Daily Way — February 15

Pruning Your Vineyard

Have you ever toured a vineyard? There is constant attention given to the condition of each vine. The gardener takes particular care of each vine and its branches. Because he is interested in producing quality grapes, he prunes the wild shoots that produce leaves and no fruit.

God is the gardener of your life. He trims the troublesome shoots so that you will be productive and fruitful for Him. Often, pruning looks and feels painful, merciless, and wasteful. But with God there is no random cutting. He trims away what is harmful and bad for you.

When self-centeredness and selfishness grow in your heart, God reaches down and begins to prune. The nutrients of God's Word bring new life. As you allow God to work, you begin to live a new life of holiness and righteousness.

How do you abide and continue to abide in Christ? The answer is by spending adequate time studying, learning, and comprehending God's Word—but not merely as words, facts, or sentiments. God's Word must be the basis for all of your actions—bringing nourishment and fulfillment.

It is easy to forget that producing fruit is impossible without the pain of pruning. Jesus said:

> I am the true vine, and my Father is the gardener. He cuts off every branch in me that bears no fruit, while every branch that does bear fruit He prunes so that it will be even more fruitful (John 15:1-2).

At the end of your days, will your life be a fruitless shell—or are you going to produce fruit? Will you be able to look in Jesus' eyes on that final day and say, "Lord, I used my time, money, talents, and gifts for Your glory?" Make it your prayer that God would prune you to produce His fruit.

From the fruit of his lips a man is filled with good things as surely as the work of his hands rewards him (Proverbs 12:14).

February 16 — The Daily Way

'I Am the Resurrection and the Life'

Just before Jesus raised Lazarus from the dead, He spoke these words to Martha: "I am the resurrection and the life. He who believes in me will live, even though he dies; and whoever lives and believes in me will never die" (John 11:25-26).

When the stone was removed, Jesus commanded Lazarus to come out of the grave, and he did. When you were dead in your sins, God called you by name. You were called to come out of your sins and to experience the power of the Resurrection.

Jesus also faced death, but God raised Him from the dead. His resurrection was physical and spiritual. It was not like Lazarus's resurrection, because he later died again.

The Bible says that Jesus died, was buried, was raised, and appeared numerous times after the Resurrection. Christ's tomb was empty then; it remains empty today. He is our risen Lord and Savior.

Even the Romans, with all their power, could not produce His body. The Jewish leaders, with all their hatred and bitterness toward Jesus, could not produce His body. And if the disciples stole His body, as some asserted, can you imagine the disciples' willingness to die for a hoax they themselves had perpetrated?

Instead, Jesus appeared to Mary and told her to "Go … to my brothers and tell them, 'I am returning to my Father and your Father, to my God and your God'" (John 20:17).

Have you experienced the power of the Resurrection? Are you living in triumph or defeat? Jesus conquered the grave, and you also can conquer eternal death—but only by placing your faith in Him. He sacrificially died on the cross for your sins and rose again that you might spend eternity with Him.

Thanks be to God! He gives us the victory through our Lord Jesus Christ (1 Corinthians 15:57).

The Daily Way — February 17

The Ultimate Triumph

The resurrection of Jesus Christ is the ultimate atonement for the sins of mankind. Whatever skeletons are in your closet, whatever dark secrets are in your memory, whatever past is shaming and condemning you, whatever memory is tormenting you—Jesus Christ offers forgiveness and redemption.

Because Jesus rose victoriously from the dead, God assures you that by His death on the cross, your sins can be forgiven. The Resurrection assures you of God's power—power to illuminate and to enlighten your heart. Power to open your eyes to receive the truth. Power to change you from a selfish person to an unselfish person.

The resurrection of Jesus Christ can change people's hearts from being spiritually dead to being alive in Christ. Because of the Resurrection, hatred can be turned into love. It is the resurrection of Jesus Christ that can change your life.

The resurrection of Christ assures you of your ultimate triumph. When you place your faith in the risen Christ, comfort and assurance of the future are yours. You will be given a body like His resurrection body. You will spend eternity with Him.

Jesus came to earth in the form of a human body. One day, He is coming back with spectacular magnificence to bring history to its fulfillment in eternity.

Not only will He raise the dead, but also He will make all things new. Jesus' resurrection is a pledge to all of those who surrender to Him—those who dwell under the shadow of His wings, those who ask for and receive His forgiveness, and those who place Him at the center of their lives.

In him we have redemption through his blood, the forgiveness of sins, in accordance with the riches of God's grace (Ephesians 1:7).

February 18 — The Daily Way

Cleansing Your Soul

When a young boy came running into the house after playing outside, his mother stopped him, asking, "What is on your right hand?"

"Oh, just a little mud," he replied.

"Are you planning to get it off your hand?" she asked.

"Sure, Mom, I'll just wipe it off with my other hand."

There was only one problem with the boy's plan. One dirty hand and one clean hand equal two dirty hands.

Many people are like this little boy. Deep down they are conscious of their sin and rebellion and of their need of cleansing, but they think that they can clean themselves by doing some good deed or charity work.

Just as the mother had to put her son's hands under running water to clean them, so you must put your life under the blood of Jesus Christ. Only the resurrected Christ can cleanse you from sin. Only the resurrected Christ can transform your destination from hell to heaven.

There is a need in each of us to do things for ourselves—to be self-reliant. If we have a problem, we want to fix it. If we want something, we try to get it. This need to be independent carries over into our relationship with Christ. But we soon discover that we cannot redeem ourselves from our sinful nature. We cannot work our way into God's favor. We must come to Him in complete surrender and obedience, seeking His forgiveness for our sins.

Without Christ, our lives are meaningless and empty. Peter reminds us, "In [God's] great mercy he has given us new birth into a living hope through the resurrection of Jesus Christ" (1 Peter 1:3).

I trust in your unfailing love; my heart rejoices in your salvation (Psalm 13:5).

God's Greatest Gifts, Part II: The Gift of His Grace

God's Grace Was in the Beginning

Grace has been defined as the second chance we did not expect.

Picture this: We hang our heads in shame because we know we blew it. We missed our opportunity to be the best. So, here we are, stuck with being second best, a far cry from what God intended for us. Yet it is with uncontrolled delight that we see God coming down the street to dry our tears and to encourage us to get back out there. He still believes in us.

What a feeling that must have been for Adam and Eve, the first people to experience the inexplicable grace God has for mankind! There they were, planted in the middle of paradise with the most perfect communion with God. They only had one rule—yet they found a way to break it.

But God is not interested in excommunicating us. Instead of getting upset and declaring the end of the world and starting over, He pursued the hearts of Adam and Eve. In the midst of their sin, God sought their hearts. And He has continued His pursuit ever since.

Many times when we sin, we wonder how God could ever love us again. However, it is the grace of God that gives us a chance to repent and to find new life. God's grace is not a pardon; rather, it is a measure of forgiveness that gives life to the broken.

As we grow in our relationship with God, oftentimes we are surprised by His love for us. But even more surprising is the amount to which He pours out His grace in our lives. When we sin, God does not cast us aside. Instead, the compassionate heart of God meets us where we are and goes to great lengths to mend our hearts and to restore our relationships with Him.

Prayer: Lord, show me Your grace today in my life.

God raised us up with Christ ... in order that in the coming ages he might show the incomparable riches of his grace (Ephesians 2:6-7).

February 20 — The Daily Way

God's Grace Will Find Us

As Adam and Eve first experienced God's grace in the Garden of Eden, they came to understand some important aspects of God's character. In learning about God, they discovered that He would not excuse sin. They also found out that He would not discard the sinner.

When we make a mistake and fall into sin, we begin to wonder what type of punishment God will issue us. Though there are always consequences for sin, there is not an excommunication from God. Instead of zapping us into the stratosphere never to be heard from again, He chases us, seeking us just like He sought Adam and Eve in the garden.

Upon the realization that they had sinned, Adam and Eve hid from God. They knew that He had given them the perfect place to live, yet they botched it by falling to the oldest lie of the enemy: God is withholding His best. So they hid, hoping that God would not find them.

However, God and His grace always find us—not because we are terrible at hiding, but because He is so good at seeking. He does not hunt us down to scold us; rather, He chases our hearts so that we can see how much He loves us.

God's grace gives us an opportunity to allow Him to change us. It gives us a moment in which we encounter God and His awesome grace, and we surrender. We stop running from God and start running to Him.

It may be painful at times as He roots out some of the strongholds of sin in our lives. But the difference He makes in our lives in the end will be worth it.

Prayer: Lord, show me how You desire to change my heart and reveal those areas You want to see transformed in me.

From the fullness of his grace we have all received one blessing after another (John 1:16).

The Daily Way

February 21

God's Grace throughout Our Lives

As God pursues us with His wonderful grace, something magnificent takes place in our lives. Before God's grace was extended to us, we were dead in our sins and powerless to overcome them. We were in bondage to the enemy, and the future never looked so dim. Then, God entered the scene, desperate to demonstrate the power of His grace.

After Adam and Eve sinned in the garden, the Bible begins to tell the unfolding tale of God's pursuit of the human heart through the goodness of His grace. And each time God catches us and reveals the power inside His grace, our once-dead souls become alive! Instead of being unable to fight sin's strongholds, God's grace gives us the power to overcome them through the Holy Spirit.

Now, we come to the battle equipped to win—not just to survive another round. God's grace empowers us to be conquerors through Christ, redeeming what once seemed all but dead.

God entered our lives to save us, not just to show up and to impress us with His omnipotence. He came to deliver us from all the bondage of the past and to bring us ultimate redemption as we follow after Him.

Through salvation, we encounter God's grace. Then one day His transformation begins in our hearts. All along, He pursues us with His grace in an attempt to get our attention. Even though at times we may have run in the opposite direction, He remains steadfast in His quest. When He captures us, the parts of our hearts that were cold toward Him suddenly warm and come to life.

Prayer: Lord, thank You for the way You pursued me and called me into relationship with You!

When he arrived and saw the evidence of the grace of God, he was glad and encouraged them all to remain true to the Lord with all their hearts (Acts 11:23).

February 22 — The Daily Way

God's Grace and Our Future

As wonderful as God's grace is in redeeming our past, it is equally powerful in the way it changes our future. No matter how far we strayed before God's grace arrested us in our sin, His plans for us remains. God wants to see us following after Him, living lives full of love and compassion for Him and for others.

The apostle Paul, a worthy vessel to convey the power of God's grace, writes: "For we are God's workmanship, created in Christ Jesus to do good works, which God prepared in advance for us to do" (Ephesians 2:10). All along, God has been waiting on us to turn to Him and to receive His love. All along, God has been waiting for us to express His love to others through our lives.

In pondering God's grace for our lives, we must realize that it changes both our past and present. He has redeemed us from the bondage of sin, and He has given us a new destiny. When our lives intersect with His grace, He places us on new paths—ones He planned for us to travel all along.

When we get to know God better, we discover He has created us to live lives of grace—and devoid of sin. We begin to understand He has plans for our lives that include following His paths and existing in a rich, deep relationship with Him.

God's grace is for our past, present, and future—transforming us into the people He has intended for us to be from the beginning of time.

Prayer: Lord, help me to walk daily in Your grace, taking hold of Your best for my life.

Since we have been justified through faith, we have peace with God through our Lord Jesus Christ, through whom we have gained access by faith into this grace in which we now stand. And we rejoice in the hope of the glory of God (Romans 5:1-2).

The Daily Way

February 23

God's Grace Alone

As we take a deep look at what it means to be a believer, we must realize how God's grace is the starting place—and the place where we return again and again. His grace is more than a gesture of goodwill to a soul mired in sin. It is the one thing that provides a way for us to escape temptation. Once we become accustomed to living in the light of God's grace, we will never want to live apart from it.

God's grace is necessary for us to experience the life-changing power we so desperately desire. The biggest mistake we can make is acting as though we have the ability to earn anything in God's Kingdom. The currency in God's Kingdom is grace—something we can never exhaust.

Oftentimes, in our desperation to have the heavenly Father smile upon us, we adhere to a strict list of do's and don'ts. Although legalism may prove our loyalty, it never changes our hearts. We can dot every "i" and cross every "t", but if we do not allow God's grace to flow through our lives, then we have done nothing but put on a show for the world.

God desires our allegiance as we desire His favor. However, earning favor from God is impossible. You can preach the greatest sermons. You can serve as a missionary in the jungle. You can pray until you run out of breath. But if you refuse to find your salvation in God's grace, then you will miss out on the greatest gift He bestows upon His children.

God's grace is free. It is unmerited favor from heaven, poured out on His children. No one deserves it, but we should all desire to walk boldly in it.

Prayer: Lord, help me to cease striving to earn Your favor. Help me to learn to walk in Your grace.

The law was added so that the trespass might increase. But where sin increased, grace increased all the more (Romans 5:20).

February 24 — The Daily Way

God's Vote of Confidence

As we examine the power of God's grace, we must be careful how we handle it. God's grace is not a free pass to commit sin and then to ask for forgiveness later. Instead, God's grace gives us the incredible freedom to passionately pursue God without fear of condemnation.

Each day, we are faced with numerous decisions—many of which are honoring to God. If we choose wisely, then we experience the blessings of God. If we choose unwisely, then we will deal with sin's consequences. However, if we do make the wrong choice, then God's love for us does not waver. He doesn't cast us aside and break ties with us. This is when God's grace and mercy shine.

In the same way a coach gives a player a vote of confidence even after he has made a mistake, God gives us a vote of confidence through His grace. All He asks in return is that we try, and that we never stop allowing the Holy Spirit to work in our lives.

In explaining how grace and works are intertwined, James writes,

> But the man who looks intently into the perfect law that gives freedom, and continues to do this, not forgetting what he has heard, but doing it—he will be blessed in what he does (James 1:25).

God knows that we are not perfect. However, He gives us the Holy Spirit to help us make the right decisions in life if we will listen to Him. In giving us this ability to choose for ourselves, we gain tremendous freedom when we choose God's path. His grace provides us with a sense of freedom like we have never known.

Prayer: When I am confronted with a decision, Lord, give me ears to hear Your voice.

When you are tempted, he will also provide a way out so that you can stand up under it (1 Corinthians 10:13).

The Daily Way

February 25

That Amazing Grace

While God's grace opens doors for us to experience freedom like we have never known, it is also the foundation for us to develop a deeper relationship with God. As we invite God into every portion of our lives, we begin to see how He wants to change us. We view those once-proud areas of our hearts in shambles, waiting to be rebuilt by the great Redeemer.

As we watch Him begin to put things into order for the first time in our lives, we understand we are mere bystanders, helpless to finish the work He so desperately desires to do in our lives. Once we reach that point of surrender, the Holy Spirit enters the construction zone of our hearts and begins to work.

So often, we want to cling to our lives instead of yielding them to the Lord. When we are worn down to the point of surrender, we cling only to Him. We realize it is God's grace that has provided the miraculous salvation of our hearts. And we are empowered through the Holy Spirit to see the transition of ownership of our lives transferred to God.

The apostle Paul underwent a dramatic conversion in his life. Everything he stood for was shattered in an instant. All the pious religious duties he carried out were rendered meaningless. He encountered God—and God made it clear it was Paul's heart He was pursuing.

As the Holy Spirit began to transform Paul from a man who oversaw the murder of countless Christians to a man who preached God's Word, Paul realized just how amazing God's grace is.

Prayer: Lord, let me experience Your freedom in my life through the Holy Spirit.

His grace to me was not without effect. No, I worked harder than all of them—yet not I, but the grace of God that was with me (1 Corinthians 15:10).

February 26 — The Daily Way

Grace Is Precious

While we always should show reverence to God, we should never fear Him the way we fear frightening things. God is love, and His love for us is unconditional. Though we do not deserve it, God freely gives His grace to us.

However, many times when we need God the most, we end up feeling as though we are least accepted by Him. Nothing could be further from the truth! Even when we fall flat on our faces due to sin, God does not turn His back on us. In fact, He does just the opposite—He opens His arms to us and beckons us to come to Him.

We do need to understand a principle concerning grace: It is not currency we carry around in our pockets, spending it at will whenever we sin. Instead, God's grace is precious because Jesus Christ paid the eternal sacrifice for our sins. His death on Calvary's cross made it possible for us to experience eternal salvation through grace alone.

It is impossible to earn God's grace. As fallen humans, we certainly do not deserve His mercy, yet He opens the windows of heaven and pours His grace on us.

As we grow in our relationship with Jesus Christ, we begin to understand that He truly cares about our lives. We learn that He wants to build intimate relationships with us. Instead of living in terror of Him, we are given the opportunity to be children of the King of kings. Suddenly, we begin to understand that He wants us in His throne room, where grace showers all who enter His presence.

Prayer: Lord, give me confidence to come to You when I have sinned, knowing You still love me.

Let us then approach the throne of grace with confidence, so that we may receive mercy and find grace to help us in our time of need (Hebrews 4:16).

The Daily Way

February 27

God's Grace Is Sufficient

How often do we feel like we have run out of steam? We feel like we cannot make it over the next hill, whose shadow looms large over us, the weary travelers. Even as we trudge in the direction of the hill—which we know we must climb—we begin to wonder if the weight of the burden we are bearing is too much.

Will we make it?

If there are two things God makes clear in His Word, they are the facts that we cannot make it on our own and that He will help us if we call out to Him. Countless times in Scripture, we read of men and women who felt as though they had reached the end. They could not go on unless God gave them hope and strength and courage. And when they called upon the Lord, He heard and answered their prayers.

While God does not promise us a life free from pain and suffering, He does promise to be our strength in our moments of greatest weakness (2 Corinthians 12:9). The apostle Paul suffered many afflictions while spreading the Gospel around the world. He was tortured, jailed, shipwrecked, and diseased. Yet he persevered—not because Paul was determined to get the Gospel out, but because God gave Paul the grace to do so.

Paul writes, "Therefore I will boast all the more gladly about my weaknesses, so that Christ's power may rest on me" (2 Corinthians 12:9). As we face hardships in life, we must remember that God is not a casual observer. He is an active participant—walking with us every step of the way. He catches us when we stumble, and He cheers us on as we pursue Him. He is the One who gives us the grace to walk through life's darkest hours.

Prayer: Lord, help me to remember that Your grace is sufficient for my struggles in life.

God is able to make all grace abound to you, so that in all things ... you will abound in every good work (2 Corinthians 9:8).

February 28

God's Grace Gives Confidence

Because we do not see God in the way we see other people—in a physical, tangible way—we often shy away from asking Him for help. Sometimes it can take us a long period of time to bend our knees and to ask God to intervene on our behalf. Deep down, we may even wonder if He even knows how difficult we have it on earth.

Jesus, God's only Son, walked on the same earth we do, and He had many of the same experiences that we face each day. Even though we may read the Bible daily, we can quickly forget that Jesus experienced life in a similar fashion to us.

When we hear the pain of others going through an ordeal that we experienced in the past, our ears perk up. Instantly, we can relate to their situation. We know what it is like to suffer like they did or to keep battling in a seemingly hopeless fight. And compassion oozes from us as we make every effort to assist them through their hardships.

Although we may not quickly think of Jesus as someone who has experienced what we are feeling, He has. All the pain we have felt, He has felt—every last twinge of it. And because of that, He wants to help us in our times of weakness.

God's grace gives us confidence as we realize that He cares about us deeply. He also wants to intervene in our lives because He has been there. He has walked more than a mile in our shoes and knows the trials and temptations we face daily. God is not a distant stranger, but an intimate friend who wants to share in our experiences. Will you trust Him with your life today?

Prayer: Lord, give me confidence to come boldly to You in my challenging times.

Whether I am in chains or defending and confirming the gospel, all of you share in God's grace with me (Philippians 1:7).

Receiving Daily Victory Over the Enemy

The Daily Way

March 1

Who Is Your Enemy?

When George Whitefield arrived in Boston, one of that city's prominent ministers told him, "I am very sorry to see you come to Boston, Mr. Whitefield." The great evangelist replied, "So is the devil, sir."

There is a real enemy at work in our world. He has sought to bring sorrow, heartache, and havoc to the hearts and minds of God's greatest saints, but he has not succeeded. Though many have faced extreme difficulty and stress, all have gained eternal victory because of the life, death and resurrection of Jesus Christ.

In his victorious hymn, A Mighty Fortress Is Our God, Martin Luther reminds us that though we face a powerful enemy, we will not taste defeat.

> And though this world, with devils filled,
> Should threaten to undo us,
> We will not fear, for God hath willed
> His truth to triumph through us.
> The Prince of Darkness grim,
> We tremble not for him.
> His rage we can endure;
> For lo, his doom is sure.
> One little word shall fell him. ...
> Let goods and kindred go,
> This mortal life also.
> The body they may kill;
> God's truth abideth still.
> His kingdom is forever.

The first step to defeating your enemy is to know your enemy. Know the truth about him, he is a defeated foe!

Your enemy ... prowls around like a roaring lion looking for someone to devour. Resist him, standing firm in the faith (1 Peter 5:8-9).

March 2

The Daily Way

Satan and His Army

Satan is your real enemy. In the book of Ezekiel, we find an outline of Satan's origin, as the prophet of God records God's words concerning the enemy:

> You were the model of perfection, full of wisdom and perfect in beauty. ... You were anointed as a guardian cherub, for so I ordained you. You were on the holy mount of God; you walked among the fiery stones. You were blameless in your ways from the day you were created till wickedness was found in you. Through your widespread trade you were filled with violence, and you sinned. So I drove you in disgrace from the mount of God. ... Your heart became proud on account of your beauty, and you corrupted your wisdom because of your splendor. So I threw you to the earth. ... By your many sins and dishonest trade you have desecrated your sanctuaries (Ezekiel 28:12, 14-18).

Satan is not alone in his mission to overthrow God's plan. He has an elaborate army of fallen angels to do his evil bidding. However, no force, no army—spiritual or human—is more powerful than God and His angelic forces.

Why is it important for us to know our enemy? Unless we know that he is a real and viable force, we will be deceived by his sinful, dark intent. While we are called by God to focus on Christ and His victory, we also must remain alert to the devil's schemes.

The way you avoid evil is by realizing that Satan is an angel of light. His beauty was equal to no other angelic being. We may not understand how something that appears innocent can be so deadly. This is the enemy's goal—deception and spiritual death. Be relentless in your quest for holiness so you will be blameless in God's sight.

For we are not unaware of [Satan's] schemes (2 Corinthians 2:11).

The Daily Way

Your Enemy's Chain of Command

In his book Prayer Shield, Peter Wagner documents how Satanists gather in different parts of the United States and Canada to pray against Christian leaders. They have identified key pastors and are targeting them for failure and destruction.

Some may find this difficult to believe. A few years ago, a professor from a noted Christian university was flying from Detroit to Boston when he noticed the man beside him praying. After the man had lifted his head and opened his eyes, the Christian professor, who also had been a pastor, leaned over and asked, "Are you a Christian?"

The man seemed shocked and said, "No. I'm not a Christian. I'm a Satanist."

The professor pushed the issue and asked the man about the nature of his prayers. The man replied, "My specific area is the pastors who live in [a certain part of the United States]." He was on his way to a convention where others like him would join together to pray against God and His people.

Satan understands hierarchy. He knows the importance of leadership. If he can entice the fall of one of God's servants, he knows the impact will be great.

You may think that when you sin, no one is hurt but you. However, the ripple effects of sin flow out in every direction. If a national leader sins, the entire nation is affected. Who can ever forget Adolf Hitler? Be assured: Satan knows the formula for failure, death, and destruction.

For the child of God, there is victory and freedom from every form of bondage. If you are struggling with a certain sin, you can be free. When you turn to Jesus Christ and place your trust in Him, a door of hope will open before you. He will provide a way of escape!

When you are tempted, he will also provide a way out so that you can stand up under it (1 Corinthians 10:13).

March 4

The Daily Way

All About Angels

Some people mistakenly believe that because we cannot see into God's heavenly realm, it does not exist. But it does, and there are at least five things that we need to know about its residents, God's heavenly host, and their abilities:

- Angels have individual personalities. They have the capacity for intellect, emotion, free will, and personality. Each one has an identity. The focus of their existence is to worship and to praise God.
- Angels never die.
- Angels do possess bodies, but not physical bodies. Their bodies are terrestrial or celestial. Heavenly bodies are incorruptible and indestructible. Concerning time and space, these bodies have no limitation. One day, we also will have heavenly bodies.
- Angels were created to live within a heavenly sphere.
- Angels are divided into different ranks. Each one has responsibilities. In Colossians 1:16, we learn that angels are divided into four different categories: thrones, powers, rulers, and authorities.

Just as there are heavenly hosts carrying out the mission of God, there are also fallen angels working to create sin and havoc among believers. Their dark commander has given them a directive. They will shadow your every footstep, follow you around every turn, attack your every plan, try to foil your prayer life, invade your thoughts with lies and temptations, hinder your testimony, and discourage you on every front.

However, God is your strong tower. He has a plan for your life. When you ask Him to save you from sin, He does. Freely, He gives new life.

He will command his angels concerning you, and they will lift you up in their hands, so that you will not strike your foot against a stone (Matthew 4:6).

The Daily Way

March 5

Your Enemy Is Deceitful

There is an underhanded way to sell products called the bait-and-switch method. Here is how it works: A retailer entices a person to purchase an item. Yet when the consumer gets ready to buy the product, he is told that there are no more in inventory.

Immediately, the deceptive retailer tries to sell the consumer another product that is inferior to the one first offered. If the consumer buys it, the retailer makes a handsome profit, while the customer is swindled.

In the same way, false teachers use biblical words to capture attention and gain the trust of someone seeking Jesus Christ. They use trusted terms to lure people away from the salvation message of Jesus Christ. Essentially, they are the masters of the bait-and-switch method.

Deception is a principal tool used by the enemy. Names such as devil and Satan are significant words because they mean "deceiver" and "slanderer."

Like the false teachers in the New Testament, those who seek to deceive us through misguided religious interpretation have one goal, and that is to keep us from establishing an intimate relationship with the Lord. Satan directs them because he wants to deceive us into believing there is another way to know God other than the one God has given us through Jesus Christ.

It has been said that Satan is not fighting churches, he is joining them! He can do more harm by sowing tares than by pulling up wheat. How do you become spiritually "in tune" to God? Ask Him to make you sensitive to His voice. Refuse to listen to or to spend time with ideologies that do not line up with the Word of God.

Watch out that you are not deceived. For many will come in my name (Luke 21:8).

March 6

The Daily Way

Your Enemy Is a Liar

Here are some of the lies Satan diabolically uses to deceive God's people:

- He interjects, "Doesn't God want every baby to be a 'wanted' baby?" Obviously, the answer is "yes." Then he whispers his lie, "Well, if a baby is not wanted, then abortion is a merciful answer."

Abortion is wrong, but the enemy consistently seeks ways to lead us into compromising God's truth.

- The enemy will say, "You're having problems in your marriage, right?" To which the person will answer, "Yes."

Then he provides his evil solution. "God wants you to be happy. The person you are with does not understand you. In fact, she doesn't love you, but your co-worker—the one who sits and listens to your every word and laughs at all your jokes—loves you. She will make you happy."

Half of all Christian marriages end in divorce, but this does not have to be true of yours. Stand firm in your faith. If you are struggling, there is help. When you seek Him, God will provide a solution to your broken life. Remember, there is never a time when adultery is acceptable.

- Satan tries to confuse us by saying, "Do you really think that a loving God will send people to hell? Go ahead, live life as you want. God is good. He will not send you to hell." It is true that God does not "send" anyone to hell. We choose between heaven and hell when we decide to either follow Jesus Christ or to be entrapped by Satan's deceitful folly.

If you feel that you have drifted from God, then you can turn back to Him right now. Tell Him that you need His help. There is hope for your future because Jesus lives.

The Spirit clearly says that in later times some will abandon the faith and follow deceiving spirits and things taught by demons (1 Timothy 4:1).

The Daily Way

March 7

Your Enemy's Camouflage

One day, a famous English art critic took his daughter to the ocean. No matter how hard he tried, he could not persuade her to join him in the chilly waters of the Atlantic. He built a fire, heated a teakettle of water, and with a great flourish, poured the steaming water into the ocean. At that point and without further hesitation, the child ran gleefully into the icy waters.

This was a father's harmless trick. However, this is exactly what the enemy does with us. He mixes small amounts of truth into an ocean of falsehood, and people wade into the icy pool, not realizing that they have been deceived.

When Satan first came to Eve, he didn't come as a result of a whim or an "out of the blue" decision. He knew what he was doing. Also, understand that before the fall of man, the serpent was not a frightening creature. In fact, it was known for being wise and prudent.

In the Garden of Eden, Satan took on the form of prudence, wisdom, logic, common sense, social acceptability, and conformity. He uses this method with us today. When Eve stepped aside to listen to the enemy's lies, she made a horrifying mistake. She fell for the tempter's plan and took the first step toward repudiating God's authority.

Today, he tempts us to question God's plan and design for our lives. However, you do not have to be trapped by the snare of the enemy. Through Christ, who lives in you through the power and presence of the Holy Spirit, you can turn away from the tempter.

God's Word provides the perfect outline for dealing with the resources of the enemy. Apply its principles to your life, and you will walk in true freedom.

When [Satan] lies, he speaks his native language, for he is a liar and the father of lies (John 8:44).

March 8

The Daily Way

Your Enemy's Masquerade

A legend is told of a fifth-century Egyptian monk. He was known as a holy man, one who lived a righteous life in a desert monastery. Satan's demons tried to tempt him—to trip him in his devotion to God or to entice him to sin—but they failed.

Satan became angry at the incompetence of his minions and became personally involved in the situation. He began by lecturing the demons. "The reason you have failed is that your methods are too crude for such a man," he said. "Watch me, and you will see a master in action."

Then Satan approached the holy man of God and whispered softly in his ear, "Your brother has been made bishop of Alexandria." Instantly, the holy man's face changed to one that reflected envy and jealousy.

A great smirk formed on the enemy's mouth as his eyes tightened with pleasure. Then he turned to his demonic forces and snapped, "You see, envy and spiritual pride are the best weapons to use against those who seek holiness."

If you are attempting to walk with God, be advised that Satan will not abandon his quest to bring ruin to your life. If you are thinking that he is only interested in "big," immoral sins, then you are in for a surprise. He is the author of envy, discord, doubt, confusion, and jealousy, along with every form of perversion.

Therefore, the apostle Paul reminds us to stay alert to God's truth. Do not be unaware of the enemy's schemes formed against you (2 Corinthians 2:11).

Forgive those who have wronged you so that you may not be tempted to cave in to bitterness or anger. Maintain a God-centered focus, and ask the Lord to reveal any form of deception that you may have entertained.

Satan himself masquerades as an angel of light (2 Corinthians 11:14).

The Daily Way — March 9

False Light

The very name Lucifer is taken from the word light or luciferous, which means "bringing light" or "illumination." In Satan's case, it is a false light—one that deceives rather than illuminates the truth.

The reason the enemy appears as an angel of light is because he has programmed himself to imitate God. Satan wants us to believe that he is as powerful as God. The Bible does describe him as the "god of this world," and there are millions of people who unknowingly follow him and his leading each and every day.

Paul, however, was intent on bringing true light to the Gospel message. He reminds each one of us that we were once "dead in [our] transgressions and sins, in which [we] used to live when [we] followed the ways of this world and of the ruler of the kingdom of the air, the spirit who is now at work in those who are disobedient" (Ephesians 2:1-2).

However, the fact is that Christ has set us free from the bondage of sin. This does not give us the occasion to boast or to drop our guard. Every gift God gives, Satan counterfeits. Every blessing God provides, Satan seeks to pervert and distort. Every miracle the Lord performs, Satan tries to imitate.

Satan appears to the naïve as an angel of light. Yet to those who are alert and discerning, he seeks to distort the truth about his nature. Godly discernment is one of the most powerful tools available to the believer. If you feel as though the enemy is deceiving you, pray and ask God to open your eyes to His truth.

Be willing to lay aside any plans that are not God's best plans for your life. He may not provide all the answers for every step you will take in the future. But there is one thing He will do: When you ask, He will provide the discernment you need for the challenges you are facing today.

God placed all things under his feet (Ephesians 1:22).

March 10

The Daily Way

A Roaring Lion

After checking with those who work with wild animals, I was told that there are three reasons lions roar:
- They roar when strange animals hunt in their territory.
- Lions sound a roar of triumph after they have captured their prey.
- Lions roar loudest when caught in a storm. They cannot tolerate the flashing lightning or the clashing of thunder.

Peter concludes his first epistle by drawing a word picture of Satan as a lion constantly on the move, prowling around and roaring each time a careless Christian falls victim to his deception.

This is why Peter admonishes us to "be self-controlled and alert. Your enemy the devil prowls around like a roaring lion looking for someone to devour" (1 Peter 5:8).

Being alert is the antithesis of being in a drunken stupor. Each week, there are reports of people who have died as a result of being hit by drunk drivers. People who drink and drive have impaired mental and physical capacities. They cannot react properly to their circumstances and end up causing deadly accidents.

Peter is telling us that sin can numb your spiritual senses to a point where you are no longer spiritually sober. Your reaction time is affected and you fall victim to Satan's ploy.

In contrast, person who is spiritually alert views life according to God's principles and values. Spiritually, alertness means being aware of approaching danger and having the determination to avoid it.

When it comes to the enemy, be very serious-minded. Don't be flippant about his intentions. His desire is clear: to destroy your testimony and life for Christ. Therefore, stand firm in your faith. Commit yourself to prayer and you will gain the victory!

Be self-controlled and alert (1 Peter 5:8).

The Daily Way

March 11

Negotiate With a Bear?

This is only a legend, but the principle is very true: There was a hunter who had taken aim at a very large and angry bear. The hunter was ready to pull the trigger of his rifle when he heard the bear speak in a soothing voice, "Isn't it better to talk than to shoot? Why don't we negotiate this matter? What do you want?"

The hunter lowered his rifle and answered, "I would like a fur coat."

The bear said, "This is good. I think there is something we can do about that. All I want is a full stomach. Maybe we can compromise."

So they sat down to talk. A little while later, the bear walked away alone. The negotiations had been successful. The bear had his full stomach, and the hunter had his fur coat!

There are many believers who think it is perfectly acceptable to enter a spiritual dialogue with the enemy. They lower their weapons and negotiate. But Peter admonishes us to be vigilant and firm in our faith (1 Peter 5:8-9).

After the successful battle of Jericho, Joshua learned a painful lesson regarding the enemy's tactics. He discovered that the consequences of sin are destruction—spiritual and physical.

The next battle on Israel's list was the little town of Ai, which should have led to an easy victory (Joshua 7). However, sin had entered the camp of God's people. Joshua, celebrating his victory at Jericho, ceased from being sober, prayerful, and alert. He did not consecrate himself or remain watchful. As a result, many of his soldiers died in battle.

The moment Joshua turned to the Lord seeking forgiveness, God revealed the problem and the solution. Are you remaining diligent in your devotion to Christ, or have you drifted spiritually?

Place God at the center of your life. Let Him be the One you turn to each day, and you will find the truth you need to handle every situation.

Be strong in the Lord and in his mighty power (Ephesians 6:10).

March 12

The Daily Way

Your Enemy's Intentions

When you have a sleepless night, what do you do? Do you get up from your bed, turn on the television, and try to avoid facing your problems? Do you allow your mind to replay old tapes of the day's events, or do you stop and pray?

Many times, Satan is the one who awakens us at night, telling us what we have yet to do or reminding us of the things we have done wrong. If God wakes you up at night, you can be sure His instruction will be swift, never condemning, and always based on the truth of His Word.

Satan, however, uses lies and temptation to work out his plan in our lives. He enjoys tempting us into doubting God's goodness. He likes to lure us away from the truth of Scripture, while getting us to respond to his lying words.

To be prepared for the enemy's attacks, it is important to remain vigilant in our spiritual walk. When we turn to Scripture, we find that King David did not take this advice. The Lord had given David victory after victory. He even proclaimed that David was a "man after His own heart."

For years, David had lived in the light of God's blessings. He was conscious of God's abiding presence and personal love. But he made a horrible mistake. He became careless in his devotion to the Lord. He fell for Satan's trap, and on a sleepless night he took a stroll on his rooftop instead of going into the temple to pray (2 Samuel 11). Adultery left its mark on his life and on the lives of his family members.

While God's forgiveness is always available to us, His greatest desire is that we avoid Satan's entrapments. Remain faithful in your worship and in your devotion to the Lord. Pray that the Lord will guard your heart in all that you do.

He who walks with the wise grows wise (Proverbs 13:20).

The Daily Way

March 13

Are You Stuck in the Mud?

There was an old farmer who frequently described his Christian experience by saying, "I am not making progress, but I am established."

One spring day he was hauling some logs and his wagon wheels sank in mud down to the axle. He tried, but could not get the wagon out. Defeated—he sat on top of the logs.

One of his neighbors saw him and said to the farmer, "I see that you are not making much progress, but you must be content because you are well-established."

Is your testimony like the farmer's? Your salvation may be established, but you may be "stuck" and unproductive. You may be a child of God, but is your Christian walk like wheels stuck in mud? You know God and have made Him a part of your life, but are you growing in your personal relationship with Him?

The devil thrives on keeping you from growing in faith, from being productive in your Christianity, from comprehending and applying the Word of God in your daily life.

Satan wants to keep you focused on your problems, pain, and worries. His goal is to prevent the effectiveness of God's Word in your life. "For the word of God is living and active. Sharper than any double-edged sword, it penetrates even to dividing soul and spirit, joints and marrow; it judges the thoughts and attitudes of the heart" (Hebrews 4:12).

Satan knows the Word of God is powerful—to change lives, to convict of sin, to judge and condemn, to encourage and strengthen, to lift and uphold, to forgive and restore, to produce fruit, and, most of all, to accomplish God's purpose. When God's Word is a significant part of your life, Satan's mission against you will be destroyed.

Today, if you hear [God's] voice, do not harden your hearts (Hebrews 4:7).

March 14

The Daily Way

Preparing the Soil

In Middle Eastern farming, there is a pathway between two fields. It is the boundary. It is the place where hard-packed earth is found. It is the strip in the field where the soil is not prepared for receiving the seed.

The parable of the sower in Matthew 13 tells us that Jesus is the sower and your heart is the soil. Satan seeks to work on the soil on which the seed of the Word is planted. If he can, he will harden the soil of your life. Many times he does this by getting you to substitute human wisdom for God's Word. Then he succeeds in snatching away the good seed of the Gospel.

Have you ever known a person to be excited about sharing his faith with others, only to have someone make fun of him? Soon he is no longer sharing his faith at all.

If Satan cannot keep the Word of God from taking hold in your life, then he will use any means to pull you away from growing your relationship with God. Unconfessed sin, unforgiveness, and bitterness will harden your heart.

When Mahmud of Ghazni invaded India, his conquering forces entered a celebrated Hindu temple to destroy its idols. The temple priests entreated Mahmud to spare a certain idol, but he refused. Instead, he struck such a blow to the image that it burst open and precious stones cascaded from the hollow interior.

In many ways, this is true in your life. When you cling tightly to bitterness, anger, resentment, and unforgiveness, elevating them above your relationship with God, they become "idols" in your life. For each idol you are willing to destroy, you will gain more than you lose. Each time you surrender something to God, you will remove another hindrance to a productive life of faith and prayer. Every idol that is demolished will bring you new treasures of grace and peace.

Some people are like seed along the path, where the word is sown. As soon as they hear it, Satan comes and takes away the word that was sown in them (Mark 4:15).

The Daily Way

March 15

God's Scrambling Squadrons

During World War II, immediately after the collapse of France, Hitler moved to invade England. His Operation Sea Lion included a massive formation of bombers and fighters covering the English sky.

The British Royal Air Force (RAF) realized that there was only one way to deal with this sinister attack—higher altitude. When the pilots would get the command to "scramble" from the radar operators, it meant for them to get above the attacking German planes. These pilots became known as the "Scrambling Squadrons."

They understood that there could be no victory without high altitude. They knew that they could not blow the enemy's planes out of the sky unless they were at a higher altitude.

Back then, for the RAF fighter pilots, there was no such thing as instant altitude. But this is not so for God's "scrambling squadrons." As a child of God, you are given the privilege and the power to have instant altitude from any and every situation. When Jesus rose from the dead, He was at the highest altitude possible. He was above Satan—high above all the forces of evil.

The Bible says that those who are in Christ Jesus are seated with Him in heavenly places (Ephesians 2:6). In Christ you have been raised to the highest altitude possible. There you have victory over Satan.

Satan's craftiness and cunning can pull you down from that position. He wants you to lose your position of faith, your posture of obedience, and your power to trust. His goal is to keep you from doing the will of God. In order to stay above the enemy, you must be sustained by God's Word and only worship Jesus Christ.

Now to him who is able to do immeasurably more than all we ask or imagine, according to his power that is at work within us (Ephesians 3:20).

March 16

The Daily Way

The World, the Flesh, and the Devil

A spoiled little boy was throwing a temper tantrum. He was angry because the housekeeper would not let him have a valuable vase from the cabinet. Hearing him cry loudly, his mother went into the room to find out what was wrong.

The boy said, "I want that," pointing to the vase.

The mother said, "Yes, darling, you shall have it," falsely thinking this was how to make her son happy. But when she put the vase in front of him, the little boy cried even louder.

"What do you want now?" asked the mother.

Between sobs, the boy said, "I want something I can't have."

The apostle John explains that Satan can attack you in three ways—the lust of the flesh, the lust of the eye, and the pride of life (1 John 2:16). His attacks have also been described as inner selfishness, envy, and pride.

Satan is not merely interested in tempting you. He knows if he can get you to see something and to desire it, then ultimately it will have your affections and loyalty.

When you find yourself facing temptation, ask: Is it appealing to my selfish nature? Is it appealing to my covetous nature? Is it appealing to my pride?

Satan tempted Jesus in the wilderness, but the enemy could not overcome the Lord. As long as you are in the wilderness and at the center of God's will, He will sustain you.

The secret of Christ's victory also is the secret to your victory. Recognize the nature of the spiritual battle facing you, and use God's Word to resist the devil. When Satan appeals to your flesh, tell him that in Christ you have all of your sufficiency.

My grace is sufficient for you, for my power is made perfect in weakness (2 Corinthians 12:9).

The Daily Way

March 17

Be a Winner

Coach Bear Bryant is known as a football legend. But more than anything else, he is remembered as a winner. At the end of his 38-season career, he held six national championships and more victories than any other coach in college football history.

In a tribute to Coach Bryant in the February 19, 1983, issue of National Review, Victor Gold wrote, "Like all authentic Southern legends, he was of the soil."

Bryant once said, "If I hadn't found football, I would have ended up behind a mule just like my daddy. But I will tell you one thing: I would have plowed the straightest furrow in Arkansas."

Somebody asked Bryant if he considered himself an innovator or a trendsetter.

"No," Bryant replied, "I'm nothing but a winner."

This winning attitude and winning career says something very important to you as a believer. When Jesus died on the cross, He declared Satan's power to be no longer invincible. As a victor in a battle takes away the spoils of victory from his enemy, Jesus took away the privileges of Satan. "Having disarmed the powers and authorities, he made a public spectacle of them, triumphing over them by the cross" (Colossians 2:15).

Because of the cross, the barrier of sin that once separated you from God has been removed. The gulf of sin has been bridged. The death that characterizes your fate has been taken away, and through Christ you have been made alive.

Wherever you are spiritually today, you can be a winner. Satan has no power over you. When Christ died on the cross and rose again, He was saying to you, "Be a winner."

I press on toward the goal to win the prize for which God has called me heavenward in Christ Jesus (Philippians 3:14).

March 18

The Daily Way

Paid in Full

In Colossians 2, the apostle Paul presents a magnificent picture of how the Roman legal system worked. Under strict legal procedure, the Roman authorities would interrogate a witness.

Then his testimony had to be substantiated before the Roman court could bring his case. When the indictment had been handed down and the case came to trial, it was necessary for the accuser to stand in the presence of the accused to give his testimony before the judge.

Your accuser is none other than Satan. The Bible says that the wages of sin is death (Romans 6:23). When Satan comes before God as your accuser, he points out your sin. His accusations are just and true. There is no one righteous, for all have sinned and come short of the glory of God (Romans 3:23).

However, Jesus came and died on the cross to take away the penalty of your transgressions.

A judge cannot dismiss an indictment if it is true. The Pharisees brought forth accusations against Jesus, and Pontius Pilate tried to wash his hands of the whole affair (Matthew 27:24).

In Christ's day, when a criminal was convicted and sentenced, an official writing was drawn up by the courts. In it would be an explanation of the crime and its penalty. That is why Pontius Pilate had written on Jesus' cross: "Jesus of Nazareth, the King of the Jews" (John 19:19). When a man finished serving his sentence and was released, his indictment would be taken down. A judge would write across it Telelestai which means, "paid in full."

As Jesus Christ hung on the cross, He cried out, "It is finished" (John 19:30). If you have committed your life to Jesus Christ and have accepted Him as your Savior, Satan has no legal right against you. You have won the victory!

Everyone born of God overcomes the world. This is the victory that has overcome the world, even our faith (1 John 5:4).

The Daily Way — March 19

The Unwelcome Guest

Suppose that one day you open the door of your house and there stands a seven-foot, 300-pound man who pushes his way into your home. Before you can say anything, he makes himself comfortable in your favorite chair. When you politely ask him why he is in your house, he avoids answering your question.

You ask him to leave, but he won't. After dinner and after he has eaten most of your food, he considers departing. Your family is waiting for him to go. Suddenly, he announces that he is going to stay and moves into your bedroom. Fed up, you decide to call the police.

If you allow Satan into your life because of weakness or sin, then he will come in, take over, and bring defeat and oppression. He will not want to leave you alone. He will be like the unwelcome guest who takes over your home and refuses to leave.

The good news is that instead of waiting for the police to arrive, you have instant access to the One who has already defeated Satan. When Jesus died on the cross, He gave you the legal right to be a winner over Satan.

To know Christ is to experience forgiveness of sin. You can be assured of eternal life. If you fail to accept Christ as your Savior, then you will undergo the constant accusation of Satan forever and ever. Our subtle enemy knows that he has no authority to defeat you unless you give him that authority.

When Satan tempts you to feel sorry for yourself, when he tries to defeat you by having others attack you or criticize you unfairly, when he tries to get you to do your will and not God's will—tell him no. It is finished—paid for and canceled.

Satan cannot harass or push his way into your life. You are a winner. God desires for you to be a winner, and He has made it possible.

May the God of hope fill you with all joy and peace ... so that you may overflow with hope by the power of the Holy Spirit (Romans 15:13).

March 20

The Daily Way

The Day I Died

George Müller, an esteemed evangelist and prayer warrior of the nineteenth century, was once asked, "What is the secret of your victorious life?"

His answer was simple. "It was the day I died, utterly died."

As he spoke, Müller bent down until he reached the floor and then continued:

> Died to George Müller—his opinions, preferences, tastes, and will. Died to the world—its approval or censure. Died to approval or blame—even of my brethren and friends. Since then I have studied only to show myself approved unto God.

Until you learn to die to self, you will live your Christian life in defeat. Until you learn to die to sin, you will live in bondage. Until you learn to die to pride, you will live in slavery and servitude.

If any believer feels defeated, it is because he has bought into the lie of believing that Satan has invincible power over him. As a child of God, you do not need to be in bondage. James 4:7 commands, "Submit yourselves, then, to God. Resist the devil, and he will flee from you."

When James says, "Resist the devil, and he will flee from you," it does not mean that you are standing in the battle arena and being beaten. Rather, it is a picture of a general who has defeated his enemy and calls out to his officers to clean house.

Your commanding general arose from the dead, ascended into heaven, and is at the Father's right hand—with angels, authorities, and powers in submission to Him (1 Peter 3:22).

When you are joined with Christ, you have the same authority. You can break out of bondage. You can give up a sinful habit. You can be freed from an addiction—by the power of Christ.

You have been given fullness in Christ, who is the head over every power and authority (Colossians 2:10).

The Daily Way — March 21

Keep Satan Fleeing

In Matthew 8:28, Jesus entered the region of Gadarenes and confronted two demon-possessed men. Upon seeing Jesus, the demons in the men cried out, "Are you here to torment us before the time?" The word torment here means "consignment to eternal punishment."

These demons stood face-to-face with Jesus Christ. They recognized He was their judge and they were eternally condemned. Revelation 12:12 states:

> Therefore rejoice, you heavens and you who dwell in them! But woe to the earth and the sea, because the devil has gone down to you! He is filled with fury, because he knows that his time is short.

No wonder the apostle Paul could say in 2 Corinthians 2:14, "Thanks be to God, who always leads us in triumphal procession in Christ." On the cross, Jesus made salvation possible through the shedding of His blood. He came forth as the victor so that you might walk in His triumph. Christ not only provides for salvation from the condemnation of sin, but also protects you from the onslaught of the evil one.

When you are undergoing a satanic attack—whether it is temptation to sin, an attack on your emotions, oppression or depression, or a cooling off of your love for Jesus Christ—pray and ask the Lord to minister His truth to you. Your victory is not based on your net worth or who you are. Your victory is based on the death and the resurrection of Jesus Christ.

God has called you to cover yourself with the armor of God so that you can stand against the devil's schemes (Ephesians 6). He has called you to stand against Satan's attack, believing what the Word of God says about your victory. When you resist the devil and he flees from you, heaven rejoices.

Resist [Satan], standing firm in the faith (1 Peter 5:9).

March 22

The Daily Way

Your Enemy's Future

A traveler in New Mexico saw a Native American with his head to the ground as if he was listening. The traveler heard him muttering, "Wagon, one driver, two passengers, and two horses."

The traveler was absolutely amazed and said to the Native American, "You mean to tell me that you can tell all of this by listening to the ground?"

"No," was the reply. "They just ran over me a few minutes ago."

There are many believers who have been run over by Satan and do not know how to get up and fight back.

There was a camel driver who was taking a caravan across the desert for a few days' journey. One morning the driver said to his companions, "We had intruders last night." They looked at him in amazement and asked how he could tell, when they had neither heard nor seen anyone. He pointed to the tracks in the sand the intruder left behind.

If anyone does not believe in Satan, let him open his eyes to the tracks he leaves—broken homes and devastated families. As a believer in Jesus Christ, you are given authority over Satan. He is a defeated foe.

However, Jesus does not prevent him from attacking believers. In John 12, Jesus reminds His disciples that Satan is a vanquished foe. Jesus said, "Now is the time for judgment on this world; now the prince of this world will be driven out" (John 12:31).

After Jesus' resurrection, Satan's sentence was passed down. Now it is a matter of waiting for God's timing to carry out the sentence. When Jesus returns, He will execute His judgment against Satan.

While there is no mistaking Satan's future, your eternal future can be decided by committing your life to the ultimate Victor, the only One who offers eternal life—Jesus Christ.

God has given us eternal life, and this life is in his Son (1 John 5:11).

The Daily Way

March 23

The Reality of Hell

There was once a preacher by the name of Peter Cartwright. One morning before Cartwright was to preach, he was told that General Andrew Jackson was going to be in the service and was asked not to say anything to offend him.

When Cartwright got up to preach, he said: "I am told that General Andrew Jackson is in the congregation. Andrew Jackson will go to hell if he does not commit his life to Jesus Christ."

People were aghast. But after the service was over, Jackson approached Cartwright and shook his hand, saying, "If I had 100 men like you in my regiment, I could take on the world."

Satan does not want to hear preachers talking about the lake of fire. He does not want people to be told that unless they repent and believe in the Lord Jesus Christ, they will spend eternity in hell with Satan.

In Matthew 25:41, Jesus teaches about the reality of hell. He warns that hell is an eternal separation from God. It is a place of impenetrable darkness, uninterrupted pain, and unquenchable fire. He also warns that those who reject Him will spend eternity there.

The lake of fire was created by God to be the eternal destination of Satan and his fallen angels. When Adam sinned against God, his destiny changed, along with the destiny of mankind. He no longer had access to the presence of God. However, the Lord, in His infinite grace, provided a sacrifice for Adam's sin.

Today, through Christ, God has provided a way for our sins to be eradicated. When you confess your sin and accept Him as your Lord and Savior, your eternal destination changes from hell to heaven. Rejoice in the Lord, for He has been good to you.

Fight the good fight of the faith. Take hold of the eternal life to which you were called (1 Timothy 6:12).

March 24

The Daily Way

Satan's Final Destination

A group of Americans was touring Mount Vesuvius in Italy, which was active with volcanic eruptions. One woman, completely awed by the sight of the seething mass of lava and steam, shouted, "It is just like hell."

One of the Italian villagers standing nearby said to his friend, "These Americans tourists have been everywhere."

Hell is a destination like no other. Satan's future in hell is described in Revelation 20:10: "The devil, who deceived them, was thrown into the lake of burning sulfur, where the beast and the false prophet had been thrown. They will be tormented day and night for ever and ever."

Jesus spoke about the intense suffering of those who will be confined to the lake of fire. He also emphasized the fact that there will be no escape. The symbol of fire is God-given and is used to impress on our minds the horrors of hell. When hell is referred to as a lake of fire, God is accommodating our finite minds, our inability to comprehend all things, our ignorance.

Jesus compares hell to a prison (Matthew 18:34-35). Earthly prisons confine the body, but the spirit remains free. Hell is called an abyss (Luke 8:31), indicating the impossibility of escape or a second chance. It is also described as utter darkness (Matthew 22:13) and as a place where fire will not be quenched (Matthew 13:40-42).

C.S. Lewis writes, "There are no personal relationships in hell." However, God, through grace, has made provision for you to come to a saving knowledge of Him. If you have never met the Savior, today is a good day to pray and ask Him to forgive your sins and to place within your life a sense of eternal hope.

For God did not appoint us to suffer wrath but to receive salvation through our Lord Jesus Christ (1 Thessalonians 5:9).

The Daily Way

March 25

Deliver Us from Pride

Each day our prayer should be, "Lord, deliver me from evil."

Many times, this becomes a routine prayer and we forget that the evil we face is the result of Satan's handiwork. We quickly cry out to God when we are under spiritual attack or when we are the object of someone's mistreatment. However, we often forget to prepare for the enemy's assaults through prayer before they hit. You can pray, "Lord, deliver me from the evil one."

When David was young, his heart was set on godly obedience. When victory came, he honored God through prayer and praise. But after he became king, he allowed pride to find a place of residence in his heart.

In 1 Chronicles 21, David decided to number the people of Israel. It was not enough for him to know that God had given him the nation to rule; he wanted to take pride in the size of his kingdom. While Moses had numbered the people as a way of taking a census, David numbered them as a way to boast in the vastness of his empire.

Satan had devised a way to tempt God's servant to sin. But David quickly realized what he had done and rushed to repent and to seek God's restoration. His sin, however, had a major impact on the nation of Israel. Thousands died innocently because David had allowed his heart to be tempted.

Pride is a subtle but deadly enemy. When you sense that pride has you feeling smug about your life, remember that Christ died on the cross for you. Nothing you have to offer has the ability to save you from an eternal death. It is God's grace that saves you. Therefore, lay aside every hint of pride and ask God to deliver you from everything that would prevent you from receiving His true blessing.

Humble yourselves, therefore, under God's mighty hand, that he may lift you up in due time (1 Peter 5:6).

March 26

The Daily Way

Defend Your Soul

Without realizing it, many Christians have allowed Satan to establish strongholds in their lives. One of the greatest hindrances to living a godly life is carnality, which can prevent us from praying and knowing the mind of God. If left unattended, carnality can build power bases of self-centeredness deep within our hearts and minds.

When we study God's Word, we quickly discover that prayer is instrumental in dissolving carnality and the desires that go with it. In fact, prayer is the primary key to uncovering and pulling down every stronghold Satan seeks to establish in the life of a believer.

In the Greek translation, the word stronghold literally means "fortress." In other words, the enemy of our souls seeks to set up a fortress within our lives to prevent us from discovering God's will and from living for Jesus Christ. For example, worry and fear are emotions each of us has experienced. When these become obsessions, we quickly realize that a stronghold has been established. Uncontrollable lust, hate, anger, and bitterness are strongholds that can lead us further from God's will for our lives.

However, we are not without a strong defense. There is hope because we have been given a powerful weapon. Prayer equips us for spiritual victory. Therefore, we do not have to battle against an enemy greater than we are. God fights for us through prayer. As evidence of this, read what Paul has written to us in 2 Corinthians 10:3-11.

Our weapons are not carnal; they are not of the flesh. They are supernatural and powerful, able to tear down the dark fortresses of the enemy. Don't hesitate to call out to your heavenly Father who loves you with an unconditional love.

They overcame [Satan] by the blood of the Lamb and by the word of their testimony (Revelation 12:11).

The Daily Way — March 27

The "Devil's" Mail

Many times, we can lose our spiritual footing by focusing on the wrongs that have been done to us. Our prayer life suffers and we lose our sense of joy. We also can forget how to praise God because we are entrapped by our angry thoughts and insecurities.

Don't allow yourself to be snared by Satan's trickery. Instead, set the focus of your heart on Christ. Remain close to Him, and seek His wisdom concerning your situation. Don't hesitate to tell Him that you do not know how to handle the hurt you are feeling.

Many times, a result of focusing on your problems is that you will begin to "fake" your spirituality. Your devotion will not be true or sincere. God knows our hearts. He is aware of temptations we face. He knows when the enemy has whispered lies to us, telling us that others are speaking badly about us. Be aware of this profound truth: The man or the woman who seeks to hurt you or your reputation is merely the enemy's bagman. He or she is merely delivering the devil's mail. When you understand this, you will not be tempted to hate others or to become embittered.

Always guard your heart. Never allow the words of those who attempt to wound to you find a resting place in your life. In fact, by keeping your eyes set on the Lord, you will discover a way to love and to pray for your persecutors—just as Jesus asked us to do in Matthew 5:44.

Despite David's many trials and temptations, he knew in whom to place his confidence: "The Lord is my light and my salvation—whom shall I fear? The Lord is the stronghold of my life—of whom shall I be afraid?" (Psalm 27:1). In times of weakness and testing, remember that God is your strength and confidence. No one who places his or her hope in Him will be disappointed!

For in the day of trouble he will keep me safe in his dwelling; he will hide me in the shelter of his tabernacle (Psalm 27:5).

March 28

The Daily Way

The Greatest Fortress

Deep in the Arabian desert is a small fortress. It stands silently on the vast expanse of the ageless desert. Thomas Edward Lawrence, known as Lawrence of Arabia, often used it. Though unpretentious, it was most efficient. Its main commendation was its security. When under attack, often by superior forces, Lawrence would retreat there for safety.

While staying there, the resources of the fortress became his—the food and the water stored there were life-supporting. The strength of the fortress became the strength of its occupants. Old-time desert dwellers talked about how confident and secure Lawrence always felt when he was within the walls of the fortress.

Prayer is the believer's greatest fortress. It is a place we can run to any time of the day or night. The strength and protection we receive in God's presence are unmatched by this world. The name of Jesus and His blood are even more assuring than walls made of stone, iron, or concrete.

In Matthew, Jesus provides tremendous insight on how to stand against the enemy's attacks:

> I tell you the truth, whatever you bind on earth will be bound in heaven, and whatever you loose on earth will be loosed in heaven. Again, I tell you that if two of you on earth agree about anything you ask for, it will be done for you by my Father in heaven. For where two or three come together in my name, there am I with them (Matthew 18:18-19).

He has provided a supreme place of safety for you. Whenever confusion, fear, or feelings of doubt assail your mind, turn to Him. Pray for His protection to surround you and ask Him to provide the strength you need to stand firm against any and all deception.

Call upon me in the day of trouble; I will deliver you, and you will honor me (Psalm 50:15).

The Daily Way

March 29

The Subtle Sin of Compromise

"The safest road to hell," wrote C.S. Lewis, "is the gradual one—the gentle slope, one that is soft underfoot, without sudden turnings, without milestones, without signposts."

Many Christians do not believe that they can or will ever drift away from God. They see their devotion as being solid. However, compromise and a lack of spiritual discipline quickly open the door to temptation and sin.

Once we accept Christ as our Savior, the enemy knows his work of eternal destruction has been thwarted. However, he is relentless in his effort to work havoc in the lives of God's people. Therefore, he goes to work in a different way. He knows that he cannot have our souls, but he remains committed to destroying our lives.

One of his greatest weapons against the body of Christ is pride. He seeks to tell us we are complete and worthy apart from the Lord. He wants us to feel good about our talents and abilities—so much so that we begin to make decisions without considering God's purpose and plan. Before we know it, we have believed a lie and departed from our first love, which is the love of Christ.

There is nothing wrong with knowing God has gifted you and that He is the One who is using your abilities. The story, however, changes when you begin to take life into your own hands without regard to the Savior's will.

Temptation by itself is not sin, but if left unchecked, it quickly leads to sin and broken fellowship with the Lord. You can say no to the subtle sin of compromise by asking the Lord to keep you close to Himself. Be committed to spending time in prayer with Him each day.

Prayer: Lord, forgive me for the times I have compromised my love for You.

Can a man scoop fire into his lap without his clothes being burned? (Proverbs 6:27).

March 30

The Daily Way

Our Focus in Life

When we understand that the enemy is sly and that he attacks us from many different angles, we will be able to fend him off much better. When attacks are blatant against our lives, they are easy to spot.

Maybe your marriage has become rocky or you are facing financial problems. Maybe you have stopped going to church because you were hurt by someone there. Maybe you have experienced the pain of a losing a loved one who died unexpectedly.

If we hold on to the hand of God through life's most difficult trials, we have not escaped sin's assault on our soul just yet. In an attempt to quench our passion for God and slowly steal away our intimacy with the Lord, the enemy will try to lure our focus and attention elsewhere. He may tempt you to think of things that are not overtly sinful, but the problems come when your attention does not rest on God—and that can be destructive.

As we peer into our hearts, we must be diligent to rid our lives of things that do not point to God first and foremost. Is desiring to have a better life sinful? No, it is not. However, when our focus in life becomes to upgrade our lifestyles, shifting us away from God, it does become sinful.

Throughout life, we are faced with numerous decisions, many of which are costly by the world's standards if the right decision is made. Yet, nothing in life will ever be as satisfying as following the Lord.

No matter how many things we obtain in life, no matter how many promotions we get, no matter how much fame and popularity we have—these things pale in comparison to the hope and joy we find in a relationship with Christ.

Prayer: Lord, please help me to keep my focus on You and You alone.

For you are great and do marvelous deeds; you alone are God (Psalm 86:10).

The Daily Way

March 31

Whatever the Cost

In the days leading up to World War II, Britain was all but defeated. Hitler was sending his vicious calling card by repeated bombings and threats of invasions. Repeatedly, England's Prime Minister, Winston Churchill, requested help from allied forces, but no help was sent. Countries outside Hitler's reach were hesitant to enter the conflict. Undaunted, Churchill persisted by requesting a meeting with American president Franklin Roosevelt.

In 1941, Churchill finally had his chance to meet with President Roosevelt and to present his case. While the president was stirred by the burden the British people were bearing, he was not yet convinced America should enter the war.

While Churchill was disappointed, he remained steadfast. England would not surrender. As Churchill had already stated:

> We shall not flag or fail. We shall go on to the end. We shall fight in France, we shall fight on the seas and oceans, we shall fight with growing confidence and growing strength in the air. We shall defend our island, whatever the cost may be. We shall fight on the beaches, we shall fight on the landing grounds, we shall fight in the fields and in the streets, we shall fight in the hills; we shall never surrender.

Maybe you feel as though enemy forces have gathered around your life. Do you have a fixed focus on victory? Are you willing to fight for what God has given you and for what He is calling you to do for Him? The enemy has only two words for you: surrender and defeat. Churchill did not consider either of these plausible—and neither should you. With God's help and strength, go on to victory and never give up!

Prayer: Lord, I choose Your victory for my life.

The Lord stood at my side and gave me strength (2 Timothy 4:17).

Receiving Healing Through True Spirituality

The Daily Way — April 1

Love Will Lift You

Love lifts a broken heart—not just any love, but the love of God. Most of us have sung James Rowe's hymn, "Love Lifted Me." The first verse contains these words:

> I was sinking deep in sin, far from the peaceful shore,
> Very deeply stained within, sinking to rise no more.
> But the Master of the sea heard my despairing cry,
> From the waters lifted me—now safe am I.
> Love lifted me! Love lifted me!
> When nothing else could help, love lifted me!

Sometimes nothing can lift our hearts like the love of God. Friends abandon us. Colleagues try to bypass us. Even our families may fail to understand us. But God's love for us never changes.

Even when we act unlovable, God continues to love us. When we are undesirable, He embraces us. When it seems that the world has turned against us, God's love remains. He has promised never to leave us hopeless.

Difficulties in life can certainly leave us feeling broken and confused. Many times, disappointments come in order to teach us more about the depths of God's love. In desperation, we turn to God. This is when we discover that only His love can truly lift us up and restore our sense of hope.

We may struggle to find another way around our problems, hoping that someone or something will bring relief, but nothing can help us outside the love of God. Only His love has the ability to satisfy our every need.

Maybe you are wondering if God really loves you. Have you yielded to sin? Or have you allowed the world and its trappings to come between you and your Savior? Cry out to Him and He will restore the joy of your salvation. When nothing else can help, love will lift you.

Love never fails (1 Corinthians 13:8).

April 2

God Is Love

Many things have been said and written about love. Numerous songs recount stories of love—gained, treasured, and lost. Shakespeare wrote that it is better to have loved and lost than never to have loved at all.

Each one of us has been given a tremendous ability to love.

Why? Because we were created by God, and He is love (1 John 4:16). His love is the greatest. It is an eternal love—one that is unconditional—not based on what we do or don't do. Instead, the love of God is based on one event, and that is what Christ did for us on Calvary's cross.

No matter what has happened in this life or what you will face in the future, God's love for you will never fail. When you get up in the morning, God's love embraces you. When you lie down at night, it is the love of God that is standing guard over your life. Throughout the day, God is pouring out His merciful love toward you. So great is the love of God that Paul chooses to mention it first when writing about the fruit of the Spirit (Galatians 5:22).

If we truly want to be people who love others and love God fully, then we must begin by giving Christ our lives and by asking Him to teach us how to love the way He loves us. Love is a choice that many times we can't make on our own. People will say hurtful words about us. Some will seek to harm us, and yet the love of God has the ability to cover all sin. Nothing is more powerful than God's love in our lives.

Live a life of love, just as Christ loved us and gave himself up for us as a fragrant offering and sacrifice to God (Ephesians 5:2).

The Daily Way — April 3

The Fruit of the Spirit

A fruit tree will bear fruit if the tree is healthy and if the soil is good. For exceptional fruit, the tree must be pruned. Weeds need to be pulled around its base and adequate fertilizer and water must be provided.

Similarly, bearing the fruit of the Spirit in our lives requires pruning, weeding, and fertilizing. Growth comes through studying God's Word and applying His principles to our lives. Pruning and weeding remove the attitudes and actions that are not like His.

The Holy Spirit is the One who convicts us of sin and leads us to a point of repentance. Christ is the One who fertilizes our lives with His truth and love. He gave His followers a new commandment to love one another. But this love was not to be a human love. "As I have loved you, so you must love one another" (John 13:34).

It cost God everything to demonstrate His love for us—the very death of His Son. And love, if it is sincere, will cost us something, too. It may not cost us our physical lives, but it will cost us something emotionally. This is why a commitment of love should never be given lightly nor recalled without thinking through the consequences of our decision.

God's love is strong enough to teach us how to love someone who is unlovely and harsh. How do you do this? First, begin by realizing that many times the only way we can love another person is through God. He is the only One who can teach us to love and to understand those who are hurting or who are difficult.

Second, pray. This is the key to loving others the way God loves you. Even if you find it difficult to pray, God's Holy Spirit will guide you when you humble your heart before Him (Romans 8:26).

Let us love one another, for love comes from God. Everyone who loves has been born of God and knows God (1 John 4:7).

April 4 — The Daily Way

Joy from Within

Polls and surveys consistently show that the top three things people want the most in life are love, happiness, and peace. So often we confuse happiness with joy. There is a difference.

Happiness is the result of getting what we want. We tell ourselves that we'll be happy when we get a newer home. Or life will be great if we get a promotion at work and a pay increase.

However, getting what we want only offers a temporary form of happiness that fades over time. We get our new home, and we are so happy until we realize that we, in order to remain happy, must have all the furniture and decorations to go with it. This kind of happiness is dependent on our circumstances, and can be accompanied with a fear that we may lose whatever it is we feel has made us happy.

Joy, however, is a fruit of the Spirit. It comes from within and not from external conditions. Jesus said that we are to abide in Him so that our joy can be complete (John 15:9-11). We can experience the joy of the Lord regardless of our circumstances because joy is dependent on our relationship with Jesus Christ.

The apostle Paul instructed the Philippians to rejoice always in the Lord (Philippians 4:4). While this group of believers was anxious about their material needs, Paul reminded them that their joy came from God. They were oppressed and persecuted by the Romans. They suffered economic hardships. Yet they had a reason to be joyful—their lives belonged to the Lord.

The world tries to persuade us that joy is found in material possessions, worldly achievements, and social status. However, true joy comes from the knowledge that we are saved through the death and resurrection of Christ Jesus.

May the God of hope fill you with all joy and peace as you trust in him (Romans 15:13).

The Daily Way

April 5

Joy Amid Sorrow

For the child of God, joy does not mean the absence of sadness, trials, or disappointments. In fact, in some cases it can mean the opposite. There can be joy amid sorrow. This was true of the apostle Paul's life. He faced being beaten, stoned, and imprisoned, yet he had a tremendous sense of joy.

During moments of great difficulty, we can experience the joy of the Lord in a far greater way than in any other time. For some, this may be hard to believe. Many times, when difficulty comes, we immediately look for a way out. A sudden trial leaves us feeling hopeless and wondering if we have done something wrong. But we must remember that adversity is a part of life.

When he wrote about joy, Paul was in prison. He knew how it felt to be discouraged and abandoned, but he also experienced a tremendous joy—one the Lord had given him. It is the same joy we can experience today.

Paul writes, "I have learned the secret of being content in any and every situation, whether well fed or hungry, whether living in plenty or in want" (Philippians 4:12).

Contentment for Paul was reflective of the deep sense of joy he felt within his heart. He had a promise from God—and we do, too. One day, like Paul, we will see the Savior face to face. Therefore, no matter what this world tosses at us, we can experience a true sense of joy right now.

Do you feel as though you have lost your joy? Or are you searching to regain it? The joy of the Lord is one of God's greatest gifts. Take a moment to be silent before Him. Worship Him and praise Him for His faithfulness to you and for His precious gift of joy.

The precepts of the Lord are right, giving joy to the heart. The commands of the Lord are radiant, giving light to the eyes (Psalm 19:8).

April 6

The Daily Way

Envy

Imagine a man who is happily married to a woman whose physical and emotional companionship he values and cherishes. He is successful in his profession. His children are well-behaved and accomplished. He is satisfied with his life until he attends his twentieth college reunion.

This is where he makes a crucial mistake. He tells himself that many of his former classmates have achieved a higher social and professional status than he. He also mistakenly believes that they are married to more educated and more attractive wives, and that they seem to have more money and to have traveled more often than he has.

A sense of failure begins to grow in his heart. Once a happy man, he is now wrongly focused on his circumstances. He loses his peace and contentment to envy and jealousy.

Proverbs 14:30 states, "A heart at peace gives life to the body, but envy rots the bones." King Ahab of Israel had everything. But he wanted a vineyard that was close to his palace. When Naboth refused to sell, Ahab pouted and sulked until his wicked wife, Jezebel, plotted to kill Naboth and to take his field to satisfy the envy of King Ahab.

There are people who have everything and are still envious for more. Even a godly man like King David coveted what another man had. As a result of his actions, he committed adultery and murder, and lost his peace by harming his fellowship with God.

Envy always leads to strife and a loss of peace. Are you longing for what you cannot have? Look to Jesus. Only He can satisfy the desires of your heart. He alone brings peace and contentment to your life.

May God himself, the God of peace, sanctify you through and through. May your whole spirit, soul and body be kept blameless at the coming of our Lord Jesus Christ (1 Thessalonians 5:23).

The Daily Way

The Root of All Evil

Money and prosperity not only have the ability to create conflict between family members and friends, they can also wreak havoc in the Christian community. In many ways, nothing has a greater ability to derail ministry work than a rich endowment.

Some Christian leaders may balk at this statement, but the truth is not hard to discern. Many of America's universities were founded on Christian principles and values, but have since abandoned their faith. When their endowments grew larger, their commitment and devotion to godly education grew smaller. They adjusted their ethics to reflect the views of their contributors.

Both Lot and Abraham were wealthy men. However, there was a tremendous difference in their love for God. Abraham's quest was to follow God by faith, while Lot lived for the moment and to gain more than he had been given.

Have you ever been tempted to make the same type of decision? You may have waited a long time to enjoy the goodness of God's blessing, but be careful. Don't allow the temptation of self-centeredness to grasp your heart. Remember, you do not have to be wealthy to be consumed by thoughts of greed. Anyone can become entrapped by the world's lusts and passions.

Abraham refused to allow his wealth to control him. Lot, on the other hand, allowed the size of his herd and bank roll to negatively influence his worship of God. Open your life up to the Savior. Trust Him for your future and lay aside the destructive thoughts of envy and jealousy.

Prayer: Lord, teach me how to enjoy what You have given and not allow it to take Your place.

Abram believed the Lord, and he credited it to him as righteousness (Genesis 15:6).

Genuine Peace

Martha and Mary were sisters, and they both loved and wanted to please the Lord. However, they were very different in their actions. Martha was preoccupied with cooking and housecleaning, while Mary sought to spend time with Jesus. The Bible tells us that she sat at His feet, listening to all He said.

We need to be aware of the danger of anything that crowds the Lord out of our lives. Jesus chided Martha:

> You are worried and upset about many things, but only one thing is needed. Mary has chosen what is better, and it will not be taken away from her (Luke 10:41-42).

In the end, the only thing that matters or has meaning is God's Word in our lives. Martha was anxious about things that pertain to this life. She did not have a genuine sense of peace— one that comes as a result of spending time with the Savior.

Anxiety is the result of preoccupation with the things in life that do not have eternal value. It is a signal that we are seeking to derive security or peace from something other than from the Lord.

C.S. Lewis writes, "God designed the human machine to run on Himself. That is why it is just no good asking God to make us happy in our own way without bothering about Him."

We may be sincerely doing what we think will please the Lord—but all the while, we may be stressing over unnecessary events, feelings, and emotions. Like Martha, we need to recognize what is important. When God is the center of our lives, our priorities will be focused on Him, and then He will fill us with His peace, assurance, and hope.

The God of peace will be with you (Philippians 4:9).

The Daily Way

God's Peace

Some people believe that if they have a certain level of wealth, then they will have peace—or if they marry right, then they will know contentment. Others mistakenly believe that if they can just live in some ideal location or receive certain recognition at work, then they will have all they could ever hope to achieve.

However, none of these scenarios is capable of providing the peace and contentment we long to experience. True peace only comes as a result of living a life filled with the Spirit of God. It is eternal and has only one source—Jesus Christ. Charles Spurgeon writes, "The God of peace gives perfect peace to those whose hearts are fixed upon Him."

We can try to achieve peace through accomplishments and hard work. We may look for peace everywhere—thinking that new experiences, buying things, or stashing money away will deliver peace. However, apart from God, we will never find lasting peace.

In order to experience the peace of God, we first must have peace with God—which comes as the result of a complete surrender to Christ as our Lord and Savior. Once we are saved, God's peace is available to us. A famous actress once lamented that she had everything she could possibly want, but she still did not have a sense of peace. There are some things that money cannot buy, and peace is one of them.

Before His death, Jesus comforted His disciples with these words: "Peace I leave with you; my peace I give you. I do not give to you as the world gives. Do not let your hearts be troubled and do not be afraid" (John 14:27).

We, too, can find the peace and comfort we need within His eternal care.

The peace of God, which transcends all understanding, will guard your hearts and your minds in Christ Jesus (Philippians 4:7).

April 10

The Daily Way

The Bow and Arrow

Have you ever been described as an impatient person? It is easy to feel impatient. Maybe traffic isn't moving fast enough and you are going to be late for your meeting. Or you can't get through the checkout lane quickly enough to pick up your children from the babysitter. These daily irritations can zap your strength and cause you to lose sight of what really matters.

The source of true patience is the Spirit of God. His patience toward us allows us the opportunity to grow and to become more like Him. He does not give up on us. When we are stubborn and fail to learn what God wants to teach us, He continues to demonstrate His patience.

Many times, we grow impatient with a colleague, friend, child, or spouse and forget that God is patient with us and requires us to do the same with others. One of the causes of impatience is spiritual shortsightedness. Our view is limited. Therefore, many times we only see what has a direct impact on our lives. We become impatient because we can't see life from God's perspective!

God has a greater plan. While He does not always show us the details, we can know the big picture—we are in His loving hands.

Oswald Chambers writes:

> Patience is more than endurance. A saint's life is in the hands of God like a bow and arrow in the hands of the archer. God is aiming at something the saint cannot see, and He stretches and strains, and every now and again the saint says, 'I cannot stand anymore.' God does not heed, He goes on stretching till His purpose is in sight, then He lets fly. Trust yourself in God's hands.

Therefore, as God's chosen people, holy and dearly loved, clothe yourselves with compassion, kindness, humility, gentleness and patience (Colossians 3:12).

The Daily Way — April 11

Wait on God

For the believer, patience is built upon the absolute, unshakable belief that God is sovereign. We can be patient because we know we are not forgotten nor forsaken by our heavenly Father. Patience is the result of knowing that God has every detail of our lives under control. Nothing escapes His eternal care.

One day your loving Savior is coming back for you. Remember, your ultimate destination is heaven. Therefore, don't get hooked by Satan's bait and begin treating this world as your real home. If you do, you will find that you are becoming more impatient with the aggravations of life.

James gives us examples that spur us on to patience. First, we must understand some of the basic rules of farming (James 5:7). A farmer does not continually dig up the seed he has planted in order to check its growth—if he did so, he would never have a harvest. Likewise, we must trust God's timing in our lives. Just as the farmer waits for His crop, we must wait on God to complete His work in our lives. This takes patience! James goes on to tell us that even Job had to endure a fierce trial. However, he knew that God had a wonderful plan for his life, and he refused to deny the Lord.

There will be times when we feel like we are in a holding pattern in our lives. We long to move away from our difficulties, but God wants us to wait and to learn how to be patient. If you find yourself feeling impatient with your circumstances, look up into the glorious face of the Savior who loves you and has a great reward for you.

Be patient, then, brothers, until the Lord's coming (James 5:7).

April 12 — The Daily Way

God's Timing

As we choose to place our complete faith and trust in God, we must relinquish our grip on the plans we have made for our lives.

Even though we trust in God, our actions say otherwise when we grow fearful that life may not turn out the way we hoped it would. When we devote our lives to God, we quickly learn this truth: Our plans and timing do not always line up with God's. Yet it is with much frustration that we struggle to understand that His way, His plans, and His timing are better than ours.

Some of our greatest mistakes are made when we run ahead of God's plan. We not only undermine our faith in Him, but we also challenge the notion that He indeed does know best. It is an arrogance that assumes we know better than God.

However, we cannot live fearlessly under such presumptions, no matter how overt or discreet they are. To walk fearlessly through life with God, we must come to terms with the fact that God knows what is best for us when it is best for us. We are not mice in some cosmic maze, overseen by a God who enjoys our helplessness.

He has a plan for our lives, and when we seek Him, He will reveal it to us. We are loved by a heavenly Father who delights in seeing us become the fullness of who He created us to be.

Our shield is our faith. Our shield says, "We believe God's Word and we trust Him. We know that He knows what is best for our lives."

Prayer: Lord, we give You our plans and our dreams to do with them as You will.

He has made everything beautiful in its time. He has also set eternity in the hearts of men; yet they cannot fathom what God has done from beginning to end (Ecclesiastes 3:11).

The Daily Way

April 13

Kindness

While traveling from one city to the next, a man was overtaken by robbers. Taking his clothes and possessions, they left him badly beaten. Not long after the attack, a priest traveled the same road. He passed by without stopping. Then another traveler saw the man but did not offer to help.

Finally, someone stopped—a Samaritan. He put bandages on the man's wounds and took him to an inn for the night. The next day he gave the innkeeper money and instructions to take care of the wounded man.

The parable of the Good Samaritan in Luke 10 is a wonderful example of godly kindness. It also demonstrates that kindness often requires something of us—time, plans, privacy, and desires. The Good Samaritan interrupted his travel plans to help a stranger. What better example to follow than that of Christ? He gave us the ultimate gift of kindness—He died that we might live.

However, we cannot learn to be kind simply by disciplining ourselves. Kindness can be hard work, and from time to time, this may mean that we have to face difficult situations that drain us emotionally and physically.

Often kindness cannot grow apart from conflict and strife. We learn to be kind through the kindness of others, but we also learn a greater kindness when we are called to be kind and caring in difficult situations.

A disagreement with a co-worker, spouse, friend, or family member can tempt us to be abrupt or uncaring. Circumstances appear out of focus and God's fruit of kindness becomes lost in the battle. However, through the power of Christ we are able to act in kindness even toward those who hurt us. Is there someone who needs your kindness today?

Finally, all of you, live in harmony with one another; be sympathetic, love as brothers, be compassionate and humble (1 Peter 3:8).

April 14 — The Daily Way

Empowered by Kindness

Kindness is a characteristic of God. Out of His kindness He made a covenant with the nation of Israel. And out of kindness, He kept His side of this covenant while they rebelled and disobeyed.

It is out of kindness that Jesus left the splendor of heaven to become a man. It is out of kindness that He hung on a cross to die and pay the wages of our sin. Out of eternal love and kindness, He offers to us His precious gift of salvation.

But God's kindness did not stop at the cross. It continues today in the lives of those who accept His Son as their Savior. The more we allow Him to work in us, the more His fruit becomes evident to those whose lives we touch each day.

As we continue to live and grow spiritually, there are several things we need to know about kindness. Sometimes, kindness requires putting ourselves in another person's place. We need to view others as Christ does.

There are those of us who continually show kindness to others and yet seem to be incapable of showing kindness to ourselves. We allow past failures and sins to prevent us from growing. However, God's forgiveness is complete. When we pray and seek His forgiveness, He gives it. Therefore, we must learn to forgive others and ourselves, too.

Kindness gives birth to kindness. Love extended leads to more love. As you begin to show kindness to others, you will be set free from feelings of self-condemnation. You will find yourself being empowered by the Holy Spirit to exercise more kindness more often.

I will tell of the kindnesses of the Lord, the deeds for which he is to be praised ... yes, the many good things he has done for the house of Israel, according to his compassion and many kindnesses (Isaiah 63:7).

The Daily Way — April 15

Goodness and Sacrifice

Early in the nineteenth century, King Frederick William III of Prussia found himself in a difficult situation. His country was involved in a very expensive war. At the same time, he was seeking to transform his country into a great nation. However, the country was financially crippled.

The thought of surrendering to the enemy was unthinkable. Therefore, the king came up with a plan to replenish the country's financial wealth. He approached the women of Prussia and asked them if they would be willing to donate their gold and silver jewelry.

He explained that for each piece of jewelry they gave, he would give them an ornament of bronze in return as a token of his gratitude. The inscription imprinted into these ornaments read, "I gave gold and silver for iron, 1813."

To the king's amazement, the response was overwhelming. The women prized his tokens of gratitude more highly than their former jewelry. The reason: the emblems were the mark of true sacrifice. It even became unfashionable for women to wear jewelry.

Generosity and sacrifice for country and king became the mark of true citizenship in Prussia. Goodness and sacrifice became the badge of honor for all Prussians.

In Galatians 5:22, the apostle Paul lists the fruit of the Spirit—those characteristics that are most like Christ in us. Goodness is one of those listed—goodness without thought given to personal sacrifice.

On the Cross, God displayed His eternal goodness to each one of us. This is the same goodness we are to have for one another. The next time you experience the rebuke of another, ask God to give you the ability to demonstrate His goodness instead of anger.

Clothe yourselves with compassion, kindness, humility, [goodness] and patience (Colossians 3:12).

April 16 — The Daily Way

The Joy of Giving

Perhaps there was a time in your life when you made a bold pledge to God, vowing to give Him all that you are and all that you have. But then you were drawn off course and ended up forgetting you made this promise.

As believers intent on reflecting the goodness of God's grace, we must learn what it means to be grace givers—people who give out of nothing but love for the One to whom they give. Many Christians give because the Bible says to do it, but those who have found the secret of giving know it is more than just duty that sparks their hearts to give.

They give because God has first given to them. He is the One who gives and keeps on giving His love and so much more to us.

When we emulate God's love to others, we are doing the very thing He has commanded us to do: to love and to extend His grace and forgiveness even to those who hurt us. When we do this, His heart is warmed by our actions.

Simply modeling God's grace out of obligation will not last long. God sees the motives of our hearts. However, when we seek to live according to the model He has given us through Jesus Christ and out of pure love for Him, God is honored. When we give to God and to others out of love—not out of duty—those around us will see our hearts aflame for Christ and be changed by our testimony.

Christ gave more to the world than anyone else has given. He yielded His own pure life to be sacrificed so that others may come to know Him intimately and experience His gracious gift of salvation. And the truth is: Jesus Christ is still giving Himself to us each day.

Prayer: Lord, instill in me the passion to give as freely as Christ gave, not out of duty, but out of love.

Out of the most severe trial, their overflowing joy and their extreme poverty welled up in rich generosity (2 Corinthians 8:2).

The Daily Way

April 17

Love Your Enemies

It is easy to be good to those who are good to us. It is much harder to be good to those who harm us. However, this is exactly what Christ commands us to do. In fact, He took this thought a step further by commanding us to love those who are our enemies.

"You have heard that it was said, 'Love your neighbor and hate your enemy.' But I tell you: Love your enemies and pray for those who persecute you" (Matthew 5:43-44). Jesus admonished His followers to respond to those who hurt them with love so that His followers would become sons and daughters of God (Matthew 5:45).

If we are honest, then we must admit that often our first reaction to Christ's words is one of defensiveness. We want to proclaim our rights and demand justice. God, however, has a different route for us to take and that is one of mercy and grace. He instructs us to treat others the way we would want to be treated.

Paul is quick to remind the Galatian believers that their hearts must be set on God's goodness because goodness is an essential fruit of the Spirit. Sometimes, this means being good to those who have been bad to us. Not fair, you say?

The next time you feel as though an injustice has been committed against you, remember the Savior. He endured both rejection and insult, and He continued to demonstrate God's infinite love and mercy even to those who crucified Him.

Let Jesus' ultimate display of love be your inspiration as you respond in love to everyone you encounter today—even to those who have hurt you in the past. The evidence of Christ's life within is the outward display of His goodness, mercy, and grace. May the Lord bless you as you seek to be more like Him each day.

Love your enemies, do good to those who hate you, bless those who curse you, pray for those who mistreat you (Luke 6:27-28).

April 18

The Daily Way

Demonstrate God's Goodness

The goodness of God within our lives is often revealed through our actions. When we accept Christ as our Savior, we gain the ability to be good people—but only as we live our lives for Jesus Christ. Apart from Him we can do nothing!

The Lord told His disciples "there is only One who is [truly] good," and that, of course, is God (Matthew 19:17). Becoming a good man or woman is not something we can do on our own.

We can practice being good, but goodness that comes from the heart of God is something we gain only as we let go of our selfish wants and desires and practice being good to others. We can't cling to what we deem as our "rights" and truly be good to others.

The Good Samaritan sacrificed financial gain and personal reputation in order to help someone he did not even know. Take a moment to reread this story in Luke 10:30-37 and realize this act of goodness was born within the heart of God.

Throughout life, we will meet people who are careless with their words and actions. Everything within us will want to fight back, but we must come to a point where we level our eyes at the deepest intent of our hearts and ask, "Am I demonstrating God's goodness or my self-righteousness?"

The Holy Spirit who lives within us is our guide to godliness, which will be reflected in the love and mercy we extend to even the most unlovely person. The next time you face a difficult situation, take time to pray and to ask God to live His life through you.

Prayer: Father, it is not humanly possible for me to be good on my own, but I know that You can show me how to be both kind and good.

The good man brings good things out of the good stored up in his heart (Luke 6:45).

The Daily Way

April 19

Faithfulness

George McDonald once said, "To be trusted is a greater compliment than to be loved." Take a moment to think through this statement.

You can love a person, but do you trust that person with your life, your heart, and all that is included in your life? Many times, we are careful to say the right things and not allow those around us to see who we really are. We don't want people to see our flaws or to know about our failures because we think they may not love or approve of us.

Faithfulness is an even deeper issue because it requires being faithful even when we may not agree with the popular view. It also means being loyal to Christ and following His precepts even when the world's view is anything but His.

Today, faithfulness is viewed as an old-fashioned word. Many times, we find words like team player, champion, leadership potential, and high energy have replaced words like faithful as an important factor in the employment world. If you step into a marketing meeting of a large corporation, more than likely faithful will not be a buzzword used for a new campaign.

There was a time when a man's word was his bond—when trustworthiness was more important than wealth, fame, or popularity. It seems that the days are gone when promises were kept and friends were faithful.

Yet, God calls each one of us to be faithful to Him and to one another. Faithfulness is evidence of a humble heart that is turned toward God in adoration and devotion.

Are you seeking to be faithful to God first and then to what He has given you here on earth? Learn to be faithful and His love and goodness will also flow from your life.

Let love and faithfulness never leave you. ... Then you will win favor and a good name in the sight of God and man (Proverbs 3:3-4).

April 20 — The Daily Way

Closer than a Brother

Whether we realize it or not, faithfulness is at the heart of all relationships. It is the very thing that prevents families and societies from falling apart. And it is the one element that has the ability to encourage us to persevere in times of failure and heartache.

The psalmist writes, "The Lord preserves the faithful, but the proud he pays back in full" (Psalm 31:23). Therefore, it comes as no surprise that the apostle Paul lists faithfulness as one of the fruits of the Spirit.

In fact, one of the first things we learn about God is that He is faithful. When we were young, we often sang the song "Jesus Loves Me," and we know He does. No matter what we have done in the past or what we will do in the future, God's love for us never changes. It is eternal, it is infinite, and it is faithful.

This fact is not a license for sin. Instead, it is the evidence we need to repent and to accept God's love for our lives. There is nothing you can do to make yourself more acceptable to the Lord.

He accepts you just as you are, and He loves you fully and completely. His love and faithfulness never change; they are yours for eternity.

When life becomes difficult for someone you know, are you the type of friend who "sticks closer than a brother" (Proverbs 18:24)? Jesus is this type of friend. He remains at our side even when others abandon us, and the same should be true of us.

Far too often, we walk away when a friend needs us the most. At the end of his life, Paul writes and asks Timothy to come to him because everyone had left him except for Luke. Through Jesus Christ, you also can learn to be a faithful friend like Timothy.

But the fruit of the Spirit is love, joy, peace, patience, kindness, goodness, faithfulness, gentleness and self-control. Against such things there is no law (Galatians 5:22-23).

The Daily Way

April 21

Meekness and Courage

We often believe that perception is reality, but many times it is not.

The enemy is swift to tempt us to believe something about another person that may not be true. Remember, God created us for fellowship—first with Himself and then with others.

Once we have accepted Christ as our Savior, the enemy knows that he can no longer capture our souls. We are saved by the grace of God.

However, he never backs away from a challenge and sets new goals to disrupt and, if possible, to destroy our fellowship with God and with those we love.

When conflict arises, it is extremely important for us to listen only to the voice of God. While there is benefit that can be gained from the counsel of godly friends, there is also a great danger of missing what God wants us to see and learn on our own.

Therefore, before you react to a situation, ask the Lord to make His truth apparent to your heart. Set a goal to be meek and forgiving. He has given us the Holy Spirit, who is committed to leading and guiding us at every turn in life.

Wrong perceptions have been the cause of many misunderstandings. This is one of the reasons we view meekness as a weakness. In actuality, a meek person is not weak or timid. In fact, biblical meekness or gentleness is synonymous with courage, confidence, and strength under control.

God wants us to enjoy meekness as a fruit of the Spirit. When we learn how to rest in Him and allow Him to work through us, His meekness will rise to the surface of our lives. The inner need to be noticed professionally or socially will fade, and we will find that the glory of the Lord is ours to enjoy.

Be completely humble and gentle; be patient, bearing with one another in love (Ephesians 4:2).

April 22

The Daily Way

Send Someone Else

Imagine standing before the Lord and finding the strength within you to say what Moses said: "O Lord, please send someone else to do it" (Exodus 4:13).

Hard to imagine? Think you would never have the nerve to say these same words? We often do just that. We essentially tell God no by refusing to do what He has directed us to do.

Two verses earlier, Moses had admitted his weaknesses: "O Lord, I have never been eloquent, neither in the past nor since you have spoken to your servant. I am slow of speech and tongue" (Exodus 4:10).

There was no doubt that Moses had a problem with his self-esteem. However, he quickly decided it was in his best interest to obey the Lord. Although he had limitations and inabilities, he refused to allow these to prevent him from answering God's call.

There are times when we look at others and think we could never do what they are doing. Although we long to step forward and lead, we often fall back with feelings of inferiority and defeat.

We also allow pride to skew our view of those around us. We see someone who is either physically or mentally challenged and wonder why God has chosen that person for a particular task. He often chooses to use the "foolish" things of this world to do a mighty work (1 Corinthians 1:27).

While Moses was a meek man, he certainly was not weak. He had a tremendous inner strength and discernment that was God-given. In the end, the Lord used his meek spirit to lead Israel out of bondage and to the doorstep of the Promised Land.

Have you made meekness a personal goal of your life? If you have, then you are in store for a tremendous blessing.

The meek will inherit the land and enjoy great peace (Psalm 37:11).

The Daily Way — April 23

Pride Undercover

Would you consider yourself a meek person? Or are you still unsure of what true meekness looks like? It may be helpful to know that most of the men and women who were biblical heroes of the faith had to learn meekness.

Meekness is not something that comes naturally; instead it is learned under the direction of the Holy Spirit. When Peter first met Jesus, he was not meek. Instead, he had his heart set on selfish ideas, but life with the Savior changed that. He never lost his sense of courage or confidence. However, Christ molded Peter's personality so that he began to reflect the strength and mercy of God.

Another important aspect we need to consider is that godly meekness is different from human modesty. False meekness can be far more dangerous than bragging about all you have and all you can do. A false sense of meekness or modesty often is hard to detect. It is pride undercover and will usually be found in the lives of those who find it hard to accept God's grace for their lives.

True meekness comes as a result of sincere devotion to the Lord. It is a fruit of the Spirit that He wants to develop in each of our lives. However, there is only one way to begin this journey and that is through prayer and personal dedication. It may also require facing a time of testing. Before Peter could serve, he had to learn how to be meek and humble.

Prayer: Lord Jesus, I realize I need Your gift of meekness in my life. My greatest desire is not to serve myself but to serve You. My prayer is that You will develop in me a true sense of meekness so that others will see You living in me and be drawn closer to You.

Blessed are the meek, for they will inherit the earth (Matthew 5:5).

April 24 — The Daily Way

A Remote Control Attitude

A father asked his daughter, who spent too much time watching television, to begin memorizing Scripture. He chose the verses in Galatians concerning the fruit of the Spirit as a place for her to begin.

When she was sure she had reached her goal, she began to list the fruit of the Spirit to her Dad, "Love, joy, peace, patience, kindness, goodness, faithfulness, gentleness, and remote control!"

When it comes to the subject of self-control, many of us would like to dodge the issue. Maybe we would like to think there is a way to put our minds, wills, and emotions under God's "remote control." Instead of having to take responsibility for our actions and decisions, we think it would be easier for God simply to control us.

However, God has a more creative plan in mind. He designed us with a limited free will. This means we have the ability to choose right over wrong and self-control over emotional response.

Paul warns:

> Be very careful, then, how you live—not as unwise but as wise, making the most of every opportunity, because the days are evil. Therefore do not be foolish, but understand what the Lord's will is. ... Be filled with the Spirit. Speak to one another with psalms, hymns and spiritual songs. Sing and make music in your heart to the Lord, always giving thanks to God the Father for everything (Ephesians 5:15-20).

Don't set your heart on having a "remote control" attitude. Dig deep into God's Word. Learn what it means to be self-controlled. Pray that you always will reflect His love and self-control to others whose lives are spinning out of control.

Make every effort to add to your faith goodness; and to goodness, knowledge; and to knowledge, self control (2 Peter 1:5-6).

The Daily Way

April 25

Walls of Protection

When Nehemiah first heard of Jerusalem's destruction, he wept and was emotionally shaken. He wrote, "For some days I mourned and fasted and prayed before the God of heaven" (Nehemiah 1:4). Nehemiah suddenly realized the walls around the city of Jerusalem were in ruins. Through all of this, he had mistakenly thought they had remained in place. But when the news arrived of their destruction, he became even more burdened.

In Old Testament times, walls around a city were a symbol of strength and security. Without these, a town would be left defenseless, vulnerable, and open to attack. This was the plight of Jerusalem. It was a city without protection against even wild animals. It had lost its identity and was on the verge of being totally reduced to a mound of rubble.

A person who has an undisciplined spirit or no self-control is like a city without walls. He or she is open to enemy attack at any given moment. When we fail to exercise a spirit of self-control, the wild animals of jealousy, rage, frustration, gossip, bearing a false witness, and more can enter our lives easily and unopposed.

The lack of self-control is Satan's way of preparing us for destruction. However, you do not have to fall victim to the enemy's schemes. You have all you need to stand firm in your faith. God is the One who strengthens you. When you fall in battle and cry out to Him, He rushes to your side and lifts you up.

If you have allowed sin to come into your life, then your spiritual walls of protection are down. However, God will repair them, but you must turn to Him, confess your sin, and seek His forgiveness. When you do, He will restore His walls of holy protection around your life.

Like a city whose walls are broken down is a man who lacks self-control (Proverbs 25:28).

April 26

The Daily Way

A Higher Law

It is easy to view the fruit of the Spirit as part of a nice Sunday school lesson. We read through Paul's words in Galatians and think that he is writing about how we should live the Christian life and how we should relate to others.

This is true, but there is a deeper lesson to learn from applying the fruit of the Spirit to our lives. For example, when trials and difficulties come, the fruit of God's Spirit are the very tools that will help us deal properly with these and much more.

However, if God's fruit has not matured in our lives, then there will be even more problems for us to face. We see the evidence of this in how we demonstrate our love for others. Many times, we fail to love the way Christ loves us.

We can be abrupt, harsh, or unforgiving when we know that God calls us, and even commands us, to love others the way He loves us. In fact, we are to love and to have a sense of joy and peace within our lives so others will want the same for their lives. We also are to be patient because God is patient with us, and we are to be kind, good, faithful, gentle, and self-controlled. Each of these reflects the true nature of God and His grace toward us.

Paul writes, "Against such things there is no law" (Galatians 5:23). In other words, when we act like Christ, we are not obligated to fulfill the law of this world. Instead, we are operating under a higher law—one based on God's immeasurable grace.

Refuse to take Satan's bait by becoming angry, frustrated, or bitter over life's blows. Instead, seek to display God's fruit of the Spirit and know that you will be blessed.

Those who belong to Christ Jesus have crucified the sinful nature with its passions and desires (Galatians 5:24).

The Daily Way

April 27

Putting It All Together

If we are living by the Spirit, then we will know how to respond to life when it turns upside down. We won't give up when it becomes rough and we feel disillusioned. Instead, we will remain faithful to the course God has set before us.

When David faced a tremendous threat from his enemies, he cried out to God and the Lord answered him.

> For in the time of trouble He shall hide me in His pavilion; in the secret place of His tabernacle He shall hide me; He shall set me high upon a rock (Psalm 27:5, NKJV).

If David had abandoned all self-control, his enemies would have overthrown him. Instead, he waited on God's deliverance. He knew that the Lord was his Rock and his Redeemer.

The fruit of the Spirit is God's instructional toolset given to us so we will know how to face life's problems and sorrows correctly. Paul reminds us to "keep in step with the Spirit. Let us not become conceited, provoking and envying each other" (Galatians 5:25-26).

The fruit of the Spirit teaches us how to stay alert to Satan's schemes. Pride is one of his favorite snares. Oswald Chambers writes, "Always remain alert to the fact that where one man has gone back is exactly where anyone may go back."

When we yield to pride, we set ourselves up for a fall. But if we practice the fruit of the Spirit—love, joy, peace, patience, kindness, goodness, faithfulness, gentleness, and self-control—then the enemy will not be able to set up strongholds in our lives.

Therefore, be alert and submit your life to Christ. No matter what this life may hand you, God has given you all that you need to handle it perfectly and from His perspective.

Commit your way to the Lord; trust in him and he will do this: He will make your righteousness shine like the dawn (Psalm 37:5-6).

April 28   The Daily Way

Take Action

As we pursue God, we discover a difficult truth: Living out the principles in the Bible is not as easy as we may think. Loving God and loving our neighbor sound like simple enough commands, but when it actually comes to showing love to a difficult neighbor, our true colors begin to show. We must ask ourselves if we truly love God as much as we say we do.

Throughout the New Testament, Jesus revolted against the notion that being religious meant you loved God. The piety of the Pharisees was a mockery of what it meant truly to follow God—and Jesus went to extremes to prove this. In explaining this fact, Jesus said, "Out of the overflow of the heart the mouth speaks" (Matthew 12:34).

Regardless of what our best intentions are, sometimes our actions don't align with our words. While we know we should follow God and trust Him in every situation, we can succumb to worry and anxiety. Instead of placing our faith in Him, we panic and try to solve the situation ourselves.

While God has patience for an eternity, He does not want us to remain broken down along the roadside while we try to repair our faith. His desire for us is that we would be ever nearing a place of greater faith and unity with Him. But that process is delayed when our actions are not aligned with God's Word.

As people committed to following God, we must learn that believing means taking action. It means that we take God's Word for what it truly is: His Word. The Bible is the foundation of what we believe—and we must strive to live accordingly.

Prayer: Lord, help me to live out Your Word today in everything that I do.

And without faith it is impossible to please God, because anyone who comes to him must believe that he exists and that he rewards those who earnestly seek him (Hebrews 11:6).

The Daily Way

April 29

Hard Work Is Not Optional

While we may wish the rules were different, there are a few time-tested truths about growing and maturing. They take work. And they also involve patience, persistence, and sacrifice.

No Olympic champion ever found his way to the gold medal stand by eating a diet of candy bars and taking naps every day. To attain a high level of achievement, we understand that hard work is not optional.

Our walk with God is no different. In order to be the type of Christians who truly personify the hands and feet of Christ in every aspect of our lives, we must work hard.

The apostle Paul explained why he insisted on being a disciplined Christian:

> Therefore I do not run like a man running aimlessly; I do not fight like a man beating the air. No, I beat my body and make it my slave so that after I have preached to others, I myself will not be disqualified for the prize (1 Corinthians 9:26-27).

When we are not stretching ourselves, when we are not growing, we are stagnating spiritually. We miss out on God's best for us at that moment. To obey God at every turn is to honor Him to the fullest. Yet, it is not easy.

Making the conscious decision to disobey God shows how prideful we really are. Conversely, deciding to obey God exemplifies a spirit of true humility.

Even though we may think God's plan looks impossible, through faith and trust in Him, we will arrive at the conclusion that He indeed knows best.

Prayer: Lord, help me resist the temptation to do what looks easiest, and always obey Your voice.

And anyone who does not take his cross and follow me is not worthy of me (Matthew 10:38).

April 30

The Daily Way

Don't Play the Blame Game

When life begins to fall apart, we may realize that there was something we could have done differently. However, we refuse to acknowledge this to the Lord and to others. While God doesn't want us to feel as though we need to confess every mistake to those around us, He does want us to take responsibility for our actions.

Far too often, we shift the responsibility off of ourselves and on to someone or something else. We blame others for our mistakes by claiming, "If only he or she had not made me do it."

Yet if we are truly responsible for an error, we must be willing to say, "Yes, I did that, and I want you to know that I am sorry and have taken the necessary steps to ensure that it will never happen again." The last thing we need to do is to try to slide out from under a difficult situation by blaming others. Blame just doesn't work with God's plan for our lives.

Jesus never said, "If you had not been so hardheaded, I could have avoided the cross." He knew the responsibility God had given Him, and He was determined to be faithful. Through Him, we have been given eternal life. Therefore, we need to learn how to live as incredibly free men and women.

When we shift the blame to others so that we appear blameless, we are not really free at all. We are in bondage to the deed and to those whom we have betrayed and harmed. Forgiveness is a miraculous act whereby we come to God and confess the wrong we have done and if need be, we are willing to say "I'm sorry" to those we have harmed.

Prayer: Lord, I want to live a free life—one that is only tied to You and not to the sins of this world. Teach me Your way that I may walk in it.

Teach me your way, O Lord; lead me in a straight path (Psalm 27:11).

Discovering the Power in Praise

The Daily Way

May 1

Expressions of Honor

Have you ever thought about what the angels and the believers who have gone before us are doing in heaven? One thing for sure is that they are praising God!

The prophet Isaiah records a wonderful scene of praise:

> In the year that King Uzziah died, I saw the Lord seated on a throne, high and exalted, and the train of his robe filled the temple. Above him were seraphs, each with six wings: With two wings they covered their faces, with two they covered their feet, and with two they were flying. And they were calling to one another: "Holy, holy, holy is the Lord Almighty; the whole earth is full of his glory." At the sound of their voices the doorposts and thresholds shook and the temple was filled with smoke (Isaiah 6:1-4).

Imagine this scene and try to think how Isaiah felt in God's presence. Human words cannot express the glory his eyes witnessed. While we live in a visible, tangible world as children of God, we are only sojourners on earth. Our eternal destination is with God—praising Him. Therefore, praise is vital to our spiritual well-being.

Isaiah had an opportunity to witness God's glory, but we also can enjoy praise and worship to the Lord. In times of praise, God becomes the focus of our hearts. We see Him as the source of our hope and strength. Praise changes our attitudes and prepares us for the manifestation of God's power in our lives.

The Bible tells us that praise is a garment (Isaiah 61:3) we can put on each day. We do not have to live with feelings of doubt and fear. We can opt to live a life of praise! The psalmist writes: "But as for me, I will always have hope; I will praise you more and more" (Psalm 71:14).

Let everything that has breath praise the Lord. Praise the Lord (Psalm 150:6).

May 2 — The Daily Way

A Full-time Job

During a mid-week prayer meeting, an elderly man prayed, "Lord, we will praise You with our two eyes, by looking only to You. We will exalt You with our two ears by listening only to Your voice. We will praise You with our two hands by working in Your service. We will honor You with our own feet by walking in the way of Your statutes. We will magnify You with our tongues by bearing testimony to Your lovingkindness. We will worship You with our hearts by loving only You. We thank You for Your faithfulness that never wavers or ceases to be a blessing to us."

Praise always exalts God. And if we take time to think about it, praise should be a full-time job. However, there may be times when you wonder, "How can I praise God for sorrow and disappointment?" One way we do this is by setting our minds and hearts on God's grace and mercy. Even in times of deep sorrow and frustration, God remains faithful. He has a plan for our lives, and He will accomplish it.

David was the anointed king of Israel, yet for years he was forced to live life on the run from King Saul. From a human perspective, David had very little, if anything, to praise God for. However, he did just that. He wrote a wonderful testimony of praise to God:

> I love you, O Lord, my strength. The Lord is my rock, my fortress and my deliverer; my God is my rock, in whom I take refuge. He is my shield and the horn of my salvation, my stronghold. I call to the Lord, who is worthy of praise, and I am saved from my enemies (Psalm 18:1-3).

When you lift your voice to God with words of praise, you declare His goodness and faithfulness to an unbelieving world. Therefore, praise the Lord with all your heart!

I will praise you among the nations, O Lord; I will sing praises to your name (Psalm 18:49).

The Daily Way

May 3

Gain God's Attention

In 2 Chronicles 20, Jehoshaphat and the nation of Israel had to make a defining decision. They were about to be attacked by two formidable enemies and, from where Israel stood, there did not appear to be a way of escape.

Jehoshaphat immediately declared a season of fasting and prayer. The entire nation gathered to seek help from the Lord. They prayed:

> O Lord, God of our fathers, are you not the God who is in heaven? You rule over all the kingdoms of the nations. Power and might are in your hand, and no one can withstand you. ... For we have no power to face this vast army that is attacking us. We do not know what to do, but our eyes are upon you (2 Chronicles 20:6, 12).

Israel turned their hearts to God and he answered swiftly:

> You will not have to fight this battle. Take up your positions; stand firm and see the deliverance the Lord will give you. ... Do not be afraid; do not be discouraged. Go out to face them tomorrow, and the Lord will be with you (2 Chronicles 20:17).

The next morning, instead of marching into battle with bows drawn, Jehoshaphat and the nation of Israel marched forward with a song of praise on their lips. God confused their enemies to such a degree that the Israelites never had to fire one single arrow.

Satan hates to hear words of praise spoken to the Lord. He knows His defeat is sure each and every time we praise God. Are you praising God for His presence and power in your life?

Give thanks to the Lord, for his love endures forever (2 Chronicles 20:21).

May 4 — The Daily Way

Life Goes Better with Praise

Years ago, a soft-drink company came up with a slogan that claimed "things go better with" their product. Who can say what the positive effects of a soft drink are? But certainly we know that life goes much better with praise!

When we fail to praise God, frustration builds. God is grieved, and we miss a great opportunity for blessing. When we take time to praise Him, feelings of fear, doubt, and frustration fade.

The psalmist writes: "May the peoples praise you, O God; may all the peoples praise you. ... Then the land will yield its harvest, and God, our God, will bless us" (Psalm 67:3, 6). Praise is the prelude to blessing!

Henry W. Frost, a veteran missionary to China, discovered the power of praise amid dark and difficult circumstances. He writes: "Nothing so pleases God in connection with our prayer as praise and nothing so blesses the man who prays as the praise which he offers."

Frost goes on to explain just how he learned this truth.

> A deep shadow had covered my soul. I prayed and I prayed, but the darkness did not vanish. I summoned myself to endure, but the darkness only deepened.
>
> Then one day, I went to an inland station and saw on the wall of the mission home these words: 'Try praising the Lord.' I did, and in a moment every shadow was gone, not to return. Yes, the psalmist was right; it is a good thing to give praise unto the Lord!

Praise does not reduce the seriousness of the problems facing us, but it can certainly lift our downcast eyes to the One who has the power to lift our hearts and to offer us eternal hope.

When trouble increases and the stress of the day seems too much for you to bear, try praising God, and you will experience His wondrous joy.

I will ever praise you (Psalm 71:6).

The Daily Way

The Pride Factor

If praise is such a good idea, why do we resist doing it? There are two apparent reasons.

First, Satan tempts us to complain rather than to praise God. In fact, the enemy will do all within his power to stop us from glorifying the Lord by filling our thoughts with images of fear and defeat. He also knows that when we exalt the Lord, God quickly exposes his dark deception.

Carnality is the second reason people fail to praise God. The unregenerate human mind discredits praise as not being logical or intellectual.

We praise God when we are willing to submit:

• Ourselves to the Lord. Praise overflows from our lives once we yield ourselves to the Lord and stop resisting His will. We can't praise Him if we are trapped in disobedience.

• Our intellect to the Lord. Praise involves faith. It is only when we trust Christ fully that we learn to praise Him for His goodness and mercy.

• Our social status to the Lord. Many times, the greatest hindrance to praise is our position within the community or a company. God wants us to come to Him in humility desiring only His honor and fellowship.

• Our reputations to the Lord. When our eyes are set on ourselves, we cannot praise God. The only way to practice the joy of praise is by setting the focus of our hearts on Jesus Christ. When we do this, our lives will overflow with His goodness and mercy. We will become men and women of praise who are filled with God's love and mercy.

God opposes the proud but gives grace to the humble (1 Peter 5:5).

May 6

The Daily Way

Praising the Name of God

History books tell us of an incident in the life of Napoleon. A man once approached the French emperor and said, "I am very pleased to meet you! You see, my name is the same as yours."

Knowing that the man had a poor reputation, Napoleon was incensed and exclaimed: "Either live up to your name or change it!"

We may not take names very seriously in our culture, but in the Middle East, a person's name is given in honor of a beloved relative, or because it has been in the family for generations.

In Bible times, a name was chosen very carefully and very deliberately in order to indicate what kind of person the child would be. Also, a name was reflective of a person's character, personality, and abilities.

This is why some of the names of the people in the Bible were changed. Peter's original name was Cephas, but Jesus changed it to Peter, meaning "the rock." Abram was changed to Abraham, which means "the father of many." From God's perspective, a new name is consistent with a new mission.

God's name, however, never changes. He is Jehovah, which means "the self-existent one." He is self-sufficient. He does not need anything nor anyone in order to exist. However, He desires our worship, praise, and fellowship. He loves us with an everlasting love.

The more we learn about Him, the more we understand His faithfulness, justice, and mercy. When we grasp the depth of God's sovereignty, we also realize His wondrous gift of grace was given with a purpose. Not only do we receive salvation, but we also receive His name! We become members of His family—joint heirs with Christ. Now that is worthy of all our praise!

Praise the Lord, O my soul; all my inmost being, praise his holy name (Psalm 103:1).

The Daily Way

May 7

A Turn for the Better

God's glory is revealed in the praises of His people. When we lift our voices of praise to God, He is honored, and we are blessed.

However, God's blessings are not always material in nature. The richest people are those who have developed an intimate relationship with the Savior through personal prayer and praise.

Praise was a hallmark of David's life. As a young man, he learned to worship God through songs of praise that expressed his deep devotion to the Lord. While his brothers may have enjoyed the comforts of home, David was confined to tending to the family's sheep. But it was there, in a lonely pasture, that David wrote his greatest songs of praise to the Lord.

King David wrote:

> Where can I go from your Spirit? Where can I flee from your presence? If I go up to the heavens, you are there; if I make my bed in the depths, you are there. If I rise on the wings of the dawn, if I settle on the far side of the sea, even there your hand will guide me, your right hand will hold me fast (Psalm 139:7-10).

Christ knows when we rise in the morning, and when we lie down to sleep at night. He is the revelation of our heavenly Father—the one person who knows us completely and loves us unconditionally.

Perhaps you feel as though you have come to a dead end in your career, a relationship, or your spiritual life, and there is no way for your life to make a turn for the better. Maybe you think that God has forgotten you. Lift your eyes up to the Lord. Praise Him! He is your salvation, and He indwells the praises of those who love Him.

He will not forget His promises to you.

Because your love is better than life, my lips will glorify you. I will praise you as long as I live, and in your name I will lift up my hands (Psalm 63:3-4).

May 8

The Daily Way

Give of Yourself

One of the high points of a worship service should be the time the offering is collected. Many people, however, fail to realize the great blessing that is theirs through giving to God. They withhold their time, talent, and money from the Lord and, by doing so, miss a tremendous blessing.

True praise incorporates giving. In fact, we cannot praise God adequately without giving something of ourselves to Him through prayer or praise.

In Exodus 23:19, God admonishes us to honor Him with the "firstfruits" of our crops. We give to God because we know He loves us and has given more of Himself to us than we could ever give back.

Giving is an integral part of worship and praise, but it is not restricted solely to the area of finances. Jesus explained this to His disciples in the Parable of The Sheep and The Goats: "I tell you the truth, whatever you did for one of the least of these brothers of mine, you did for me" (Matthew 25:40). We actually praise and honor God when we show kindness and care for someone else.

You may be wondering if God really cares whether or not you give. He does—but not because He needs your gift. What He desires is your declaration of faith in Him.

Through giving, we acknowledge God as the One in control of all things. We also testify to our dependence on Him, and that we are only stewards of what He has given to us. Regardless of your financial status, God is the One who has provided for every need you have. He is totally faithful. Therefore, He is worthy of your praise, honor, and worship.

Each of us can give a portion of our time, talents, and wealth to the Lord. When we do, we acknowledge Him as the source of all blessing.

Bring the best of the firstfruits of your soil to the house of the Lord your God (Exodus 23:19).

The Daily Way

May 9

Praise through Giving

A group of Christians approached another believer about making a major contribution to a particular campaign. They did not know that this man had a serious problem with giving. He found it difficult to praise God with the money the Lord had given to Him.

After this group of men told him what the need was and challenged him to give a certain amount, he responded: "I understand why you think I can give this large sum of money. I own a large company, but there is something you do not know. My mother is in an expensive nursing home. My brother, who had no insurance, died and left a wife and five children. My son is deeply religious, and he is working with the poor and makes less than the national poverty level."

The men responded humbly by saying that they did not know any of this. "Well, then," the man said, "you also need to know that I have not given them a penny. Why would you think that I would give to your project?"

Only God can soften the hardened heart of the person who refuses to give to others. After reading this account, the image that comes to mind is one of a person who is bitter and void of true peace and contentment.

Praise and giving go beautifully together because both honor the Lord. They also teach us to set our heart's devotion on God and not on ourselves. The way to blessing is a way that is outlined by sacrificial giving.

Charles Spurgeon writes, "To bless the Lord is never unseasonable. Our thankfulness is not to be kept secret. What a blessed mouthful is God's praise!"

Our ability to praise God through giving is our personal testimony to His faithfulness. Do you trust Him enough to give all that you are and all that you have?

My heart is steadfast, O God; I will sing and make music with all my soul (Psalm 108:1).

May 10 — The Daily Way

A Heart Commitment

Giving was a major emphasis of Paul's ministry, especially during his third missionary journey. He understood that generosity naturally led to praise and worship of God. Unfortunately, when Paul thought of the Corinthian believers, he had to acknowledge that they had failed to keep their promises in the area of giving.

The Corinthian believers made a commitment to God. They had promised to support the poor through their gifts and offerings. However, when it came to doing this, they had not fulfilled their promise (2 Corinthians 8).

Praise always requires a heart commitment. Giving requires the same action. If we fail to complete the promises we have made to God, our hearts will be saddened, and we won't feel like praising Him.

Therefore, before you make a commitment to give, ask God to show you what He wants you to do, along with how much he wants you to give. Paul appealed to the Corinthians to fulfill their promise by reminding them of the grace that had been given to them by Jesus Christ.

God's mercy, love, and forgiveness had been poured out on their lives. He admonished them to "finish the work!"

Like us, these believers had been given much, and it should not have been a burden for them to give back a portion of what God had given to them. Every occasion we have to give to God needs to be viewed as an opportunity to praise Him for all that He has done for us.

Whoever sows sparingly will also reap sparingly, and whoever sows generously will also reap generously (2 Corinthians 9:6).

The Daily Way — May 11

Entering God's Presence through Praise

What is praise? It is adoration, thanksgiving, appreciation, and worship of our Lord and Savior. Praise flows from a relationship of love and devotion from us to the Lord. Praise brings us closer to Him. It changes us and helps us grow in our faith. Praise reminds us of who God is. A life filled with praise places us in a position to receive God's blessings.

C.S. Lewis said:

> Only in acts of worship and praise can a person learn to believe in the goodness and the greatness of God. God wants us to praise Him not because He needs or craves in any sense our flattery, but because He knows that praise creates joy and thankfulness.

Praise is not something that we do for God. Nor is it something that we do in order to get God's approval so that He will grant our desires. When we praise God, we are changed—even if our circumstances are not. While God is present everywhere, all the time, He is present in a special way when His people praise Him.

Words are the expressions of our hearts. The Bible says, "Out of the overflow of the heart the mouth speaks" (Matthew 12:34).

What happens to the person who continually complains about the problems and challenges of life?

If he only focuses on those things, he will lose sight of his eternal destiny. He may become pessimistic, even depressed. We all have tiring days, minor setbacks, and unexpected expenses. As believers, we can choose to find strength by praising God, or we may sink into despair.

Regardless of our problems or difficulties, when we praise God our focus shifts. We become aware, once again, of who He is and His love for us. Why wait? Praise God now and experience His power, which is capable of handling anything you might face.

You are enthroned as the Holy One; you are the praise of Israel (Psalm 22:3).

May 12

The Daily Way

Transforming Your Life

When a person does a job well, we find ourselves wanting to praise him. But what about our praise to the Lord for who He is and what He has done for us? Charles Spurgeon writes:

> The Lord always deserves to be praised for what He is in Himself, for His works of creation and providence, for His goodness towards His creatures, and especially for the transcendent act of redemption.

Praise is a constant reminder of God's unconditional love, His all-knowing wisdom, and His unchanging power.

Spurgeon goes on to say, "It is always beneficial to praise the Lord; it cheers the day and brightens the night; it lightens toil and softens sorrow."

Praise reminds of us of who God is, and who we really are—sinful human beings, redeemed and saved solely by the grace of God. Without Christ we are nothing, but in Christ we have every good thing.

Because Jesus Christ died on the cross for the sins of mankind, those who believe in Him have newness of life and the promise of eternity with Him. But we don't have to wait for eternity to enter God's presence. Through praise we can enter His presence every minute of every day.

As we praise God, He begins to work in our lives, conforming us to His image. Our prayer should be, "Lord, make me into the person You desire me to be." His power will transform your life and give you strength and hope for what He has called you to do.

Whatever your past difficulties may be, there continues to be many reasons to praise the Lord. For it is through our praise that we enter His presence—into His very throne room.

I will praise you as long as I live, and in your name I will lift up my hands (Psalm 63:4).

The Daily Way

May 13

Networking with Heaven

Every generation has a buzzword. In the 90s, the word was networking. It was not really what you knew, but rather who you knew that was important.

The ultimate form of networking in the kingdom of God is developing a life of praise. Praise is a direct connection with our heavenly Father.

Take a moment and ask yourself: "Do I delight in praising God? Am I networking with heaven or am I tangled up in the world's demands and pressures?"

The Bible tells us the angels are praising God, singing, "Worthy is the Lamb, who was slain, to receive power and wealth and wisdom and strength and honor and glory and praise!" (Revelation 5:12).

Praise demands us to change—from focusing on ourselves to focusing on God. However, many times we resist change for various reasons. We think change will be too hard or too painful.

We may fear the unknown and prefer to stay in our comfort zones. However, praising God has a positive impact on our lives. Our attitudes, relationships, perceptions, and even our desires change. When we take time to praise our Savior, we will find it nearly impossible to harbor anger, bitterness, and resentment toward others.

As we praise God, He takes our anger and replaces it with compassion. He destroys our bitterness and replaces it with mercy. When we praise God in the midst of our difficulties, we find our eyes turned toward the Lord. We find healing for our discouragement, despondency, and grief.

Our eternal destiny is in heaven with our magnificent Lord and Savior, who desires our praise and worship. You don't have to wait until eternity to network with God. You can do this right now as you rejoice in His love and delight yourself in His presence.

I will be glad and rejoice in you; I will sing praise to your name, O Most High (Psalm 9:2).

May 14

The Daily Way

Wearing a Spiritual Garment

The prophet Isaiah writes:

> The Spirit of the Sovereign Lord is on me, because the Lord has anointed me to preach good news to the poor. He has sent me … to bestow on them a crown of beauty instead of ashes, the oil of gladness instead of mourning, and a garment of praise instead of a spirit of despair (Isaiah 61:1, 3).

Garments or clothing are things that we wear every day. They are not made just to hang in our closets.

We also have a spiritual garment to wear—praise. If we leave it hanging, we will fail to grow in our relationship with the Lord. There are many reasons we have for praising the Lord—salvation, mercy, grace, family, health, and provision for our needs. When things are going well and we feel happy, it is easy to praise Him. However, when times are hard, often we don't feel like praising God or reading the Bible.

Regardless of how we feel, if we lift up the name of Jesus, He will remove the cloud of discouragement surrounding us and give us His power and strength.

It is when we fix our eyes on Christ through praise that He changes us. Our circumstances may stay the same or even grow more difficult. We may not see an end in sight, but because we know our future is in heaven with the Lord, we can continue to praise His name.

May the words of Fanny Crosby be your prayer every day:

> Praise Him! Praise Him! Jesus our blessed Redeemer! Sing, O earth—His wonderful love proclaim! Hail Him! Hail Him! Highest archangels in glory; strength and honor give to His holy name!

As for me, I will always have hope; I will praise you more and more (Psalm 71:14).

The Daily Way

May 15

Praise: The Ultimate Cure for Pride

Pride asks, "How do others perceive me?" and "What impression am I making on other people?" When there is pride in our lives, it makes us self-conscious. Pride wants to be praised.

While we all need encouragement, only God deserves praise.

Pride can blind us to any feeling of gratitude toward the Lord. Unchecked, it will ultimately separate us from God and those we love. The only cure for pride is surrender to the Lord Jesus Christ—making a commitment to Him and then choosing to let the Spirit of God work in our lives on a daily basis.

After David was anointed as king over Israel, he and his men brought the ark of God back to Jerusalem (1 Chronicles 15).

David appointed musicians and singers, and the ark of God entered the city with shouts, trumpets, and the playing of harps. In exuberance and excitement, David took off his royal robe and began to dance before the Lord (2 Samuel 6:14). But his wife Michal watched and later criticized David's actions. She was proud and thought David's actions were not kingly (2 Samuel 6:20).

Placing undue importance on our self-images and the opinions of others are just two of the distractions that Satan uses to discourage us. However, God wants us to have healthy self images based on His unconditional love for us. Once we accept Christ as our Savior, we become children of the King of kings and are made members of His royal family.

David was not concerned about his image. He was praising God. He was focused on the Lord and not on himself. Are you concerned about your appearance before others? Don't withhold your worship of the Lord because of fear of what others will think.

Praise frees you from the hold of pride.

Those who walk in pride he is able to humble (Daniel 4:37).

May 16

The Daily Way

Praise and an Untrue Heart

Pride is not the only thing that can keep us from praising God. An untrue heart can squelch both the desire and the ability to develop a life of praise. An untrue heart is a heart that is insincere, hypocritical, or filled with doubt. The writer of Hebrews said:

> Let us draw near to God with a sincere heart in full assurance of faith, having our hearts sprinkled to cleanse us from a guilty conscience and having our bodies washed with pure water (Hebrews 10:22).

There are some people who try to honor God with their lips while their hearts are full of anger, bitterness, or envy. However, God knows the status of our hearts and our weaknesses.

We cannot develop a life of praise alone or in our own strength. Instead, we must surrender our intellect, feelings, and will to the Lord. As we do this, God will empower us to develop a habit of praising Him—regardless of our circumstances.

In Genesis 22, when God asked Abraham to sacrifice his son, Isaac, He was asking him to surrender the object of his love. He was asking Abraham to give up something that meant more to him than anything else.

Did God want Abraham to sacrifice Isaac? No. God wanted to be certain that Abraham was willing to surrender everything to Him. Like Abraham, God wants us to surrender to Him. He wants us to praise Him. Praise is a sacrifice that costs us our pride, our plans, and our desires. True praise requires that we place everything on the altar to the Lord.

Don't let pride or an untrue heart keep you from a life of praise. Yield to the Lord, come before Him in humility, and God will give you His strength and power to live a victorious life.

Praise be to God, who has not rejected my prayer or withheld his love from me! (Psalm 66:20).

The Daily Way

May 17

Everything's in a Name

In biblical times, a name often represented a person's character or calling. The same can be true for us today. Our names can reflect who we are, and what character traits we have.

If names are important to us, they are even more important when it comes to our understanding of the Lord. His names are a revelation of His nature, identity, and sovereignty. If we really want to know God, we have to know His names and what they reveal about Him.

He wants us to know Him intimately and to praise Him completely. He desires a deep, abiding relationship with each of us. Hebrews 13:15 states, "Through Jesus, therefore, let us continually offer to God a sacrifice of praise—the fruit of lips that confess his name."

The sacrifice of praise that the writer of Hebrews is talking about is speaking the names of Jesus. Some of the names of the Lord are: Jehovah Jireh, our provider; Jehovah Rapha, our healer; Jehovah Nissi, our banner; and Jehovah Shalom, our peace.

God delights in the praises of His people. Praise Him when you are happy. Praise Him when you are lonely or worried. Call out to Jehovah Shalom. He will give you His peace. Praise Him when you have a specific need and don't know how it is going to be met. Seek Jehovah Jireh and trust in His unfailing provision.

When we praise the names of God, we begin to know our Savior more and we see His work in our lives.

Praise be to his glorious name forever; may the whole earth be filled with his glory. Amen and Amen (Psalm 72:19).

May 18

The Daily Way

God Knows Your Name

Have you ever wanted to change your name or wondered who you would be without a name?

Names are important. It is by our name that other people identify us and that we identify ourselves. In biblical times, parents gave their children names with descriptive meanings such as strong, trustworthy, and leader, in hopes they would embody these traits when they grew up. Ecclesiastes 7:1 states, "A good name is better than fine perfume."

The words we use to describe other people can either hurt or encourage them. There was a teacher who asked her students to tell what they wanted to do when they grew up.

For the most part the students gave the usual responses—doctor, lawyer, policeman, nurse, pilot, and firefighter. Then the teacher asked Billy. He said, "I want to be possible."

"Possible?" she asked.

"Yes," he replied, "because my mom tells me all the time that I'm impossible. So I want to grow up to be possible."

As believers, we are adopted into the kingdom of God. We are given a new identity, a new name, and a life filled with possibility. We are called the children of God. No matter what our past and regardless of our mistakes, the Lord knows our name and desires our worship and praise.

As a son or daughter of the King of kings, there are many reasons why we should praise Him. He does not change. He is mightier than any problem we might face. He is all-wise and loving. He will never leave us. He is our hope. So whether we like the name on our birth certificate or the nicknames we have been given by those who know us, we can find joy in knowing that we are called by God and that our names are written on the palms of His hands (Isaiah 49:16).

Sing to God, sing praise to his name, extol him who rides on the clouds (Psalm 68:4).

The Daily Way

In the Name of God

There was a day when a person's name meant everything—more than all the money and prestige in the world. The Bible tells us that because names have incredible meaning and importance, there were times when they were changed. These name changes were an indication of a new identity and significant of a new calling of God.

God changed Abraham's name from Abram, meaning "the father is exalted," to Abraham, which means "the father of a multitude."

But there was another reason God made the change. Abraham's parents probably were worshipers in the moon cult of Ur.

They named their son Abram, suggesting that his name may have represented a moon god or another pagan deity. God wanted Abraham to have a name that reflected His plan for Abraham's life. He also wanted him to have a clear break from his old pagan lifestyle.

When you worship God, take time to consider His names and how each one applies to your life. Reflect on a few of God's names:

- Elohim—majestic Lord
- El Shaddai—all-powerful, all-sufficient, transcendent, sovereign God
- Yahweh—the proper name for God, which means "self-existing one." I Am!
- Yahweh Nissi—our banner
- Yahweh Rapha—our healer
- Yahweh Rohi—our shepherd
- Yahweh Jireh—our provider
- Yahweh Shalom—our peace
- Adonai—master, ruler, Lord
- Abba—our father who intimately cares

As you spend time worshiping the Lord, remember God's name reflects His attributes and nature. He is your Peace, Provider, Healer, Shepherd, Lord, and Eternal Savior!

I will ... sing praise to the name of the Lord Most High (Psalm 7:17).

May 20

The Daily Way

Praising God through Giving

Some believers make the mistake of thinking that how they use money can illustrate the totality of their lives before God. But there is no way for money exclusively to represent the true nature of our hearts. Only the Lord knows where we stand with Him.

We can give to spiritual causes, but our giving does not buy a favorable position in God's kingdom. This is why Jesus was so quick to point out that we should give to God according to our faith and love for Him, not so others will see and be impressed.

Luke writes:

> As he looked up, Jesus saw the rich putting their gifts into the temple treasury. He also saw a poor widow put in two very small copper coins. "I tell you the truth," he said, "this poor widow has put in more than all the others. All these people gave their gifts out of their wealth; but she out of her poverty put in all she had to live on" (Luke 21:1-4).

When we fail to give back to God, we miss a tremendous blessing and overlook the fact that He is the One who gives us the ability to make a living. He also provides for those who have very little or who have great financial needs. God has commanded us to tithe a portion of our income—not so He can have more money, but so that our priorities will be right: God first and above all else.

Giving proves that:
- We trust God completely.
- God is the Lord of our lives and finances.
- We are willing to submit to His authority.
- We acknowledge that He is the owner of everything, and we are stewards of His provision.

When we give, God sets us free to receive His blessing and to enjoy the goodness of His protective care.

Give to Caesar what is Caesar's, and to God what is God's (Luke 20:25).

The Daily Way

May 21

Praising God through Generosity

Andrew Carnegie's wife was so fond of classical music that at the end of every year, she insisted that Andrew pay any outstanding debts incurred by the New York Philharmonic Symphony. Finally, Andrew became weary and faced the symphony's board of directors with this challenge: "I can't keep doing this year in and year out. You need to go out and raise half of the money needed and I will give the other half."

Within a few days the board members called him with good news. "Mr. Carnegie, we have met your request. We have half of the money we need."

Carnegie was pleased, applauded their efforts, and said he would fulfill his end of the agreement. Before he hung up the telephone he asked, "Where did you get the other half?"

There was a pause and then the answer: "Mrs. Carnegie!"

Some people have a spirit of generosity and that generosity is the fuel that keeps them going each day. In Luke, Jesus reminds us of a simple, yet basic truth: "Give, and it will be given to you. A good measure, pressed down, shaken together and running over, will be poured into your lap. For with the measure you use, it will be measured to you" (Luke 6:38).

If we are stingy and withhold our tithes and offerings in support of God's work, then we can expect the same in return. Our motivation for giving to God's work should be to praise, worship, and honor Him.

When you do give, make sure that you are motivated by God and not guilt. No price tag can be placed on Christ's death on the cross. It was there God gave to us His greatest gift—salvation through His Son. Therefore, ask God to teach you how to give generously, as it was given to you.

A generous man will prosper (Proverbs 11:25).

May 22

A Heart of Thanksgiving

As the enemy attempts to lure us subtly away from God's best plan for our lives, we begin to compromise in many areas. And the trick that the enemy has used since the beginning of time is trying to convince us that we are getting a bad deal.

Human nature does not like to get taken by anybody or anything—and the enemy knows this. So, once Satan convinces us that God is robbing us of some of life's greatest pleasures, we begin to plan and to plot how we will get what we think we deserve. It is dangerous to venture down such a path.

However, there is a way to combat such tempting thoughts. To have a heart of gratitude means that we appreciate what God has given us. In fact, life itself is a gift from God to us for our enjoyment and pleasure.

When Paul and Silas were tossed into prison, they sang praises and hymns to God. These grateful hearts prepared the way for God to do something incredible in that Philippian jail. Had they been murmuring and grumbling about how a loving God could let them land in such a place, they would have missed an opportunity to lead a man and his entire family to the Lord.

As we seek God more and more, we discover that for every temptation the enemy presents, there is a greater blessing God wants to give. We must remain faithful to the Lord in those trying moments, pressing ahead with the knowledge that God will not withhold His best plan for our lives as long as we are putting Him first.

Prayer: Lord, please help me realize when I have an ungrateful heart and give me a heart of thanksgiving.

The Lord is my strength. ... My heart trusts in him, and I am helped. My heart leaps for joy and I will give thanks to him in song (Psalm 28:7).

The Daily Way

May 23

Heaven on Earth

Have you ever known anyone who went to the airport to catch a flight and decided to live in his new destination permanently? Sound crazy? Unfortunately this is the attitude many Christians have regarding heaven. Without much thought given to our eternal destination, how many of us spend most of our time, energy, and money planning our future for this life on earth?

Many who recite the words of the Lord's Prayer, "Our Father who is in heaven," never stop and think about heaven. In Psalm 19, heaven is used to describe the unending realm of the constellations. In 2 Corinthians and the book of Revelation, heaven is referred to as a definite place, a new Jerusalem, and a home prepared for God's children.

Our heavenly Father is very much in heaven, but we can experience a little bit of heaven on earth right now because our Lord walks and talks with us. Nothing escapes His watchful eye. He is especially interested in us and dwells in the hearts of those who trust and believe in His Son.

When the apostle Paul thought of heaven, he longed to be there. He said, "I am torn between the two: I desire to depart and be with Christ, which is better by far; but it is more necessary for you that I remain in the body" (Philippians 1:23-24).

Can you honestly say today that you share Paul's sentiment? Are you longing for the time when you will be face-to-face with the Savior? If you find this question difficult to answer, stop and reflect on the goodness of God. Imagine being in His glorious presence, apart from all sorrow, pain, and strife. Now, lift your praises to Him for His unending love and incomparable faithfulness.

Prayer: Lord help me to turn my thoughts away from the troubles of this world and toward my incredible future with You.

Devote yourselves to prayer, being watchful and thankful (Colossians 4:2).

Our Eternal Destination

Some day, we who belong to Christ will experience firsthand the splendor and the magnificence of heaven. Our earthly lives are temporal, what is most important is our eternal destination.

In heaven, we will finally be free from Satan's assaults of temptation, deception, and division. There will be no separation or dissatisfaction. All of our restlessness and discontentment will be over.

We will be made complete in God's presence. There will be no tears or anguish in heaven. There will be no more death because we will be home forever. There will be no sorrow or remorse.

How often do we find ourselves regretful because we have said unkind words, harbored selfish motives, or had wrong attitudes? In heaven, there are no painful memories—no nightmares, flashbacks, baggage, or broken hearts. Anger and pain will not exist.

As believers, we have a daily challenge to live this life to the fullest—as we share the good news of the Gospel, obey the call of God on our lives, and grow in our walk with the Lord. Everything we do impacts eternity.

The apostle Paul told Timothy:

> Command them to do good, to be rich in good deeds, and to be generous and willing to share. In this way they will lay up treasure for themselves as a firm foundation for the coming age, so that they may take hold of the life that is truly life (1 Timothy 6:18-19).

As you go about your day, ask God to help you look beyond the trials of this life. No matter what pain you are experiencing, it will not exist in heaven. Remember, God is your hope and your strength!

We fix our eyes not on what is seen, but on what is unseen. For what is seen is temporary, but what is unseen is eternal (2 Corinthians 4:18).

The Daily Way

May 25

Who Is the Unknown God?

Our society is fascinated with power. In fact, many people crave it to such a degree that they would do anything to gain more of it. More than likely, these are the very people who have never tapped into the infinite power that has been given to us through a personal relationship with the Lord Jesus Christ.

During the "dot com" boom of the late 90s, many people became overnight millionaires. Their newfound wealth gave them an incredible sense of power, that is, until the stock market crash that followed soon thereafter. Those who have bought into this type of "instant power" have never experienced true power—the power of God. While many may appear to have power from the world's perspective, they really are weak from God's viewpoint. This is because they lack God's power in their lives.

There is a great difference between real power and the mirage of power. In most settings and circumstances—even on the national and international stage—power is fleeting. It rises suddenly and dies just as quickly. There is a great difference between power that is permanent and self-giving, and power that is fleeting and self-serving. Very often, temporary power is visible, while lasting power is invisible because it has its source in God alone.

The power that is ours through Jesus Christ is a power like this world has never known. It is power to do God's work God's way. There may be times when the world will look at you and think that you are weak because you are not fighting or wrestling with an issue.

Instead of fear and anxiety, there is a calm sense of sure peace deep within your heart and mind, telling you that God will make your way straight. All you need to do is to trust in the One who has given you life and to know that He who loves you is faithful.

Whatever this life holds, you have the endless resources to face it victoriously. What a blessing!

"Not by might nor by power, but by my Spirit," says the Lord Almighty (Zechariah 4:6).

May 26

The Daily Way

Our Powerful Advocate

We probably would not believe the number of people who are seeking to know the future. They worry about tomorrow because they feel out of control today. While they may not be world leaders or CEOs of large companies, they are on a personal power quest, devising ways to gain more power and to keep from losing the power they presently have.

Unless a person is trusting Jesus Christ with every area of his life, having more of the world's power will do him no good. Position on a corporate ladder will not save him from death. But true power—the power that only God provides—saves us from an eternal death and from making some very poor decisions.

When we place our faith in God's Son and trust Him to hear our prayers for forgiveness, we are saved by His wondrous grace. He forgives our sins and enables us to live a very powerful life. This is because when we accept Christ as our Savior, God sends His Holy Spirit to live within our lives.

We no longer have to face life alone. Someone very powerful is facing it with us. When you need guidance for your life, God will provide the wisdom you need as you pray. Trust Him and you will find that He will guide your every step. This is a powerful truth, and it is the reality of God's power at work in your life.

The power that God infuses into your life is the same power that He used to raise Jesus from the grave. He has given His Spirit to you so that you might have authority and influence in your world. Therefore, don't get bogged down by the circumstances of life. You have a powerful advocate through prayer. Jesus Christ is our personal source of life-changing power.

Prayer: Lord, thank You for the hope that You have given me through Your Son, Jesus Christ. Help me to remember that all the strength and power that I need is available through You.

We have one who speaks to the Father in our defense—Jesus Christ (1 John 2:1).

The Daily Way — May 27

Moments of Weakness

Sometimes our vision fails us. We look at the muck and mire of our own lives, the shambles that lie at our feet, and wonder aloud how God could do anything with us. We are a mess and we know God knows it. Yet, over and over in His Word, He promises to use us for His glory.

At times, it is difficult for us to see beyond ourselves. We see what we are, while God sees what we can become. However, all our striving, all our determination, all our energy will not complete the transformation process. It is through God's grace alone that we become what He has envisioned for us to be all along.

Paul had many trials and tribulations while delivering the Gospel message to his world. He even had a constant nagging affliction of some sort. While many scholars have speculated as to the source of this affliction, Paul never says what it is. He does not want us to miss what is most important about our moments of weakness.

Paul writes, "That is why, for Christ's sake, I delight in weaknesses, in insults, in hardships, in persecutions, in difficulties. For when I am weak, then I am strong" (2 Corinthians 12:10).

From the thorns in our lives, God brings forth roses. When we are hanging by a thread at the end of our rope, God gives us the grace to hang on—He gives us the grace to scurry to the top of the rope. He does not want us to just make it; rather, His desire is to see us succeed by finding our strength in Him.

It certainly takes time and maturity to—like Paul—praise and thank God for our weaknesses. Yet, when we are willing to humble ourselves before God, He will exalt us (James 4:10). In the midst of the trials you may be facing today, cry out to the Lord.

Prayer: Lord, as I face difficulty in my life, give me the strength to continue, knowing that through Your grace You will accomplish Your will for my life.

I became a servant of this gospel by the gift of God's grace given me through the working of his power (Ephesians 3:7).

May 28   The Daily Way

He Will Move Mountains

As we face challenges in our lives, there are a number of reasons we might not pray. We may tell ourselves that we are too busy to pray. We may think we can solve the problem on our own. Or we may think God does not answer our prayers. And even if we eventually pray, we sometimes do it out of duty more than faith that God will answer us.

Yet, God hears our prayers. Jesus told His disciples that faith only the size of a mustard seed was needed to move mountains. It is clear that it does not take much for us to put our trust in God and to allow Him to do the spectacular in our lives. His grace surpasses all our expectations in life.

As we begin to pray with faith, emboldened to believe God will do the impossible in our lives, He shows up and His glory is revealed. He answers our prayers in one way or another. It is not always the way we imagined Him answering them, but His best is revealed for us.

When this occurs in our lives, we begin to approach God's throne of grace confidently. While we should never demand that God do things our way, we should recognize He wants us to seek Him on both the easy and tough issues in our lives. He wants us to come before Him with confidence that He loves us and He desires to help us.

All our cynicism begins to vanish in the wake of God answering our prayers. When heaven opens up and pours out miracles into our lives, we realize the truth. We realize He loves us so much that He will move mountains for us. Hallelujah to the King of kings!

Prayer: Lord, give me confidence to go before You in prayer, knowing that You desire to meet me where I am in life.

Let your conversation be always full of grace, seasoned with salt, so that you may know how to answer everyone (Colossians 4:6).

The Daily Way

May 29

God's Work of Art

Have you ever had a hero—someone you knew you could count on when life turned dark and stormy? Have you ever played sports and had one teammate who you knew could win the game for you, no matter how far behind you were? Have you ever experienced someone meeting your biggest need when you least expected it?

Just when we thought we were finished, God was beginning to work on us. We looked at our lives and thought we had created a mess not even God could clean. However, we did not realize these types of messes are His specialty. He delights in redeeming the forsaken.

God's grace gives us confidence because He does things in our lives that we could never do. He transforms and changes us into new people. He takes the messes we make and converts them into works of art. Suddenly, we are not helpless people, limping through life without hope or purpose—we are people with vision, racing down God's perfect path for our lives.

Paul knew this as well as anybody. Before he came to Christ, he was a scoundrel, a murderer, and a hypocrite. He was full of the law and knew nothing of grace. But God so transformed Paul's life that this pious aristocrat became God's mouthpiece during the birth of the new church. Paul went from condemning Christians to walking side-by-side with them.

Today, as you think about the change God has caused in your own life, praise Him for doing what no one else could do. He rescued you from eternal death. He cleansed the stains of sin from your heart. And now He has an incredible plan for your future.

Prayer: Lord, show me places in my heart You desire to change in me today.

For the grace of God that brings salvation has appeared to all men (Titus 2:11).

May 30

The Daily Way

Saved from Drowning

A group of young men was meeting by a river. During their usual horseplay, one of the men fell into the water. Immediately, this fellow began to thrash around, and it became obvious that he could not swim.

Another member of the group, a strong swimmer, stood by and watched as his friend fought to stay afloat and alive. Those on shore began to shout at the one who was a good swimmer and demanded that he jump into the water and save his friend.

However, he waited a few more seconds. Once the drowning man stopped his wild struggle, his friend dove in and pulled him to safety.

When the rescue was over, the rescuer explained why he had waited to save the drowning man: "If I had jumped in earlier, he would have been too strong for me and possibly both of us would have drowned. Only by waiting until he was too exhausted to try to save himself could I save him."

There are times when our self effort can prevent us from being saved. This is especially true concerning our spiritual salvation.

There is only one way to be saved and rescued from a sure death, and that is by stopping all human efforts and crying out to the Lord Jesus Christ for His forgiveness and mercy.

The more a person seeks to devise ways of saving himself, the deeper he will sink into fear and disillusionment. Salvation is a gift, not the result of our good works. It is a gift that is given graciously by God, who loves us with an eternal love. Truly, there is no greater gift we can receive!

Do you feel as though you are drowning and want to give up?

Jesus is your Savior. Call out to Him and He will save you. Praise to the Lord Jesus Christ who died so that we may experience eternal life.

I tell you the truth, he who believes has everlasting life (John 6:47).

The Daily Way

May 31

Enter the Door of Hope

What is the focus of your life? Christ's focus was the redemption of mankind. His gaze was set on your salvation. In fact, this was the only reason He came to earth. If you had been the only person in need of His gracious gift of eternal life, He would have left heaven and endured the heartbreak of rejection, and ultimately death on the cross, so you could have eternal life.

None of us will ever be required to do what Jesus did at Calvary, though God will demand that we deny ourselves and follow His Son. There is no room for self-centered thinking. There is only room for holy devotion to the One who loves us with an eternal love. He gave His life, so we might have life.

The psalmist writes, "Better is one day in your courts than a thousand elsewhere; I would rather be a doorkeeper in the house of my God than dwell in the tents of the wicked" (Psalm 84:10).

Psalm 84 is a reminder that even before Christ came, men and women longed to experience God's love and protection. We have no idea what the circumstances of this writer's life were like.

However, we can know from reading his words that he was facing extreme difficulty and stress.

Yet, he found hope and comfort in God's presence. He knew that there was a door standing before him—one of hope and not defeat.

God had a plan for his life, and the Lord has a plan for your life, too. You can pray with the psalmist: "Hear my prayer, O Lord God Almighty; listen to me, O God of Jacob. ... Better is one day in your courts than a thousand elsewhere" (Psalm 84:8, 10).

Jesus is your door of hope. When you enter His presence, you will discover true intimacy and peace.

O Lord Almighty, blessed is the man who trusts in you (Psalm 84:12).

Looking Up When Life Knocks You Down

The Daily Way

June 1

God's Scouts

As the voice of the Holy Spirit calls us to do courageous things for the Kingdom of God, we sometimes wonder if we are really hearing His voice. We may shy away from walking down a certain path in faith and boldness for fear of ruining God's reputation when, in fact, it is His glory that rests at the end of the road.

Paul found God's grace in the unlikeliest of places—on a dusty road to Damascus. Yet, he was more than simply arrested by God's splendor and glory. In a matter of days, as Paul regained his vision, he saw God's vision for his life. Basking in the glow of God's glorious grace, Paul found himself venturing into something that less than a week before no one would have conceived possible.

More than trail blazers, God is looking for trail scouts—people who are willing to head down the paths God has already cleared for them. Whenever God asks us to do something that seems impossible, He does not expect us to do it in our might. He does not ask us to make it happen; He asks us to participate in a small portion of His plan of grace for mankind.

As believers whom God has captured with His love, we must be willing to obey the voice of the Holy Spirit, no matter how impossible the situation seems. Even if His leading seems to be taking us down an improbable path, we know we can count on Him because He has already prepared the way. Every heart that needs prodding, every mind that needs changing, every eye that needs opening—they all have been touched by God. All we have to do is obey and watch His grace unfold before our eyes.

Prayer: Lord, whenever life seems impossible, please give me the strength to trust You and the faith to go forward.

For everyone born of God overcomes the world. This is the victory that has overcome the world, even our faith (1 John 5:4).

June 2

The Triumph of Grace

Reading about the apostles of the New Testament, our views can be skewed somewhat by knowing the entire timeline of their ministry. We read highlights and letters, dramatic bits and pieces of lives that proclaimed the resurrection of Jesus along with the power of the Gospel. The days, months, and years they spent waiting for God to do the impossible in a post-resurrection world seem but mere pauses in a flurry of God-orchestrated activity.

Regardless of the vision we may have for our lives or the direction we have been led by the Holy Spirit, we cannot expect to get ahead of God's timeline. After Jesus left the earth, the disciples spent a substantial amount of time waiting for prayers to be answered as well as wondering when God was going to rescue them from dire situations. We, too, must be willing disciples, waiting patiently for God to work in our midst.

God's plan oftentimes has curves we never expected. Ten years passed from the time Paul encountered the risen Christ to the time God commissioned him to ministry. Ten years! During that time, the Lord was preparing him—softening his heart and positioning him so that he could be used to impact the church in the first century and for generations to come.

Waiting on God can be difficult at times. In our anxiousness to see Him move, we have a tendency to try and prod God along. We want to see His glory here and now. Yet, God does not let us venture into new territory alone. He prepares the hearts and minds of those we are to encounter on our journey so that the fullness of His plan becomes apparent in the aftermath.

Prayer: Lord, quiet my heart and help me to remain patient as I wait upon Your plan to unfold in my life.

Wait for the Lord; be strong and take heart and wait for the Lord (Psalm 27:14).

The Daily Way

June 3

The Pattern for Revival

In the heart of every believer, a hunger should exist—a hunger to see God use us to advance His Kingdom in ways we never imagined. Christianity morphs into little more than a stale religion if we quit pursuing God. The moment we get content with where we are is the moment we stop moving toward God. He has more for us than we can ever imagine.

While God desires to turn our lives upside down and use us in His amazing plan of redemption for the world, He never forces His will on us. If our desire is not there, He will not make us do it. He will accomplish His will through other willing vessels. But who wants to miss out on the opportunity to be an integral part of God's plan?

However, before any such life-changing events can occur in our own hearts, we must surrender unconditionally to the leadership of the Holy Spirit. On the road to Damascus and in the days following, we do not read of a defiant Paul, trying to resist every directive. Instead, we find a Paul who is stunned momentarily and quickly submits to the Holy Spirit's voice in his life.

Surrendering to the Holy Spirit's leadership in our lives opens the door for God to begin shaking our world to the point we may not recognize it once He is finished. Yet, it is a shaking that takes us from awed bystanders to active participants in His plan of grace and redemption.

Taking the first step is never easy. However, relinquishing our freedom to the One who brings ultimate freedom will pave the way for a personal revival to occur in our hearts.

Prayer: Lord, empower me daily to surrender to the leadership of the Holy Spirit in my life.

For the kingdom of God is not a matter of eating and drinking, but of righteousness, peace and joy in the Holy Spirit (Romans 14:17).

June 4

The Daily Way

Your Internal Compass

There is a tension afoot in our world today. Really, it has existed from the moment mankind sinned in the Garden of Eden.

It comes as a result of our being tempted to twist the truth of God's Word so that we can live conveniently and not totally committed to Jesus Christ.

When an unbelieving friend wants to know if Jesus Christ is the only way for him or her to be saved, our answer should be an affirming "yes!" There is no other way for mankind to be saved except by faith in God's Son (John 14:6).

God's Word is a double-edged sword. It is able to cut through the dross surrounding the weak and vain arguments of those who are seeking another way to gain salvation.

It is true that sin and disbelief can keep us from speaking what we know is true. However, these cannot stop the light of God's Word from touching the blinded eyes of those who have never experienced His salvation.

Without the light of the Holy Spirit to transform them, the hearts of men would remain in darkness. Revival never falls on the casual seekers of Christ. Instead, it falls on those who are seeking the Lord with all of their hearts.

If your deepest desire is to be radically transformed by the power of the Holy Spirit via internal revival, the truth of God's Word must be written on your heart. It must become your internal compass for every road you travel and for all that you do.

Prayer: Lord, help my words and actions today to reflect the fact that Your Word is the ultimate truth.

For the word of God is living and active. Sharper than any double-edged sword, it penetrates even to dividing soul and spirit, joints and marrow; it judges the thoughts and attitudes of the heart (Hebrews 4:12).

The Daily Way

June 5

Spiritual Battles

There is an unfounded idea in some circles that when we come to Christ our lives will be fine. All the worries and problems that plagued us before we accepted Christ will disappear once we commit our lives to Him. That is far from the truth. In fact, just as a blacksmith uses fire to shape iron, God uses difficulties in our lives to shape us.

Usually when God's revival begins, an opposition arises—a spiritual battle takes place, as the enemy seeks to mount a siege on our hearts.

In order to see revival occur in the lives of men and women, we must be willing to stand steadfast in our faith and live uncompromising lives in the face of opposition. During revival, our hearts are cleansed of sin as we come to a point where conviction meets surrender. We become willing to give up things in our lives or to drastically change our lifestyles as evidence of our obedience to God's call.

The apostle Paul constantly fought opposition. Yet the revival in Paul's heart was so strong that he could not resist God's leading and direction. He made a decision that nothing the enemy did would keep him from doing God's will.

Prison, ridicule, torture, beatings, mockery—Paul endured all this opposition to see God's Word reach and penetrate the hearts of both Jews and Gentiles. As revival falls on our hearts, we must be prepared to withstand any opposition, honoring God through obedience to Him.

Prayer: Lord, strengthen me through Your Holy Spirit to withstand any opposition I may face.

The God of all grace, who called you to his eternal glory in Christ, after you have suffered a little while, will himself restore you and make you strong, firm and steadfast (1 Peter 5:10).

June 6 — The Daily Way

Keeping Your Integrity Intact

The longer we walk down the road with Christ, the more we understand what it means to put our trust in God. Despite our best intentions, it does not take long to realize we simply cannot determine in our hearts to live righteous lives. Our best striving and efforts fall short of God's glory.

Fortunately, there is hope. In the magnificence of creation, we see one detail that cannot escape us: God created us for relationship. Verse after verse, chapter after chapter, we read about the relationships of people bent on following after God. We see their triumphs as well as their failures, and we learn some valuable lessons.

One such valuable lesson is that we need people who will hold us accountable. No matter how hard we determine to make the right decision in every case, we are bound to falter at some point. And when we know that we do not have to answer to anyone in person, it becomes more comfortable to ease into what is convenient for us, even if it means we are compromising our integrity.

If we truly desire to live with integrity, honoring God in everything we say and do, we must find trusted friends who are willing to walk alongside us and hold us accountable for our actions. These people will be instrumental in our growth as believers. They will help us to move to new depths in our faith with Jesus Christ and they will love us regardless of the flaws our lives contain.

Integrity is a key trait of a committed follower of Christ. It shows that we are not living for ourselves but for God.

Prayer: Lord, show me people in my life who can help me be accountable for my actions as I seek to honor You with all that I am.

Righteousness guards the man of integrity, but wickedness overthrows the sinner (Proverbs 13:6).

The Daily Way

June 7

Possessing Godly Integrity

Finding people with integrity in this day and age is a daunting task. While many people may desire to live with integrity, they fall short when they are put to the test. They may reason away certain actions, justifying them with a twisted world view. But what is our integrity worth? Is our integrity worth an hour's pay if we lie on our time card? Is our integrity worth the office supplies we slip into our pockets on the way home? Is our integrity worth the damage of spreading a bit of juicy gossip?

Possessing godly integrity is rare in today's world because people are determined to live for themselves, with little or no intention of living for anyone else. People compromise their integrity because they are looking out for themselves instead of living for someone other than themselves. This outlook on life infiltrates behavior, which results in dishonest action.

As we look at the life of Paul, one thing is crystal clear: He lived for no one but God. Everything Paul did was for the glory of God. Paul was scorned by men. In fact, there was a period shortly after his conversion during which he was eyed cynically by everyone. The Christians did not trust him, and the Pharisees wanted to put him in prison. Yet over time, Paul proved he was not after fame and certainly not fortune.

Paul's aim in life was to live for the glory of God. When that becomes our primary purpose in life, integrity will be a natural by-product. If we are living for and thinking about God first and foremost before we act, then what follows will be activity that intentionally honors Him. Integrity will not be contrived but overflowing.

Prayer: Lord, give me the right perspective on my life, revealing to me that living for You is far better than living for myself.

Kings take pleasure in honest lips; they value a man who speaks the truth (Proverbs 16:13).

June 8

The Daily Way

Praise from the Prison of Affliction

Regardless of how many times we have experienced the fulfillment of God's promises, we seem to have short memories.

Life suddenly veers down an unexpected path, and we begin wondering if we are going to make it. We try to find a way out of our misery and realize the situation is impossible apart from God. Instead of praising the Lord and trusting Him for a way of escape, we resort to worrying and grumbling.

If there was one man who had a right to grumble and complain in the New Testament, it was Paul. After his conversion, his life seemed to be composed of one life-threatening conflict after another. He was imprisoned, shipwrecked, tortured, or threatened. So much was Paul's suffering that many of his letters were written from prison.

Yet when we find Paul in his darkest hour, he was not griping about his circumstances—he was praising God. For Paul, praising God had become a habit, a way of life. Paul wrote to the church in Ephesus:

> Be filled with the Spirit. Speak to one another with psalms, hymns, and spiritual songs. Sing and make music in your heart to the Lord, always giving thanks to God the Father for everything, in the name of our Lord Jesus Christ (Ephesians 5:18-20).

As believers determined to honor Christ with every portion of our lives, our lips should come into harmony with our actions as we praise God at every opportunity. This is how we live with a heavenly perspective—one that is set on the One who can transform our darkest situation into one of hope and light.

Lord, remind me of Your goodness and greatness today when I get discouraged, and help me make praise a regular part of my life.

Be exalted, O Lord, in your strength; we will sing and praise your might (Psalm 21:13).

The Daily Way

Be Strong and Take Heart

Though we are confident that God has the power to deliver us from any situation or circumstance in life, we often lose hope as we try to figure out solutions to our problems. The fact remains that despite our most determined efforts to make life work harmoniously for us, we need God.

When there is no hope in our lives, we become despondent. We wonder how we are ever going to make it. Despite all our knowledge of what God can do, we opt to wallow in pity and despair. When this becomes our response, we are like many characters in the Bible.

David, who experienced the pit of despair on more than one occasion, commanded his soul to praise God, even though he did not feel hopeful or encouraged. He writes, "Why are you downcast, O my soul? Why so disturbed within me? Put your hope in God, for I will yet praise him, my Savior and my God" (Psalm 42:5).

David lived as though both praise and hope were synonymous. To him, hope was not possible without praising God. He writes, "But as for me, I will always have hope; I will praise you more and more" (Psalm 71:14).

When we begin to praise God, hope begins to rise up within us. We realize that although our situation may look bleak, we are not without a Savior. What an encouraging feeling to know that someone is willing to rescue us—not only to save the day, but also to reverse our circumstances.

As we open our mouths, may our words speak what we know is true in our hearts: God will hear our prayers and our words of praise.

Prayer: Lord, reveal the power of praise to me today, helping me to experience the overwhelming hope that comes when I praise You.

Be strong and take heart, all you who hope in the Lord (Psalm 31:24).

June 10

The Daily Way

Changing Circumstances

Being in prison for something you did not do is not an ideal situation, but Paul found a way to make it a place of praise. Most people would have been questioning why they were there, wondering if living for Christ was really the right decision. Who would want this type of abuse?

However, Paul understood the power that rested within the God he served. He knew that despite the gravity of his circumstances, God could change everything in a moment. So instead of waiting until after God delivered him to sing praises, Paul took the first step. He and Silas began crooning praises to God. Then the foundations of the prison shook.

Praise is powerful because it removes our focus from the circumstances and turns us toward God. Instead of seeing a desperate situation, we see an opportunity for God to reveal His glory to everyone involved. And in this instance, God did just that. He shook the prison and the jail doors swung open, freeing all the prisoners.

Yet God wanted to use this situation to save the Philippian jailer. Paul stopped the jailer from committing suicide and led him to Christ. Eventually, the jailer's entire family accepted Christ. As we focus on Christ, praise invites God's presence into our circumstances.

In one of his many letters to those in the early church, Paul explains his firm faith in trusting God: "Give thanks in all circumstances, for this is God's will for you in Christ Jesus" (1 Thessalonians 5:18).

Prayer: Lord, help me to focus on You and not my circumstances each day.

I am not saying this because I am in need, for I have learned to be content whatever the circumstances (Philippians 4:11).

The Daily Way — June 11

Who Is the Unknown God?

In a recent radio commentary, Chuck Colson lamented over the idolatrous condition of our world. He reported that between 1976 and 1997, the belief in astrology grew from 17 to 37 percent.

During the same time, belief in reincarnation nearly tripled from 9 to 25 percent. Up to half of the American population now says they can communicate with the dead! According to Colson, only one conclusion can be drawn from the findings and that is the economics of ABC—Anything But Christianity. We have become very undiscerning about spiritual issues.

G. K. Chesterton said, "When people cease to believe in the biblical God, the problem is not that they believe in nothing. It is that they believe in everything!"

A lack of true spiritual discernment was the same problem that Paul faced in Athens. The Athenians did not believe in God. Instead, they believed in many gods, and in order to make sure that every god was represented in their temple of worship, they even erected an altar to the "unknown god" (Acts 17:23).

How miserable life must have been for these people. They were captivated by their unbelief and sentenced to finding a way of satisfying the demands of their false gods in hope of gaining eternal life. But Paul remained determined to preach the Good News of the Gospel to them.

They may have been lost in their unbelief, but they did not have to remain that way. The knowledge they were seeking was fully available to them through a personal relationship with Jesus Christ.

Prayer: Lord, open the eyes of my heart so that I can discern Your truth.

Men of Athens! ... What you worship as something unknown I am going to proclaim to you (Acts 17:22-23).

June 12 — The Daily Way

Enlightenment of the Ages

Most of the people Paul encountered in Athens were members of two opposing groups, the Epicureans and the Stoics, and both were steeped in godless philosophies. The Epicureans pursued pleasure and were materialistic, while the Stoics rejected pagan idolatry and worshiped one "World God." Their beliefs were rooted in self-discipline and human reasoning, which led to eternal enlightenment. Simply put: the Epicureans' goal was to enjoy life, while the Stoics endured it.

As maddening as this all seems, both these groups believed they had found a way to gain a sense of higher knowledge. But in truth, they had missed the opportunity to gain eternal knowledge and salvation.

The pleasures of this world are fleeting. Human reasoning, no matter how detailed and thought-provoking, cannot deliver the infinite knowledge that is ours through a personal relationship with Christ.

In his address to these two groups, Paul said:

> The God who made the world and everything in it is the Lord of heaven and earth and does not live in temples built by hands. And he is not served by human hands, as if he needed anything, because he himself gives all men life and breath and everything else (Acts 17:24-25).

If you are on a conquest for knowledge, you do not have to look any further than Jesus Christ. If you want to experience the enlightenment that has stunned the ages, turn to the Lord and seek His will and purpose for your life. He holds the keys to the universe and all that you long to have and experience.

Prayer: Lord, my only desire is to know the fullness of Your love and truth.

God did this so that men would seek him ... and find him, though he is not far from each one of us (Acts 17:27).

The Daily Way

June 13

Hang In There

In Athens, the Spirit of God empowered Paul to present the truth of God to an unbelieving audience of Greek philosophers. Standing on Mars Hill in the Areopagus—which was viewed as the seat of worldly wisdom—he brilliantly proclaimed God's Word.

However, after his proclamation, he became emotionally shaken. He had prayed that the hearts of those who heard his words would be changed, but his message had received only a lukewarm reception. By the time he sailed for Corinth (Acts 18), he was struggling with discouragement, and God knew it. Therefore, He spoke words of encouragement to His servant:

> Do not be afraid; keep on speaking, do not be silent. For I am with you, and no one is going to attack and harm you, because I have many people in this city (Acts 18:9-10).

In other words, "Paul, you are not alone. I am aware of your circumstances. I am with you, and others who know Me are with you, too."

Paul realized the key to success was not human strength or ability but faith in an unshakeable God. His responsibility was to do what God had called him to do. God's responsibility was to bring the right results from Paul's ministry at the right time.

Though he may have fought feelings of fear and discouragement, Paul knew God was faithful and the work he had been given to do would be accomplished. The message he had been called to preach would bear fruit at the proper time. Worry, doubt, and fear about the future only lead to sorrow and disappointment. Trust God right where you are and He will bless you as you praise Him.

Prayer: Lord, I give all that I am to you—all my work and all my talents belong to You.

The one who calls you is faithful and he will do it (1 Thessalonians 5:24).

June 14

The Daily Way

A Cave of Rejection

Maybe you have just heard a negative remark that someone said about you and the temptation to become fearful is gripping your heart. Waves of panic sweep over you as you wonder what you will do. David would understand your plight.

On the run from Saul, who was a vicious and relentless ruler, he wrote these words:

> The Lord is my rock, my fortress and my deliverer; my God is my rock, in whom I take refuge. He is my shield and the horn of my salvation. ... I call to the Lord, who is worthy of praise, and I am saved from my enemies (Psalm 18:2-3).

David, the future king of Israel, was forced to leave his home and the ones he loved. Almost overnight, he became a hunted criminal, though he had done nothing wrong.

Now, he was the commander of a thrown-together army, which was made up of bandits, murderers, and social outcasts. Alone and hiding out in a cave of rejection, David wondered how life had turned out so differently from what he had planned.

Today, you also may feel like a cave dweller. Friends have betrayed you, peers scorn your name, and even family members have turned against you. At night, tears stain your pillow as you wonder if God will hear your cry.

God has given you a marvelous promise: If you will seek Him, you will find He is right beside you. No matter how deep your valley may seem, God's love for you is deeper.

He is your faithful Lord and Savior, your best friend, and your eternal source of hope and encouragement. Hang in there. Don't give up. God has a wondrous plan for your life.

Prayer: Lord, I cannot imagine life without You.

He who dwells in the shelter of the Most High will rest in the shadow of the Almighty. ... He will cover you with his feathers, and under his wings you will find refuge (Psalm 91:1, 4).

The Daily Way

June 15

A Prisoner ... Yet Free

During the Second World War, Corrie ten Boom and her family realized the risks associated with hiding and protecting Jewish citizens. However, in a small hidden room in the family's home above Corrie's father's watchmaker shop, men and women found temporary refuge from Hitler's wicked pursuit. Once they secured safe passage out of the country, they would leave, but there was always a steady flow of others coming to find a place of safety.

In the book The Hiding Place, Corrie tells how most of her family was captured and sent to a concentration camp. The conditions in the camp were deplorable and beyond anything that she thought she could bear.

Watching her beloved sister waste away and then die seemed like the final blow to her heart. Had God forgotten her? She was a believer and only had done what she and her family felt He was leading them to do. How did she end up a prisoner?

From our perspective, most of life's tragedies do not make sense. Some come as a result of our fallen world. Corrie struggled to make sense of her imprisonment until one day she realized God's grace truly was her strength and salvation.

"It was dark in my cell," wrote Corrie. "I talked with my Saviour. Never before had fellowship with Him been so close. It was a joy that I hoped would continue unchanged. I was a prisoner—and yet ... how free!"

A day before her scheduled execution, Corrie was set free. Especially in times of confinement and inactivity—remember, God has not abandoned you. He is right beside you.

Prayer: Lord, I know Your love for me drives the darkness of this world away.

Even the darkness will not be dark to you; the night will shine like the day, for darkness is as light to you (Psalm 139:12).

June 16   The Daily Way

In the Hand of God

Charles Spurgeon told a story of how during a sudden storm a woman on a ship became very terrified. She was so distraught that she found her husband, who happened to be the ship's captain, and said, "I don't understand how you can be so calm while I am totally terrified."

Her husband calmly walked across his quarters and picked up his sword. He took it and aimed it at the center of her chest, but she only laughed. Then he asked, "Why aren't you afraid of this sword? It could slay you in less than a minute.

His wife replied, "I am not afraid of a sword that is wielded by the hand of my husband."

"Then neither am I," said the captain, "afraid of a storm in the hand of my heavenly Father."

In 2 Timothy, Paul writes, "For God did not give us a spirit of timidity [fear], but a spirit of power, of love and of self-discipline" (2 Timothy 1:7). This is the same Paul who allowed himself to be stoned and left for dead, who was beaten to the point of death, and who was rejected and imprisoned. Yet in 2 Corinthians, he wrote:

> For when we came into Macedonia, this body of ours had no rest, but we were harassed at every turn—conflicts on the outside, fears within. But God, who comforts the downcast, comforted us by the coming of Titus (2 Corinthians 7:5-6).

The security of God's close presence, the warmth of His words to us, and the visitation of a friend are like a cup of cool fresh water in the heat of a fierce battle. God's love brings hope to our hearts.

Prayer: Lord Jesus, I need Your words of encouragement today. The world is pressing in on me, but I know You are in total control.

The Lord upholds all those who fall and lifts up all who are bowed down (Psalm 145:14).

The Daily Way

June 17

Look Up to God

In Acts 16, Paul had "one of those days." On the way to the house of prayer, a young slave woman began following him and Silas. Her shouts were meant to draw unwanted attention to the apostle. In reality, the enemy was seeking to run Paul and his evangelistic team out of town. But Paul commanded the harassing spirit to leave this young woman (Acts 16:18).

Her owners, who made money through her fortune-telling, were not happy. Frustrations grew until the entire city of Philippi erupted into an uproar.

> The crowd joined in the attack against Paul and Silas, and the magistrates ordered them to be stripped and beaten. After they had been severely flogged, they were thrown into prison (Acts 16:22-23).

If anyone had a reason to be depressed, it was Paul and Silas. Yet they did not allow their circumstances to cause them to question the providence of God. Instead, they turned a bad situation into one of praise to the Lord (Acts 16:25).

God had a plan for their imprisonment. At midnight the door to their jail cell opened, and they were free men—but they did not leave because they knew it would mean death for the jailer who had been given the charge to watch over them. He was amazed by their commitment to God and accepted Christ as his Savior, but the story did not end here. The jailer's entire family was saved, and the next morning Paul and Silas were freed.

The next time you are tempted to be downcast, look up to God. Ask Him to use you as an instrument of truth, hope, and encouragement to others.

After Paul and Silas came out of the prison, they went to Lydia's house, where they met with the brothers and encouraged them (Acts 16:40).

June 18

The Daily Way

Standing at the Crossroads

Exodus 3:7 tells us God heard the cries of His people. He knew they were suffering in exile. Yet their promised deliverance lingered, and because days stretched into weeks and weeks into months and years, they began to wonder if God had forgotten them.

Have you ever caught yourself wondering the same thing? Maybe you have obeyed Him and followed Him faithfully, but now you are standing at a crossroads of hope and doubt.

Choose to hope in the Lord. He has not forgotten you. He has heard your cry, and He is working behind the scenes to deliver you. Timing is everything with God. He knows when you are in the right position to move on to the next step. You can be sure of this: He won't be late. ... He will be right on time!

Moses had almost forgotten what it was like to hear the distressing cries of God's people. He had been banished to the wilderness, but not to be punished. Instead, he was being trained for a greater purpose.

In the beginning, Moses thought he had to take matters into his own hands. He ended up killing an Egyptian, which was not a part of God's plan. After this incident, Lord drew him aside for 40 years—silencing his heart and tempering Moses so he would be willing to follow the Lord perfectly.

If you feel as though you have been set aside by the Lord, know that you are not being punished. You are being readied for the next step. Make sure your obedience is unconditional and your willingness to follow the Lord is sincere.

Prayer: Lord, teach me to follow only You.

I commit you to God and to the word of his grace, which can build you up and give you an inheritance among all those who are sanctified (Acts 20:32).

The Daily Way

June 19

The Promised Land

As the people of Israel stood at the doorway to the Promised Land, fear gripped the people's hearts. Moses had sent spies into the land and out of 14 men only two returned with positive reports. Joshua and Caleb filed this report: "We should go up and take possession of the land, for we can certainly do it" (Numbers 13:30).

These two men had witnessed God's deliverance at the Red Sea. They had been fed by Him in the wilderness, led by His Spirit both day and night. They believed the same God who had fought for them, delivered them from their enemies, and provided for their every need would fulfill His promises.

"We can do this," were the words that Caleb spoke to Moses.

However, the others who had gone with Joshua and Caleb filed a different report. Theirs was a chronicle of fear and dread: "We went into the land ... and it does flow with milk and honey! ... But the people who live there are powerful, and the cities are fortified and very large" (Numbers 13:27-28). Their blow-by-blow account goes on: "We can't attack those people; they are stronger than we are" (Numbers 13:31). They went on to spread "a bad report about the land they had explored" (Numbers 13:32). In other words, they kept talking until the people no longer believed God would do what He said He would do. Fear prevented them from enjoying the goodness of the Lord's blessings. Israel finally made it into the Promised Land, but not until they had spent 40 years wandering in a wilderness!

When life gets you down, and you want to give up, don't. Turn your heart to God. He has only His best for you.

Prayer: Lord, thank You that You know my future and will provide for me throughout my years.

For you have been my hope, O Sovereign Lord, my confidence since my youth (Psalm 71:5).

June 20

The Daily Way

True Peace

Though he was a hero of the Christian faith, Paul never thought of himself in this way. He knew there is only one true hero and that is the Lord Jesus Christ. If there were any challenges in Paul's life, they were these—to be obedient and faithful to the One who called him.

Usually, heroes are individualists. They are not worried about pleasing others—only the one to whom they report. Paul was not worried about being well-received or liked. He knew the way before him would be difficult because he had chosen to follow Jesus.

Christ's call to him on the Damascus Road upended his life. One day he was persecuting members of the early church; the next day he was being prepared by the Holy Spirit to proclaim God's truth to the world.

Following Christ was a matter of God-given conviction—something that would lead Paul through three missionary journeys to all parts of the known world, and finally to places of danger and terror.

Just like today, Jerusalem was a hotbed of political unrest. Yet Paul knew he was being prepared to preach the Gospel message in this city. He also knew he would be met with strong opposition and persecution.

Some people have heard God's voice calling to them. He has asked them to go in a certain direction, but they have turned and gone another way. Their conviction to follow Christ has been weakened by their desires to experience the pleasures of this world.

The truest peace you will ever experience is the peace gained from being in the center of God's will. Ask the Lord to direct your path.

Prayer: Lord, there is only one way I want to live my life and that is in the center of Your will.

And now, compelled by the Spirit, I am going to Jerusalem, not knowing what will happen to me there (Acts 20:22).

The Daily Way — June 21

Sure Hope

Until you develop a strong sense of conviction, you will not have the sure-footedness that is needed to be a follower of Christ. When faced with a crucial decision, you will be tempted to waver between right and wrong—what you know is godly and ungodly.

Those who are soft in their convictions often experience disappointment, doubt, and fear. When we are fully committed to Christ, we have a sure hope. However, when we allow temptations to lure us away from what we know is right, we miss God's blessing.

The rich young ruler wanted to follow Jesus, yet his emotional attachment to earthly treasures kept him landlocked. He was not free to join those who were a part of Christ's band of followers (Mark 10:17-23).

The apostle Paul did not have a problem with commitment or conviction. He gave his life to the Lord and in doing so left behind the very things this world deems as both impressive and valuable.

Paul had been a Pharisee—a man of social influence and position. He had been trained by one of the most eminent scholars of his day—Gamaliel, a member and former president of the Sanhedrin, the high council of Jews in Jerusalem. It was said that Gamaliel's influence was so great that he was one of the only seven Jewish scholars who have been honored by the title "Rabban."

None of this mattered to Paul. He had formed a strong conviction: "I consider everything a loss compared to the surpassing greatness of knowing Christ Jesus my Lord, for whose sake I have lost all things" (Philippians 3:8).

Prayer: Lord, I want to be able to say with Paul that the only thing I hold dear is Christ Jesus who lives inside of me.

I consider them rubbish, that I may gain Christ and be found in him (Philippians 3:8-9).

June 22 — The Daily Way

The Price of Conviction

Throughout God's Word, we read how His saints suffered greatly for their faith. Yet their lives emitted a sweetness that continues to draw us to the Lord Jesus Christ each day.

The author of Hebrews writes:

> I do not have time to tell about Gideon, Barak, Samson, Jephthah, David, Samuel and the prophets, who through faith conquered kingdoms, administered justice, and gained what was promised; who shut the mouths of lions, quenched the fury of the flames, and escaped the edge of the sword; whose weakness was turned to strength; and who became powerful in battle and routed foreign armies. ... Others were tortured and refused to be released, so that they might gain a better resurrection. Some faced jeers and flogging, while still others were chained and put in prison. They were stoned; they were sawed in two; they were put to death by the sword. They went about in sheepskins and goatskins, destitute, persecuted and mistreated—the world was not worthy of them. ... These were all commended for their faith, yet none of them received what had been promised. God had planned something better for us so that only together with us would they be made perfect (Hebrews 11:32-40).

Making a commitment to follow Christ will cost you something, but the rewards are eternal. The Old Testament saints followed God in reckless abandon and considered knowing Him far more valuable than anything this world has to offer.

Prayer: Lord, forgive me for the times that I put my desires before Your will and purpose for me. I want to follow wherever You lead.

Consider him who endured such opposition from sinful men, so that you will not grow weary and lose heart (Hebrews 12:3).

The Daily Way

June 23

Turning Oppression to Opportunity

In each of our lives, there will be times when we want to quit. Sorrow comes and the tempter draws near, whispering words of defeat and calling us to give up and to abandon the station in life God has called us to man.

Have you left your post? Only you know this for sure. Maybe you have and you wonder if you can retrace your steps back to where God first gave you your marching orders. Elijah had come through a very trying time. Few of us, if any, will ever have to face the wickedness he faced on Mt. Carmel. The prophets of Baal mocked God, and in turn, the Lord destroyed each one. Elijah's faith had held strong.

But a strange thing happened in the aftermath of the battle—the hollow threats of a wicked queen brought fear to Elijah's heart. In his distress, he ran and ended up in the desert under a broom tree, praying he would die! How could God's prophet go from the mountain top to subterranean living in such a short amount of time?

The truth is that Elijah is not alone. Many of us have done the same by allowing fear to change our focus. He was sure he was the only prophet left who had remained true to God. In reality, the Lord had preserved 300 prophets who had never bowed their knees to a foreign god. If God has shown you that you have taken a wrong turn, confess your disobedience to Him, and ask Him to show you how to get back to the point where you can serve Him fully and completely. The way you turn oppression into opportunity is through obedience.

Prayer: Lord, I only want to serve You. If I am off course, show me how to get back to the place where I belong.

When Elijah heard [a gentle whisper], he pulled his cloak over his face and went out and stood at the mouth of the cave (1 Kings 19:13).

June 24 — The Daily Way

When Shadows Gather

When trials come and frustrations build, we often look for a way out from under the pressure. We may overlook the fact that God has a plan even for our emotionally rainy days. Many times, as problems linger long and sorrows grow tense, we forget that God is right beside us. He has not left us to battle our way through this difficulty alone.

Pastor and devotional author George Matheson writes:

> O my God, teach me, when the shadows gather, that I am only in a tunnel. It is enough for me to know that it will be all right some day. They tell me that I shall stand upon the peaks of Olivet, the heights of resurrection glory. But I want more, O my Father; I want Calvary to lead up to it. I want to know that the shadows of this world are the shades of an avenue—the avenue to the house of my Father. Tell me I am only forced to climb because Thy house is on the hill! I shall receive no hurt from sorrow if I shall walk in the midst of the fire.

Some of the greatest lessons we will learn come from time spent with God in the fires of affliction and rejection. If your world seems to be spiraling down, look up! If the heartache seems too much for you to bear, pray and ask your heavenly Father to hold you close. He will, and this will make a beautiful difference in the way you view the trouble that is trying to besiege your heart.

Prayer: Father, I can see my way through the cloud that has gathered around me. I know You are near because Your Word tells me You will never leave me. Move close to my broken heart, O Lord, and tell me how to worship You in this hour of need.

The cords of death entangled me. ... I cried to my God for help. From his temple he heard my voice; my cry came before him, into his ears (Psalm 18:4, 6).

The Daily Way

June 25

The Rope of Life

An ancient monastery sits on top of a cliff in the beautiful countryside of Portugal. Visitors to this lofty retreat are rewarded with a magnificent view. However, the only way to reach the monastery is by being hoisted up a cliff in a wicker basket by an aged monk.

One day, as a visitor prepared to leave, he turned to his guide and asked nervously, "How often do you replace this rope?" The gray haired monk chimed, "Each time the old rope breaks."

Many times, this is exactly how we live. We push and shove our way through each day, worrying when the rope of life will break. Fear, doubt, and worry can paralyze us. We may mistakenly think only non-believers live this way. However, many Christians are living the same.

Here is the wondrous truth of God: He holds the rope of our lives within His infinite, loving grasp. Nothing is strong enough to remove His shelter of protection from our lives. He knows our every move, and He is constantly aware of our deepest needs.

Jesus reminds us that not even one sparrow falls to the ground apart from God's knowledge and will. "Even the very hairs of your head are all numbered," says Jesus. "So don't be afraid; you are worth more than many sparrows" (Matthew 10:30-31).

The next time you sense your anxiety level rising, stop and remember that God is aware of you. He loves you and nothing can change this. You can trust Him fully. He holds the rope of your earthly life in His infinite hands, and nothing can break it.

Prayer: Lord, thank You that You have a wonderful plan for all my days.

Do not worry about your life. ... Look at the birds of the air; they do not sow or reap or store away in barns, and yet your heavenly Father feeds them. Are you not much more valuable than they? (Matthew 6:25-26).

June 26 — The Daily Way

The Hand of Providence

What would you do if you discovered that a plot had been formed against you? Maybe the conspiracy resulted when someone misinterpreted something you said. Or perhaps it came from the overflow of jealousy.

Regardless of how it originated, the fact remains that you are under attack. In Acts 23, Paul had been arrested because of his witness of Jesus Christ. The Jews were so incensed over Paul's defense of the Gospel that the commander of the Fortress of Antonia in Jerusalem "was afraid Paul would be torn to pieces" (Acts 23:10).

Soldiers were sent to rescue Paul from the hands of the angry mob and to bring him back to the fortress. In the next verse, we read: "The following night, the Lord stood near Paul and said, 'Take courage! As you have testified about me in Jerusalem, so you must also testify in Rome'" (Acts 23:11).

Paul needed this encouragement because the next day he received word that the Jews had formed a conspiracy to kill him (Acts 23:12). More than 40 men were involved in the plot. However, God in His providence allowed Paul to discern their motives and to realize that no harm would come to him. As Paul's enemies drew near, the commander transferred the apostle by night under heavy guard to Rome. Paul was on his way to accomplishing what Christ had given him to do—he was unharmed because his trust was in the One who could save him from all danger.

It is heartbreaking to learn that we have enemies—people who seem bent on our destruction. But remember, when your faith is in Christ, He is your refuge and strength.

Prayer: Lord, thank You that You see the way before me and that You will make a way for me to travel— even when it appears that way is blocked.

You, O Lord, keep my lamp burning; my God turns my darkness into light (Psalm 18:28).

The Daily Way

June 27

Vision Adjustments

Have you ever had a dream that you could accomplish something great for the Lord? But before you could see it unfold, obstacles appeared, blocking your way and tempting you to give up your dream.

One moment you were on top of the world, the next you were in a valley of hopeless thoughts—all because you listened as someone spoke a careless word of discouragement. It was as if someone had poured a pitcher of cold water over your red-hot vision. Now the fire is out, the ashes are smoldering, and the stench of death is choking your senses.

God is the One who helps us cast our vision, and He does not want us to give up. No matter how trying your situation becomes, never give up and never give in to the enemy's suggestions that you will never realize your dreams for the Lord.

Paul envisioned himself preaching in Rome. In Acts 24, he begins to make a turn in that direction. By the grace of God, Paul arrived safely in Rome—though he never thought he would arrive as a prisoner.

Because Paul's faith was placed solely in God, his testimony in Christ was preached not only in the city but throughout the palace guard. If that were not enough, his witness resulted in the spreading of the Gospel throughout the world.

As you continue to pursue your vision, at times you may not understand why your life takes sudden turns. But be patient—God has a plan. He was faithful to Paul (Acts 23:11), and He will do the same for you, so be encouraged!

Prayer: Lord, I bow in humble adoration to You. You are my Savior and my living Lord.

The Lord is near. Do not be anxious about anything, but in everything, by prayer and petition, with thanksgiving, present your requests to God. And the peace of God, which transcends all understanding, will guard your hearts and your minds in Christ Jesus (Philippians 4:5-7).

June 28   The Daily Way

He Will Set You Free

More than likely, when Paul was a young man he had a dream to know God fully. His quest for knowledge led him to study under one of the greatest rabbis of his day.

As he grew in knowledge, he became a Pharisee and then was elected to the Sanhedrin. Only the most noted of Jewish scholars held these positions. Paul was one of them. His heart, though charged with the wrong motivation, longed to worship God. Then one day, God revealed Himself to Paul through the life of His Son, the Lord Jesus Christ.

There is only one way to interpret what happened to Paul on the Damascus Road and that is to say it was life-changing (Acts 9:1-9). Christ did not just appear to Paul; He embraced him. Only the Lord knows what rested deep in Paul's heart—but like Moses, once he turned aside to study the things of God, it was enough to move God into action.

Maybe you are feeling the weight of your circumstances closing in on you. You have longed to be free, but you have remained shackled to this world in ways that only God knows and understands. If you seek Him, He will set you free from the sin of worry, doubt, fear, hopelessness, lustful feelings, and more. When you pray with a sincere heart, the Lord will be found by you. Then your witness and testimony will become a way to glorify God and lead others into His throne room of mercy and grace.

Prayer: Lord, I confess that I need Your purifying touch on my life. There are things I have done and said that do not honor You. Forgive me as I mention each one to You and receive Your forgiveness and eternal love.

I am the way and the truth and the life. No one comes to the Father except through me (John 14:6).

The Daily Way

June 29

Forgive and Forget

Some people understand God's redemptive plan for their lives, and yet they fail to see how He can use them for His kingdom work. They feel as though their lives have been stained too deeply by sin, and they are not useable. This is not true.

God's plan for our lives is one of hope. He never looks back and reminds us of our past transgressions. He never says, "If only you had not done this or that, then I could use you." These are words the enemy uses to discourage us and to keep us from being all that we can be for the Lord.

God's purpose in saving us was not just to save us from eternal death and torment. His purpose was to save us so that we could learn to love Him the way that He loves us. Once He forgives our sins, He forgets them. What a glorious reminder of God's unconditional love.

However, just like Paul, we were not saved merely to enjoy God's love. We were saved with a purpose in mind: to tell others about His saving grace. This is what Paul did. Once Christ saved him, once Christ returned his earthly sight, and once Christ had prepared him, Paul began to do some serious kingdom work. And you can, too.

Maybe you have struggled with an emotional problem and have received God's deliverance. Won't you be available for God to use you in someone else's life? You may think, "No one could possibly struggle with the sin that I have fought." Many have—and many need to know there is a way through the darkness. That way is through Jesus Christ.

Prayer: Lord, it is hard to understand how You could possibly use me for Your glory, but I know this is exactly what You want to do. I give my life to You and ask that You would use me so that others will experience Your wondrous grace.

If anyone is in Christ, he is a new creation (2 Corinthians 5:17).

June 30

The Daily Way

The Victor's Crown

Most of us know that it is one thing to set out to reach a certain goal and another thing to actually complete it. Some people have a hard time visualizing how to begin a project, while others just jump right in.

Many more may begin only to find their progress halted by one obstacle after another. Soon the enemy whispers words of defeat and failure—and they begin to wonder if they will reach the goals God has helped them to set.

During his life, the apostle Paul faced many challenges, but he also enjoyed many victories and successes. Over the years, he developed a strategy that kept him grounded in his faith. He writes:

> Endure hardship ... like a good soldier of Christ Jesus. No one serving as a soldier gets involved in civilian affairs—he wants to please his commanding officer. Similarly, if anyone competes as an athlete, he does not receive the victor's crown unless he competes according to the rules. ... Reflect on what I am saying, for the Lord will give you insight into all this (2 Timothy 2:3-5, 7).

Hardships will come. Difficulties will arise. Sorrow and disappointment are a natural part of our lives, but we have been given through Jesus Christ a supernatural way overcoming. We do not have to lose our vision or cast aside the goals God has given us. Paul kept the eyes of his heart and mind focused on Jesus Christ. He reached his goal because he was not drawn off course by feelings of doubt, criticism, or fear.

When your vision becomes cloudy, ask God to help you to see your situation from His perspective.

Prayer: Lord, thank You for reminding me that when You are involved, all things are possible.

I can do everything through him who gives me strength (Philippians 4:13).

Developing Your Faith Muscles

The Daily Way

July 1

Stand Firm in Your Faith

Paul tells us not to conform to the ways of this world (Romans 12:2). However, many times our beliefs and morals are challenged to a point beyond anything we have known. It is so easy to get caught up in a quest for more money, freedom, and material possessions.

What does nonconformity mean in today's world? It means standing firm in our faith—no matter what the cost. 2 Timothy 3:12 reminds us, "In fact, everyone who wants to live a godly life in Christ Jesus will be persecuted." John Calvin said, "It is in vain to try to detach Christ from His cross and it is only natural that the world should hate Christ, even in His members."

Throughout the Bible, those who followed Jesus Christ endured much persecution and hardship from those who despised the Lord and His followers. But the saints of God never gave up.

Though it ultimately cost them their lives, their physical death meant being in the presence of God. Jesus said, "Whoever tries to keep his life will lose it, and whoever loses his life will preserve it" (Luke 17:33).

Even in the midst of persecution, the godly will go forward, grow upward, and receive victory. When you feel overwhelmed by life's temptations, turn to the Lord. His strength will protect you so that you will be able to continue on the path He has ordained for you.

Winston Churchill challenged the students at Harrow:

> Never give in. Never, never, never, never—in nothing, great or small, large or petty—never give in, except to convictions of honour and good sense. Never yield to force; never yield to the apparently overwhelming might of the enemy.

May he strengthen your hearts so that you will be blameless and holy in the presence of our God and Father when our Lord Jesus comes with all his holy ones (1 Thessalonians 3:13).

July 2

The Daily Way

God's Unconditional Love

Has someone ever told you that he or she is ashamed of you? Perhaps you have told someone that you are ashamed of him. Words carelessly used can hurt the heart and quickly stir up feelings of guilt and shame.

They also can be used by the enemy to attack our position in Christ. Satan is quick to whisper words that lead to doubt and insecurity. Shame is at the top of his list of effective tools to use against the believer.

Few people actually take time to stop and to ask, "Why am I feeling shameful?" Only God has the right to know our past sins and mistakes. When we allow dark secrets to pursue us, we usually end up hiding our emotions from one another and, ultimately, God.

What dark secret do you have? What embarrassment have you hidden from others? One thing you can be sure of—God is not ashamed of you. His love for you is unconditional and eternal.

Many times, He allows us to experience shame so we will turn away from sin and seek His forgiveness. Then we can come to Him freely, confessing our sins and receiving His forgiveness and grace.

Many people today treat the gift of God's grace shamefully by living immoral lifestyles. There are also believers who act as if they are ashamed of God's Word. They give an approving nod to sin so that they appear politically correct. How this must hurt the heart of God!

Be strong in your faith. Christ died for you and has given you an opportunity to live a life free of sin and shame. There may be times when you suffer man's rejection, but your heavenly Father will never turn His back on you.

I thank Christ Jesus our Lord, who has given me strength, that he considered me faithful, appointing me to his service (1 Timothy 1:12).

The Daily Way

The Journey of Faith

Paul's purpose for writing to Timothy was to encourage him and to remind him never to give up. The early church faced all kinds of trials and temptations. There were many who challenged Paul's teaching. They also challenged Timothy's spiritual leadership.

Religious teachers then, just like many today, sought to weaken God's Word and truth. Paul writes:

> God did not give us a spirit of timidity, but a spirit of power, of love and of self-discipline. So do not be ashamed to testify about our Lord, or ashamed of me his prisoner. But join with me in suffering for the gospel, by the power of God, who has saved us and called us to a holy life (2 Timothy 1:7-9).

There are many who attend church and are involved in religious work, but they remain afraid to speak God's truth—especially when facing moral and spiritual issues.

Paul reminds Timothy to be strong, firm in his faith and steadfast in his devotion to God. When we refuse to compromise our convictions, we experience a God-given strength throughout our lives. But when we waver between what we know is right and wrong, we become unstable in all we do.

How do you avoid becoming fearful and doubting? Begin by refusing to compromise your convictions. Don't sell out to the world's deception. Then you will remain strong in your faith. If Timothy had taken his eyes off Christ, he would have weakened and his ministry would have been ineffective.

Refuse to dilute the truth of the Gospel so that it will be acceptable to fallen men. Don't deny God's truth so that you may feel popular. Never be ashamed of God's Word. Cling to it because it is a light unto your path.

I am not ashamed, because I know whom I have believed (2 Timothy 1:12).

July 4

The Daily Way

Our Identity Crisis

Several years ago, a popular women's magazine surveyed 3,000 Protestant clergy concerning their views on Christianity. The result of the survey was disheartening. A considerable number rejected the idea of a personal God. Many said God was nothing more than a "force of life, a principle of love, and the ultimate reality."

There was no mention of Jesus Christ or His death on Calvary's cross as an atonement for mankind's sin. No promise of salvation by grace was recorded. No thought was given to the resurrection of Christ as a matchless demonstration of God's power over sin and death.

There is an identity crisis at work—not just in our lives but also in our churches. It comes as the result of our being willing to accept and even embrace other religions as being equal to Christianity. This false view has weakened our faith and has caused us to give up what we once held as dear—our godly convictions.

So many in our society who claim to be Christians are suffering from an identity crisis because they are confused about their Christian faith. However, the Bible makes it clear.

A Christian is a person who has repented of his sins, surrendered his life to the lordship of Jesus Christ, and acknowledged that without Christ's death on the cross, he would have gone to hell for eternity.

How do we avoid confusion and deception, especially when our world paints such pleasant pictures of sin and compromise?

Begin by being committed to the study of God's Word. Then, make sure the church you attend is one that teaches God's truth without compromise. Finally, demonstrate Christ's love to those who have repented and turned away from sin. God forgives and restores us when our hearts are turned toward Him.

Do your best to present yourself to God as one approved, a workman who does not need to be ashamed (2 Timothy 2:15).

The Daily Way

July 5

Reap What You Sow

If you are diligent in your commitment to the Lord, one way to test your Christian identity is to ask yourself the following questions:

- Are you willing to invest your time and effort in the lives of others?
- Are you willing to be a soldier on active duty?
- Are you willing to run the race of endurance according to God's rules?

Most farmers are very hardworking people. They know that in order to have a bountiful harvest, they have to remain committed to their crops and to their land. They can't begin a project, stop halfway through it, and expect to be successful. If you want to reap a harvest, you must be committed.

Farmers can't allow their machinery to fall into disrepair. They can't say, "Well, I don't feel like planting this year," or "I don't feel like harvesting my fields." Instead, they must be willing to get up before sunrise to plow their soil and sow their seed. This is why lazy people never make good farmers. You have to be diligent and persistent.

The weather is not always fair. There will be hardships—times when you want to give up, but you must not. If you feel you are not growing in your walk with the Lord, ask yourself whether it is because you have failed to cultivate fields of godly character and desire.

We must never forget that we reap what we sow. If we don't till the soil of godly character and plant the Word of God in our hearts, then we will harvest emotional and spiritual thorns and thistles. There is no harvest unless you labor with a willing heart in the things of God. Ask Him to show you how to apply His principles to your life. The Holy Spirit will grant you the understanding when you pray and seek God's face.

If we endure, we will also reign with him (2 Timothy 2:12).

July 6

The Daily Way

The Workman Approved by God

There was a time when people took pride in doing a good job and in sacrificing their lives for someone else. Now, the reverse of this principle has become acceptable behavior. We have become a society that rewards laziness and dependence instead of diligence and commitment. We also are faced with a generation of people who demand rights and privileges without accountability.

A story is told about a man who was driving along a lonely road on a summer's day. He noticed a car pulled off to the side with a flat tire and a woman struggling to change it.

He decided to be a "good Samaritan" and to help change the tire. In the process, he grew hot, sweaty, and dirty. The woman only stood by and watched. Just as he finished, she said to him, "When you let the jack down, be careful. My husband is sleeping on the back seat, and I don't want to wake him."

We have abandoned our foundational work ethic. Today, when life becomes too difficult, we check out, drop back, and let someone finish the work for us. Paul's message to us in 2 Timothy is this: We are to be "approved" workmen of God (2 Timothy 2:15).

As Christians, we are called to finish the course God has set before us. Nowhere in His Word do we read where it is acceptable to give up and walk away from difficulty. When life becomes tough, we are to keep our eyes set on Christ and move toward the finish line.

Have you been lazy in your devotion to the Lord? Now is the time to change this habit. Have you leaned back and failed to be conscientious in your love for Him? He is faithful and totally devoted to you. Turn every area of your life over to Him and prepare for a tremendous blessing.

Flee the evil desires of youth, and pursue righteousness, faith, love and peace (2 Timothy 2:22).

The Daily Way

July 7

The Slippery Slope

Paul did not want Timothy to suffer the same identity crisis that was filtering through the Christian community in Asia Minor.

Just as Paul preached that there was only one Gospel, there were false teachers teaching that there were other ways to know God. Paul wrote to Timothy to admonish him not to be ashamed of God's truth. He was to preach the Word of God "in season and out of season" (2 Timothy 4:2). In other words, Timothy was to be prepared to teach God's truth regardless of the circumstances and without compromise. He was to teach it according to what had been given to him through the apostle Paul. There was no provision for false doctrine. Timothy was to preach God's Word with conviction no matter who stood up against him.

Are you standing strong for what God has taught you? Or are you wavering in your faith? The moment you question the faithfulness of God, you begin to slide down a very slippery slope to ruin and failure.

Just like Timothy, we are certain to encounter false teachers among us today. There are people who claim to be teaching from God's Word, but instead they speak falsely, saying that "all religious roads" lead to God.

There is only one way to God and that is through Jesus Christ. We cannot work our way into heaven. We cannot buy salvation. It is a free gift given to us by God as result of His grace.

Timothy understood that preaching God's truth would bring alienation, discrimination, and persecution. He was faithful to the call God had placed on his life. Are you faithful? Are you doing what God has given you to do?

For [God] has rescued us from the dominion of darkness and brought us into the kingdom of the Son he loves (Colossians 1:13).

July 8 — The Daily Way

Godlessness in the Last Days

A few years ago, a newly elected politician proclaimed, "We are the children of the modern age!"

If this is true, a good question for us to ask is, "What has the modern age given us?" The answers that come to mind are disheartening: crack cocaine, satanic cults, instructions on safe sex, misdirected individuals who would rather save a spotted owl than an innocent baby inside a mother's womb.

Difficulties like these should not surprise us. Paul told Timothy that in the last days:

> People will be lovers of themselves, lovers of money, boastful, proud, abusive, disobedient ... ungrateful, unholy, without love, unforgiving, slanderous, without self-control ... lovers of pleasure rather than lovers of God—having a form of godliness but denying its power (2 Timothy 3:2-5).

Then he cautions us, "Have nothing to do with them" (2 Timothy 3:5). Despite what the world is doing, we can live in victory because we serve a mighty God who provides the wisdom we need for every situation.

When the winds of adversity blow hard against your life, take shelter in the Lord. When the world turns dark and lonely, place your trust in Christ, and you will receive the victor's crown!

Remember this the next time trials come your way: It is a natural first reaction to ask God to remove any form of adversity from your life. However, it is often hardship and difficulty that provide the right atmosphere for spiritual growth.

You then ... be strong in the grace that is in Christ Jesus (2 Timothy 2:1).

The Perfect Solution

Human nature is sinful—unholy, proud, and in need of redemption. Without Christ, we are self-centered, unforgiving, ungrateful, abusive, and boastful.

However, God has not abandoned us to sin. He has provided a way for each one of us to experience His eternal grace and salvation. Christ's death on Calvary's cross was God's perfect solution for our sin.

Charles Spurgeon writes:

> No matter what level of unworthiness we find in our hearts, out of the depths, out of the dungeon of self-loathing, we still cry out to God, for His salvation rests in no measure or degree upon you or upon anything that you are or have been or can be. It is your responsibility to be empty so that Jesus may fill you, yours to confess your uncleanness that He may wash you, yours to be less than nothing that Jesus may be everything to you.

The Bible tells us that every person who calls on the name of the Lord will be saved (Acts 2:21). When you accept Christ as your Savior, you become a new person. "Therefore, if anyone is in Christ, he is a new creation; the old has gone, the new has come!" (2 Corinthians 5:17). God desires a personal relationship with you. He also wants you to be obedient to His Word—to respect and revere Him. You can trust God. He knows your future and the plans He has for you.

God is in control. "The eyes of the Lord are on the righteous and his ears are attentive to their prayer, but the face of the Lord is against those who do evil" (1 Peter 3:12).

We demolish arguments and every pretension that sets itself up against the knowledge of God, and we take captive every thought to make it obedient to Christ (2 Corinthians 10:5).

July 10 — The Daily Way

A False Sense of Security

The prosperity of the 1920s came to an end with the beginning of the Great Depression. The collapsing stock market triggered severe economic decline. Intoxicated with the optimism of the times, a false sense of security had left people unprepared for the difficult years that would follow.

Those who lived through the depression learned their lives could change quickly. One day, they had plenty—money, a home, a job, and plans for the future. The next day, all of this was gone.

Many were without work. Some lost their life's savings. Countless people were homeless and struggled to find enough money to buy their next meal.

It is natural to be concerned about our daily lives. We think about our jobs, our homes, our families, and our friends. We track our retirement funds and make vacation plans. But unless we keep our focus on God, we are living with a false sense of security.

The Bible reminds us that before Christ returns, many people will be doing what they want to do. Just as it was in the days of Noah and Lot, few will follow the ways of God (Luke 17:26-30). There will be a lack of godly love, affection, gratitude, and respect for others. Giving little thought to eternity, people will be self-centered and lack self-control. They will be "treacherous, rash, conceited, lovers of pleasure rather than lovers of God" (2 Timothy 3:4).

Are you prepared for His coming? Don't be caught unaware as were those during the Great Depression. Keep your heart and mind focused on God and His Word. Do not be a lover of self, money, or pleasure. Rather, love God and seek Him above all else and you will discover true prosperity.

[He] gave himself for us to redeem us from all wickedness and to purify for himself a people that are his very own (Titus 2:14).

The Daily Way

Storms of Life

With all the modern-day weather instruments, meteorologists can predict where a hurricane is likely to strike. Over the years, those living in areas with a high probability of being struck by a tropical storm or a hurricane have learned to be prepared.

In the same way, we must learn how to face the "storms" of life. God's Word is our best source of instruction. In it we learn that appreciation, reverence, and obedience are three principles that lead to victory in times of trial.

One thing we quickly discover is that life contains a variety of storms—some are furious and some are subtle. One of the more deadly storms—deception—can blow into our lives without warning. The greatest protection against this formidable storm is to cling to the truth of God's Word.

Have you made a commitment to study the Bible each day? Do you apply it—to the problems, crises, fears, and decisions you face? When you do, you will quickly discover that you are able to face the difficulties of today and the uncertainties of the future with a sense of strong assurance—all because you are grounded in God's Word.

Charles Spurgeon said, "When a home is ruled according to the Word of God, angels might be asked to stay a night with us, and they would not find themselves out of their element."

The Bible is our compass through the difficulties of life. Its text originated in God's mind and was communicated by the Holy Spirit to men who were God's messengers (2 Timothy 3:16).

Make a habit of spending time reading and applying His Word to every area of your life. When you do, you will find hope, encouragement, and strength to face the storms of life.

As for you, continue in what you have learned and have become convinced of, because you know those from whom you learned it (2 Timothy 3:14).

July 12 — The Daily Way

Consequences of Deception

Cults and heresies flourish because sincere people are looking for answers. Many are willing to turn to anything other than God. As a believer, you have been given the source of all truth through God's Word. However, we must be on guard when it comes to deception.

If a pastor or preacher teaches something contrary to the Bible, disregard it. In Matthew 24:4-5 Jesus warned his disciples, "Watch out that no one deceives you. For many will come in my name, claiming, 'I am the Christ,' and will deceive many."

Satan is the source of all deception. He wants us to wander off course by compromising the convictions God has taught us. At first, we may wander just a few steps to the left or the right, but before we know it, we have fallen into sin.

Deception breeds distrust in God—His leadership, His authority, and His Word. When we reject His truth, all we have left to stand on is a handful of lies.

There are consequences of deception. Paul writes:

> In the presence of God and of Christ Jesus, who will judge the living and the dead, and in view of his appearing and his kingdom ... preach the Word; be prepared in season and out of season; correct, rebuke and encourage—with great patience and careful instruction (2 Timothy 4:1-2).

Life is hopeless without Christ. But He is alive, and He is willing to fill every void in your life. You can look to Him for all the right answers to your every question. Jesus will meet you right where you are. God knows you, and He loves you. He knows your deepest needs. Keep His Word close to your heart, and you will not be deceived.

Resist [Satan], standing firm in the faith, because you know that your brothers throughout the world are undergoing the same kind of sufferings (1 Peter 5:9).

The Daily Way

July 13

Fight the Good Fight

With the stroke of a pen, Emperor Constantine issued the edict of Milan in 313 A.D., and Christianity became fashionable instead of a source of persecution. As a result, thousands joined churches, professing faith in Christ. Only God, the searcher of hearts, knows how many remained pagan at heart.

A life lived for Jesus Christ is not usually outlined with popularity or ease. Salvation cannot be earned or received by any other way than by coming to the Lord and seeking His forgiveness of sin. You can do nothing to earn God's gift of grace.

> For it is by grace you have been saved, through faith—and this not from yourselves, it is the gift of God—not by works, so that no one can boast (Ephesians 2:8-9).

Are you, like Asaph in Psalm 73, feeling as if you are the only person suffering and sacrificing for the cause of Christ? Be patient. Don't give up. God will reward your faithfulness and honor your perseverance. Paul said:

> I have fought the good fight, I have finished the race, I have kept the faith. ... We are hard pressed on every side, but not crushed; perplexed, but not in despair; persecuted, but not abandoned; struck down, but not destroyed (2 Timothy 4:7, 2 Corinthians 4:8-9).

Be content to trust God for your deliverance. Take a moment to consider these words written by a martyr: "I won't give up, shut up, let up till I have stayed up, stored up, prayed up for the cause of Jesus Christ."

Always give yourselves fully to the work of the Lord, because you know that your labor in the Lord is not in vain (1 Corinthians 15:58).

July 14 — The Daily Way

Final Words

Many times, the last words of great people contain very important messages.

They are often a summary of that person's life. D.L. Moody's last words were, "Earth is receding, heaven is coming." John Wesley said, "The best of all is God with us." Charles Wesley's last words were, "I shall be satisfied with thy likeness, satisfied ... satisfied."

There are some who maintain their sense of humor all the way to their dying moments. A story is told about a man named John Drew. As he was dying, his family gathered around his deathbed and one of his daughters asked, "Is he dead?"

Another daughter said, "Feel his feet. No one ever dies with warm feet." Upon hearing this, Mr. Drew opened his eyes and said, "Joan of Arc did." Then he died.

Some of the apostle Paul's last words were "Don't ever give up." There was no tinge of bitterness, no measure of regret, no anguish, and no remorse. Paul obviously had kept short accounts in his life, so when the time came for him to die, he was ready.

Paul writes, "Godly sorrow brings repentance that leads to salvation and leaves no regret, but worldly sorrow brings death" (2 Corinthians 7:10).

We can be prepared for the time when we meet Christ in heaven; it is only a heartbeat away. Ecclesiastes 3:1-2 says, "There is a time for everything, and a season for every activity under heaven: a time to be born and a time to die."

Paul lived his life in readiness. He was accountable to others and lived in peace. Even when he was imprisoned, he did not harbor bitterness toward his captors. Paul was forgiving. Those who harmed him, he forgave.

Are you keeping a short account? What will your final words be?

Each of us will give an account of himself to God (Romans 14:12).

The Daily Way — July 15

Alone with God

Have you ever felt like the little boy who was told he should not be afraid of the dark because the Lord was with him? The boy said, "I know that, but I want somebody with skin on."

Sometimes when we feel lonely, we find ourselves wanting to talk with someone who has "skin on." But God never slumbers or sleeps. He is closer to us than any brother (Proverbs 18:24).

Maybe you feel alone because you refuse to compromise your biblical convictions. Your friends make fun of you and challenge your faith. Noah would have understood your feelings. When God gave him the seemingly absurd instruction to build an ark, he probably felt as though he needed to talk with someone who had "skin on." Instead, he listened to the invisible God who was and is the great I Am.

During the years of construction of this huge vessel, people laughed at Noah. They felt sorry for his family and wrote him off as being insane, until it began to rain and rain and rain.

When you think about true loneliness, remember the Garden of Gethsemane. Nothing we face can compare to the depth of loneliness Jesus experienced. Not only did His friends and disciples abandon Him, but, for one brief moment, the Father turned His face away from His Son because Jesus bore the sins of the world. The psalmist writes "My God, my God, why have you forsaken me? Why are you so far from saving me, so far from the words of my groaning?" (Psalm 22:1).

If you feel like the psalmist, take comfort; you are not alone. "God has said, 'Never will I leave you; never will I forsake you'" (Hebrews 13:5). Christ experienced the deepest level of loneliness so you might have eternal fellowship with the Father who loves you perfectly.

My soul finds rest in God alone; my salvation comes from him. He alone is my rock and my salvation (Psalm 62:1-2).

July 16 — The Daily Way

The Journey of Faith

Abraham's life was one of obedience. While he was not perfect, he certainly was a man who wanted to obey God. He went from worshiping many gods to worshiping only one—the Lord God.

In Genesis 12:1, we read that the Lord said to Abraham, "Leave your country, your people and your father's household and go to the land I will show you."

Immediately, Abraham answered God's call. His love for the Lord was so great that he responded by packing up his family and setting out for a new home—one known only to God! Most of us would never consider a move like this. We usually want God to lay out every detail before we make a decision.

We pray that He will reveal His will to us, and then we ask Him to provide the evidence we need in order to step forward. We never read, however, that Abraham did this. In fact, his faith was so pure that when God said go, he went.

There will be times when God will require us to do things that from our perspective do not make sense. We may struggle with our decision and long for God to repeatedly make His will known to us. However, if the Lord calls us, we must go. If He instructs us to take a certain route, make a certain decision, or work toward a certain goal, we had better get busy doing it.

Obedience is the doorway to blessing. Abraham became the father of a great nation. God fulfilled every promise He made to His servant, and He will do the same for you. Before He does, He may require a step of faith on your part. Are you willing to step forward into His blessing?

I will make you into a great nation and I will bless you (Genesis 12:2).

The Daily Way

July 17

Obedience: The First Step of Faith

You may be facing a situation that calls for a step of faith. You have considered trusting God, but you are not sure of His response. Questions that could lead you down a pathway of doubt begin to fill your mind. "Does God know my needs? Is He aware of my situation? Does He understand what I am feeling?"

Everything we do in this life requires a step of faith—from getting up in the morning to making important decisions regarding our jobs or our families. Faith is a part of life. We seldom lie down at night and wonder if our beds will support us. We trust that the bed frame will hold us up. While the challenges we face in life are more complex, the same simple faith is at work.

Abraham trusted God. When he heard the Lord's voice, he knew he had only one choice to make and that was one of obedience. God told him to pack up his belongings and leave his friends and family, and he did.

When we resist God's call, our lives can become clouded with feelings of doubt and confusion. This was not going to happen with Abraham. He made a decision to trust the Lord and to do what God had asked him to do. He also had taken time to know God and to learn that God could be trusted.

Through prayer and the study of God's Word, you will discover all that you need to know about the heart of God. When you are linked to Him through a heartfelt devotion, you will not hesitate to trust Him fully.

Prayer: Lord, teach me to love and trust You with my whole heart.

I will praise you with the harp for your faithfulness, O my God (Psalm 71:22).

July 18

The Daily Way

Separate from the Past

Have you ever wondered why God instructed Abraham to leave his home (Genesis 12:1)? This request meant packing up all that belonged to him and leaving behind those he loved—his mother along with other family members and friends. It was not an easy request, but it was a necessary one.

When God calls you to Himself, the first thing He does is separate you from the immorality of the past. He gives you a new life and a new standard of living. The power of sin is broken in your life.

However, we have a choice to make. Either we obey God and move away from sin or we continue to fall prey to its temptation. Abraham made a decision to obey God and to leave the very things that once held him captive.

We can do the same. We can leave the addictions of the past behind. We can say no to habits that seek to prevent us from enjoying our fellowship with Christ just as we can step away from the very people who remain involved in sin and idolatry. However, this will require a step of faith.

You may be a young Christian who has an unbelieving spouse and wonder how you will continue to grow spiritually. God will make a way as you pray for your loved one and ask that he or she would be saved.

Abraham's obedience and faith were motivated by a deep love for God. He never would have been able to step away from the familiar things of the past were it not for God's love and commitment to him.

When God calls you to do something, He provides the strength and wisdom you need to get it done. Therefore, you can step out in faith without fear or dread.

Prayer: Lord, help me to follow You wherever You lead.

God said ... Go to the land I will show you. So [Abraham] left the land of the Chaldeans (Acts 7:3-4).

The Daily Way

July 19

A Test of Faith

The fact that you are in the middle of God's will does not mean that your faith will not be tested. It will. No sooner had Abraham made a commitment to obey the Lord than he found himself facing a heart-stopping test of faith. We might be surprised to read that he failed the test miserably. Abraham, like us, needed to learn how to travel the road of faith.

In Genesis 12:10, he found himself in the middle of a serious problem. Therefore, he made a decision to go "down to Egypt to live there for a while because the famine was severe." Before entering the country, Abraham looked at his wife, Sarah, and realized that her beauty could lead to trouble.

Afraid that Pharaoh would take her to his household or harem, Abraham devised a plan to save himself and his wife. He decided to tell the Egyptians that Sarah was his sister. He knew that in most cases anyone interested in making Sarah his wife would have to ask his permission. If this happened, he would quickly leave the country.

However, he did not realize that this code of ethics did not apply to Pharaoh. When Sarah ended up in Pharaoh's household, God became involved and sent a plague on those in the royal palace.

Often, when temptation draws near, we fail to consider the consequences of sin. Had God not stepped in, His covenant to Abraham and future blessing for the nation of Israel would have been derailed and the entire course of Israel's future changed. But God is sovereign. Abraham's faithless actions were revealed and the promise of God preserved. Even when we are faithless, God remains faithful.

Prayer: Lord, direct my steps and teach me your principles so that I may become a true person of faith.

O Lord, I lift up my soul; in you I trust, O my God. Do not let me be put to shame, nor let my enemies triumph over me (Psalm 25:1-2).

July 20

The Daily Way

God's Timetable

When we go through times of trouble, God remains at our side. When we face difficulty of any kind, He provides the strength and wisdom we need to remain steadfast and hopeful.

Feelings of uncertainty fade when we pray and seek His will. The Lord promised Abraham that he would become the father of many people. Like us, Abraham could not imagine how this would happen, especially as he grew older and Sarah became barren.

Many times, God impresses a certain promise on our hearts and minds, but what we fail to realize is that it may take years for this to come to pass. We may even sense Him preparing us for a future blessing, but as time moves on and the blessing is not realized, we begin to wonder if we misheard the Lord. This is what Abraham and Sarah did.

We may even find ourselves wondering if God has forgotten us or if we have done something wrong to miss His blessing. But God is not slow in fulfilling His promises to us (2 Peter 3:9).

He knows the promises He has spoken. Our responsibility is to remain faithful and to remember His timetable is not ours. Years are like moments to the Lord. Therefore, be patient, and you will experience His goodness in a tremendous way.

When God makes a promise, He fulfills it. Just as the Lord promised, Abraham and Sarah had a son. Make a commitment to wait faithfully for God's blessings. Also, be willing to surrender every area of your life to Him. God may be waiting on you to commit yourself fully to Him. When you do, the blessing will come at the right moment.

Prayer: Lord, I want to be faithful in all that I do in this life.

For the word of the Lord is right and true; he is faithful in all he does (Psalm 33:4).

The Daily Way

July 21

Self-Centeredness: The First Step Back

Most disputes and arguments come as the result of selfish ambitions. We quarrel over professional ideas, children, political views, relationships, and, especially financial issues.

Though Abraham strayed from God's will by traveling to Egypt, he managed to leave the country a rich man. This was the first cue we are given that problems existed between him and his nephew Lot.

> Now Lot, who was moving about with Abram, also had flocks and herds and tents. But the land could not support them while they stayed together, for their possessions were so great. ... And quarreling arose between Abram's herdsmen and the herdsmen of Lot (Genesis 13:5-7).

Feelings of jealousy, envy, and selfishness can divide the best of friends. They also can cause us to take a step back in our journey of faith. This is what happened between Abraham and Lot. Both men had always enjoyed a relationship that was as close as one shared by a father and son. Therefore, when feelings of envy grew between them, rather than quarrel, they went their separate ways (Genesis 13:8-12). In reality, their lives should have been focused on caring for one another and pleasing God. But money drove a wedge between them.

When arguments develop between you and another, be sure to take time to pray about the situation. Ask God to help to see if and when you may have made a mistake. Then, be willing to apologize for your wrong actions—and mean it.

In our day and time, true friendship is hard to find, but when we discover it, we need to preserve it through the love of God.

Prayer: Lord, let nothing come between You and me and those I love.

Let's not have any quarreling between you and me ... for we are brothers (Genesis 13:8).

July 22

The Daily Way

A True Reflection

There is a children's story that tells of a dog with a big juicy bone crossing over a small footbridge. He stops long enough to gaze down into the pool of water beneath the bridge and sees what he believes is another dog with an even bigger bone!

Instead of being happy with what he has been given, he drops his bone and lunges forward to take the other dog's bone. But there was no other dog and no other bone. What he saw was his own reflection in the water below. His entanglement with greed and deception caused him to lose what was precious to him.

Many people live their lives in a state of comparison. They look at what others have and want more than what they have been given. Discontentment and jealousy fill their hearts and the result of their attitudes is disastrous.

Lot was jealous of Abraham. This is obvious because when the men parted, Lot insisted on settling in the cities of the plain near Jordan. The fertileness of this area could be viewed from where these two men stood (Genesis 13:10-11). Abraham humbly accepted the physically challenging land of Canaan.

Lot's choice was one motivated by his self-centered desires, while Abraham was motivated by a sincere desire to please God. Once we open a door to temptation, the enemy is quick to respond. Selfishness, envy, and jealousy have one end: sorrow and defeat. If you have allowed any one of these attitudes to set up shop in your life, ask God to tear down the stronghold and forgive you for your faithlessness. He has a marvelous plan for your life, and you do not have to envy the life of another.

Prayer: Lord, cleanse me from all thoughts of envy and jealousy. Teach me to be satisfied with Your blessings in my life.

I am your shield, your very great reward (Genesis 15:1).

The Daily Way

Fearlessness: Walking with the Shield of Faith

Sometimes life can give us more than we can handle. There are moments when our burdens topple the smooth plans we have made for our lives. Our natural tendency is to hold on to what we have, clutching tighter than before. But God says we should do something different.

To walk truly fearlessly in the face of life's threatening storms, we must fully place our trust in God. He wants us to see if we really believe what He says in His Word. And it begins with our simply releasing our lives into His hands.

When your life's boat begins to rock upon the waves, God wants you to focus on Him more than ever. To walk fearlessly, upholding faith as your banner and shield, you must know who you are following.

God does not lead us down dark alleys only to abandon us. But He may take us through some of life's most tumultuous storms, holding our hands every step of the way.

After hearing about the kidnapping of Lot and his family, Abraham rounded up 318 men and went on a rescue mission. Abraham was fearless—not because he had 318 men to back him up, but because he was walking under the shield of faith. He trusted God and desired to obey Him no matter what.

Walking fearlessly with our heavenly Father means that we have come to a place of complete dependency upon Him, a place where we know He has His best in mind for us no matter what. The challenges that come our way can be conquered when we place our faith in Him. As our trust in God grows, we realize that while He will not shield us from life's challenges, He will shield us from defeat.

Prayer: Lord, help me to live free from fear as I fully place my trust in You.

When I am afraid, I will trust in you (Psalm 56:3).

July 24 — The Daily Way

Disobedience: The Trail to Spiritual Stagnation

There are times when we confuse our happiness with God's will. When everything is running smoothly and we are as happy as can be, we presume that we are in the center of God's will. However, when things take a turn for the worse, we tend to presume just the opposite: we are not in God's will.

Our initial reaction to friction in our lives is to change something. If everything looks unsettled, then we must be doing something wrong. Yet, if the unsettling is taking place around us and not in our spirit, God wants us to turn to Him and hold on.

As Abraham dealt with what he viewed as a delay in receiving God's promise for his life, he tried to change his own circumstances. If God was not going to open Sarah's womb, Abraham sought an alternative way to fulfill God's promise for his life.

God desires to fulfill His promises for us. He never intends for us to hear His promises and then go and try to make them happen ourselves. When our lives reach a point where there seems to be no way out, we must be obedient at all costs. Disobedience delays God's promises for our lives.

Anyone can obey God when life is easy. When obeying God means helping someone with minimal effort on our part, we joyfully oblige. But when obeying God means there is sacrifice or waiting involved, we must not turn about-face and run.

God may ask you to do some difficult things throughout the course of your life. However, when you follow His lead, all that you do will be for your best and for His glory.

Prayer: Lord, help me to be obedient today, no matter how easy or difficult it might be.

If you are willing and obedient, you will eat the best from the land (Isaiah 1:19).

The Daily Way — July 25

Our Transformation

Throughout God's Word we discover promise after promise of how He desires to care for us and look after us. God wants the best for our lives and nothing less. However, along life's journey, our faith might sometimes be shaken. If suddenly everything in our lives begins to take a turn for the worse, we wonder, "is this really in God's plan for me?"

If we are walking closely with the Lord and life deals us a blow that knocks us down, that does not mean we need to abandon our faith. In fact, those are the days when we need to turn to Him even more. It does not necessarily mean we are doing something wrong or that God is unhappy with us; rather, we should approach such circumstances as an opportunity for the Lord to do the amazing through our lives for His glory.

God is most interested in transforming us into His likeness. And if we allow Him to do so, He will use every event and circumstance—no matter how difficult or easy—to achieve that transformation in our hearts. Our belief that God is who He says He is, and that He will do what He promises to do, opens the gateway for Him to work through us in incredible ways.

Just as unbelief can cause us to miss out on seeing God work the impossible in our lives, devout faith and belief that He will do as He has promised allows Him to do the impossible. Instead of a destination of disappointment and defeat, our destination is one where God works His changing power in our lives, demonstrating His love and glorifying His name.

Prayer: Lord, help me to remain steadfast in my faith in You today.

Now faith is being sure of what we hope for and certain of what we do not see (Hebrews 11:1).

July 26

The Daily Way

Lessons of Impatience

In fervently seeking God's will for our lives, there are moments when we clearly hear God's voice. And there are moments when we do not wait around to let Him finish His sentence. We may hear what God is saying, but we do not listen to every part of His direction for us. Following God completely means there must be a total commitment to obedience—no matter how long it takes.

Hailed as a hero in the realm of faith, Abraham had his moments of weakness, which proved to be costly. Even though he heard God's promise that his offspring would be innumerable, Abraham struggled to wait; mistakenly supposing that maybe God meant his offspring would come through his maidservant, Hagar.

God fulfilled His promise to Abraham; Sarah had a child. However, he almost missed the blessing of the Lord. Even when we make mistakes, God still sticks by His Word—He never fails us. However, we must be ever diligent to prove faithful to what God calls us to do in our lives. Our impatience in God usually proves to delay the timing of His best for our lives. God does not choose to make us wait because He enjoys making us suffer—we wait because His timing is always the best for us.

Oftentimes, we don't see how disaster was averted by waiting on God. Or we might know all too well how our impatience resulted in a costly lesson. Waiting on God's best for our lives proves we believe Him. It demonstrates our faith in who He is and what He says about our lives. Learning to wait on His perfect timing results in greater joy when His promises are fully realized in our lives.

Prayer: Lord, teach me to have patience in following You today.

Those who know your name will trust in you, for you, Lord, have never forsaken those who seek you (Psalm 9:10).

The Daily Way

July 27

Let Truth Be the Light

One of God's greatest desires for us is that we come to know Him intimately. He made the ultimate sacrifice so that we may have constant fellowship with Him, laying the foundation for a powerful relationship that transforms our lives and causes us to become who we were created to be. However, in relating to God, we must be honest about living and walking in the truth.

Getting what we know as truth actually to become real in our hearts takes work. We have heard all the right answers and know the correct response, but we act as if we do not really believe it at times. The truth of what we believe is more determined by how we live than what we say.

To walk in the truth is to walk in the light, unashamed of how we live before both God and man. When we are walking in the truth, living out God's Word in our everyday lives, there is no need to deceive. The truth needs to make no apologies or excuses for its deeds.

In our journey with God, walking in His truth must be the standard by which we live. It is in God's Word that we find His truth. And if we trust Him and His Word, we will be people who not only hear His truths but who incorporate them into who we are.

The book The Day America Told the Truth reports that two out of three Americans believe that there is nothing wrong with telling a lie. To thrive in our journey of faith, we must be people who swim up the stream of modern culture and let truth be the light that declares who we serve—a Holy God who uses truth to bring us out of the darkness and into the light of His perfect plan for us.

Prayer: Lord, help me to live out the truth of Your Word in all that I do.

But whoever lives by the truth comes into the light, so that it may be seen plainly that what he has done has been done through God (John 3:21).

July 28 — The Daily Way

Truth: Freedom in the Journey

At times, it may seem impossible to span the chasm between who we really are and who we know God desires for us to be. In the distance, we see who we can become, yet we get discouraged when we look at who we are and realize how far we have to go.

But God does not want us to grow disheartened on this journey, which is why He desires for us to live and walk in the truth. When we try to deceive others about who we really are, it becomes more difficult to reach the destination God has chosen for us. We cannot put on masks and pretend our spirituality is much deeper than it truly is. Our masks may fool others, but God is not deceived. James encourages us to be honest with each other:

> Therefore confess your sins to each other and pray for each other so that you may be healed. The prayer of a righteous man is powerful and effective (James 5:16).

There is something freeing about coming clean and being honest. Those little secrets that we try to hide from others so they will not know what is really in our hearts become more of a burden with each passing day. We deeply desire to be known and loved for who we are, yet we struggle to allow anyone to see the truth for fear of how he or she may react.

However, when we learn to walk in the truth, freedom reigns in our lives. We also discover an exciting truth about being honest: We find others struggling just like us in areas where we thought we were all alone. God's truth will transform your life when you shirk conventional thought and are honest about who you are.

Prayer: Lord, let me see Your love for me today and know the freedom of Your truth.

Jesus said, "If you hold to my teaching, you are really my disciples. Then you will know the truth, and the truth will set you free" (John 8:31-32).

The Daily Way

July 29

The God of Me-ism

Of all the false gods of this world, the one that is the most dangerous is the god of "me-ism." When we place our desires above the desires of God, we are yielding to the pressure of "me-ism."

When we begin to look at a project or a goal and think, "I am in control of this as well as my destiny," we take another huge step toward bowing down before the god of this world—the god of senseless pride whose goal is to entrap us in the lustfulness of "me-ism."

One of Satan's greatest desires is to tempt us to doubt God. He loves to twist God's Word by telling us that we don't need to rely on the Lord's wisdom because we have all that we need within us.

The bottom line to faith is being willing to trust God with our lives. He is the One who calls us to live lives of personal sacrifice—being willing to give all that we are to Christ to be used for His glory. The enemy of our souls tempts us to stop and think about what our sacrifice will cost us. He tells us we don't need to make a deep commitment because that would be too costly and embarrassing.

Abraham lived a life of faith. He was not concerned with what his sacrifice would cost him. He was only concerned with his love and devotion to God. Therefore, he learned to follow the Lord, and we can do the same. There will be times when we make wrong turns but God will quickly restore us and direct us back to the place where His blessings are.

Have you been afraid to commit your entire life to the Lord?

You may know Him as Savior but now you can know Him as your living and eternal Lord.

Prayer: Father, help me to know how to follow You and not be drawn aside by the temptations of this world.

So [Abraham] built an altar ... to the Lord, who had appeared to him (Genesis 12:7).

July 30

The Daily Way

Test of Faith

If we are going to live lives of faith, we must realize that our faith will be tested—not just once but many times over the course of our lifetime. We will experience great joy, but we also will have to face defining moments when the intent of our hearts is revealed and the level of our faith checked.

Abraham loved Isaac. Almost every time he looked at his son, he was reminded of the fulfillment of God's promise to him. He had chosen to believe the Lord even at a point in his life when it seemed impossible to have a solid sense of faith.

Then came the day when the Lord made a request of him that did not seem to fit the nature and character of God.

> Take your son, your only son, Isaac, whom you love, and go to the region of Moriah. Sacrifice him there as a burnt offering on one of the mountains I will tell you about (Genesis 22:2).

Few of us would know how to respond to a command like this one. More than likely, we would pray, "Surely God, You have made a mistake." But Abraham never questioned God's reasoning or judgment. Once again he made preparations to obey the Lord.

Early the next morning, he saddled his donkey, gathered two of his servants and his son, and headed out to do what the Lord had asked him to do. Most of us know the conclusion to this story. God provided a ram as the sacrifice.

There may be times when the Lord requires you to be willing to give up something that you love deeply. However, He will never require you to harm another. He simply wants to know that your love for Him is not outweighed by something or someone else.

Prayer: Lord, You, and You alone, are my first love.

To obey is better than sacrifice, and to heed is better than the fat of rams (1 Samuel 15:22).

The Daily Way

July 31

Sacrifice: The Gift of Giving Your All

François Fénelon writes:

> Whatever spiritual knowledge or feelings we may have, they are all a delusion if they do not lead us to the real and constant practice of dying to self. And it is true that we do not die without suffering. Nor is it possible to be considered truly dead while there is any part of us which is yet alive.
>
> This spiritual death (which is really a blessing in disguise) is undeniably painful. It cuts swift and deep into our innermost thoughts and desires with all their parts, exposing us for what we really are. The Great Physician, who sees in us what we cannot see, knows exactly where to place the knife. He cuts away that which we are most reluctant to give up. And how it hurts! ...
>
> He wants you to live abundantly, but this can only be accomplished by allowing Him to cut into that fleshly part of you which is still stubbornly clinging to life. Should you resist? Certainly not! You must learn to suffer all things! The death of self must be voluntary, and it can only be accomplished as far as you allow.

Abraham was not the only one of God's saints who had to make a choice concerning self-sacrifice. David, the prophets, the disciples and the apostle Paul came to a point where they willingly laid down their lives—their personal desires, goals, and dreams—for the love of God.

Jesus willingly sacrificed His life for you so that you would have the opportunity to know Him personally.

Prayer: Lord, teach me how to live each day as a living sacrifice for You.

Therefore, I urge you, brothers, in view of God's mercy, to offer your bodies as living sacrifices, holy and pleasing to God—this is your spiritual act of worship (Romans 12:1).

Champions Are Made, Not Born

The Daily Way

August 1

A Devoted Heart

Once while visiting President Roosevelt in the White House, Wendell Willkie asked, "Mr. President, why do you keep that frail, sickly man—Harry Hopkins—constantly at your elbow?"

Without hesitation, Roosevelt replied, "Through that door flows an incessant stream of men and women who almost invariably want something from me. Harry Hopkins only desires to serve and to do that well. He must stay near me."

The same thing can be said of David. When Samuel first saw him, he almost questioned God's judgment. The Lord's choice for Israel's future king was the youngest of Jesse's sons. He was ruddy in appearance and did not look like kingly material. But Samuel wasn't able to see David from God's perspective.

Many times, for us to gain God's perspective we have to be willing to let go of our limited and often personality-skewed viewpoint. David was a man whose heart was devoted to God. He wanted nothing more than to worship the Lord and be close to Him.

Most of the book of Psalms was penned by David. Many entries were written while he tended his father's sheep. He was a content man because he had learned how to practice the presence of God. It was there in his father's fields that he realized God's hand was on his life.

God has a plan for your life, but before you can see it unfold, you have to be willing to allow Him to test your faithfulness.

David was loyal and faithful. And God knew that whatever happened in this young man's life, he would never abandon his godly faith.

Prayer: Lord, make me like David—a person with a heart devoted only to You.

He who dwells in the shelter of the Most High will rest in the shadow of the Almighty (Psalm 91:1).

August 2

The Daily Way

A Champion for the Lord

Have you ever thought of your devotion to God as being fair weathered? Many believers are not in this category. They are committed to finishing the course God has laid out before them (2 Timothy 4:7). Countless others barely make it across the finish line.

David was a champion for the Lord—but not because he was a gallant warrior. He did not find glory in the fact that after he defeated Goliath, the people shouted words of praise to him. In reality, David lived a very difficult life. In many cases it was tragic, lonely, and filled with broken dreams.

After the prophet Samuel anointed him king over Israel, David probably thought he would be going to Jerusalem, but instead, he ended up shivering in a dark and lonely hillside cave. Instead of accolades and praise, David had to settle for a life lived on the run from a king who was bent on killing him.

Here is what is noteworthy about David's life: He never gave up. He never lost his confidence, and He always believed He would experience God's victory. It did not matter to David if he realized the victory here on earth or in heaven. Though he sinned and stumbled in his witness for God, he never gave up and he never yielded his life of devotion to anyone other than the Lord.

He writes, "As a deer pants for streams of water, so my soul pants for you, O God" (Psalm 42:1). What do you do when sorrow comes? When disappointment fills your soul? David responded by being available to God. He never abandoned his devotion to the Lord. He sought humility over bitterness, repentance over resentment.

Prayer: Lord, may I live my life the way David did—in love with You.

Blessed is the man who does not walk in the counsel of the wicked. ... But his delight is in the law of the Lord (Psalm 1:1-2).

The Daily Way

August 3

Champions Have Faith Above Fear

Life's furious pace can be overwhelming, and the problems we encounter during those days can seem consuming. We scheme to solve our problems, yet they only grow larger and larger. One situation after another arises, and we feel as if we cannot face another trying moment. In fact, we respond by retreating because we are so afraid of another dilemma.

If ever there was a man who had his share of problems, it was David. As a shepherd for his father's flock, David always seemed to be addressing some sort of problem.

There was the problem of wild animals who wanted to kill his family's sheep. So, David killed a lion and a bear. Then there was the problem of King Saul, whose fits of rage sometimes resulted in spears being hurled at David while he played the harp.

Courage is not the absence of fear; rather, it is the conquest of fear. Surely, David was afraid as he faced death on a regular basis. However, he faced his fears by doing whatever was necessary to conquer them. Though he had been anointed to replace Saul as king of Israel one day, David never gave up. Instead, he placed his faith in God, knowing He never allows us to go into circumstances from which He cannot deliver us.

As problems arise, we must learn to face our fears with faith—faith that God is going to deliver us. David writes, "God is our refuge and strength, an ever-present help in trouble" (Psalm 46:1). In order to conquer fear, such as the fear of mounting problems, we must lean on God's promises, knowing He will help us overcome any obstacles placed in our paths.

Prayer: Lord, increase my faith as I trust You in facing my fears.

For great is your love, reaching to the heavens; your faithfulness reaches to the skies (Psalm 57:10).

August 4

Our True Champion

Fear can paralyze us—leading us to believe that moving in any direction will result in something bad. In fact, we can become afraid to face our fears mostly because we are afraid of facing them alone.

As the Israelites faced the daily boasts of Goliath, they cowered at his challenge. He loomed over the Israelite army—standing taller than everyone else in their camp. Day after day, Goliath challenged the Israelites until a man stepped forward, one who was brave enough to stand up to him—even if he was only half Goliath's size.

David, who refused to use King Saul's armor, could not believe the boasts of this man. Though Goliath towered over him, David saw no need to hide in fear from this gargantuan mortal.

Despite what seemed to be a one-sided challenge, David knew that he was not alone. As we read his writings in Psalms, we come to an understanding that he had a keen awareness of God's protective presence. Standing in front of Goliath would be no different for David than facing a bear or a lion bent on killing one of his father's sheep.

While Goliath struck fear in the hearts of many men, David was brave enough to accept his challenge, knowing the Lord would be with him. A true champion knows he never faces any challenge or difficulty alone; God is with him.

As we face the challenges of this world, we must remember that God is our true champion. The victories we obtain come as a result of God's power at work in our lives. In every circumstance, He desires the best for us.

Prayer: Lord, as I face my fears, help me to realize You are always the source of my victory.

Love and faithfulness keep a king safe; through love his throne is made secure (Proverbs 20:28).

The Daily Way

August 5

Champions Have Courage, Not Contempt

Whenever we experience any level of success in life, it is tempting to revel in our own glory, soaking in the praise as if we were the sole reason for our success. Undoubtedly, David faced the same temptation. Yet because of where his faith rested, he never yielded to these urges.

As a young man, David was anointed to become the next king of Israel by the prophet Samuel. You would think that hearing such a prophecy and then receiving an anointing to affirm God's call would be enough to drive David to go out and make it a reality.

David reacted differently. Instead of marching up to the palace gates and telling Saul that his days as king were over, David decided to act as a true champion: He let God fulfill the calling on his life by placing him in the right place at the right time.

David was a courageous young man, facing many fears with great resolve. Yet he never took his courage too far, and he never challenged God's timing. So often in life, whenever we get a whiff of success, we proceed ahead of the Lord. But God often uses a delay in timing to prepare our hearts and minds for what He desires to do through us.

David never usurped God's timing, despite his bold and courageous demeanor. He fully trusted God, which was why David experienced the level of success that he did.

He knew the Lord was the source of his every victory. So, instead of trying to venture into challenging places alone, David waited for God's timing. To be truly courageous in God's Kingdom, we must be servants willing to wait on Him.

Prayer: Lord, instill in me the patience necessary to wait upon You to fulfill the calling You have on my life.

Those who know your name will trust in you, for you, Lord, have never forsaken those who seek you (Psalm 9:10).

August 6

The Daily Way

My Way or God's Way?

The song "My Way" is a snapshot of how many people view life. They do not want to be told what to do, scoffing at any suggestion of submission. To many people, freedom means doing whatever they want, whenever they want—but true champions do not share this view.

As David neared his coronation as king of Israel, his life was getting extremely dangerous. King Saul knew David's popularity was growing—and he begrudged David for it. So much so that he decided he would kill David to end this problem. So Saul set out on a manhunt through the mountains in search of David.

Despite being the object of a heated pursuit, David refused to do things his way. Twice David had opportunities to kill Saul, yet he would not do it. Resisting the urging of a traveling companion, David said, "But the Lord forbid that I should lay a hand on the Lord's anointed" (1 Samuel 26:11).

David knew this was not God's pathway for him to the throne of Israel. He had so much respect for God's anointing Saul to be the king of Israel in the first place that David refused to meddle with God's plan. There was not a contemptuous bone in his body.

As true champions, we must realize God is the One who brings victory, and we must fulfill our roles as humble servants, submitting to His plan for our lives. Though the temptation may be to do things our way—especially when we know that God is leading us in a certain direction—we must resist that temptation and trust His plan. Doing things God's way is the only way to go.

Prayer: Lord, help me to follow Your ways and Your plans as You have laid them before me.

Some trust in chariots and some in horses, but we trust in the name of the Lord our God (Psalm 20:7).

The Daily Way

August 7

God's Calling for You

Obeying God is the most courageous act we will do. In our society today, rebellion seems to be the status quo. So many people are going against the grain of our cultural norms that their actions have become the norm. When this type of thinking seeps into the way we view God, we begin to venture down a very dangerous path—one of disobedience.

God has a special calling on each person's life. However, our response to His calling determines whether we will be courageous followers or rebellious children.

Many times, we resist God's calling because we fear what He might make us do. We forget that His plan is the best possible plan for us. His calling on our lives does not mean we are doomed to a lifestyle we loathe; rather, it is a calling to experience the fullness of life as we have yet to know it.

There were many moments in which David could have wandered down another path. After all, King Saul was chasing him across the countryside—wanting nothing less than to take David's life. Yet during this difficult time in his life, God's man chose to remain faithful and obedient to the Lord.

If we want to become courageous champions for Christ, we must remember that obedience to God is the cornerstone of our love for Him. While we may praise God with our mouths, what we do with our lives demonstrates where our hearts truly rest. God's calling on our lives awaits our obedience, and our decision to follow and obey Him—no matter what—will mold and shape us into true champions.

Prayer: Lord, show me what it means to walk in true obedience to the call You have placed on my life.

Commit your way to the Lord; trust in him and he will do this (Psalm 37:5).

August 8

The Daily Way

Champions Know How to Fail

In His infinite love, God watches as we stumble along the path of life, opening His arms wide again and again to us. However, many believers are stranded along life's narrow road because they do not know how to recover from failure. Falling into sin and disobedience leads to dangerous territory, yet God wants us to know He is the Great Redeemer. He can transform our most dismal failures into victories.

Sin has dangerous consequences. However, when we do stumble, we must remember that the shame we feel is miniscule in comparison to the love God has for us.

Our guilt should drive us to the Cross where we are reminded of God's amazing plan of redemption. Real champions know how to get up off the ground and keep going. No matter how strong we are or how determined we are, our faith will be challenged.

Looking at our failures as being unforgivable is an injustice to the life and death of Jesus Christ. Once we have asked God to forgive us, we must view each failure as a teachable moment—a time where we gain God's wisdom and understanding.

When we humble ourselves before Him, we must remember that God can take the weakest moments of our lives and turn them into stepping stones on the path to spiritual transformation. And as we approach our heavenly Father with open ears to hear His direction for our lives, we must remember that He can carry us from the darkest valleys to the mountaintop.

Prayer: Lord, help me to learn from my mistakes, changing me as I submit my life to You.

Do not conform any longer to the pattern of this world, but be transformed by the renewing of your mind. Then you will be able to test and approve what God's will is—his good, pleasing and perfect will (Romans 12:2).

The Daily Way

August 9

Champions Focus on God

Everyone loves to pull for the underdog. Whether in sports, business, or the movies, we always like to see the character with the most obstacles to overcome conquer them. It stirs our souls because we secretly wish we could have the courage to accomplish something extraordinary.

There always is one consistent trait that moves even the weakest person on to triumph, and that is true focus. The men and women in the Bible who accomplished great things for God's Kingdom had great focus. Abraham, Moses, David, Solomon, and even Samson trained their eyes to stay put on the Lord.

Taking your eyes off God can result in failure, just like keeping your eyes firmly fixed on Him can bring some of the greatest victories you will ever know. In your weakest moments, ask yourself if you are focused on God or on your situation. Whenever self-pity sets in, know that failure is lurking nearby. Bemoaning about difficulty demonstrates that your faith has been rocked. Confidence in God can vanish when you try to solve your problems apart from Him.

Keeping our focus on the Lord keeps us from repeating past failures. As we realize that He is the One who leads us through impossible situations, we rely less and less upon our own strength and more on His.

Trusting Him for direction and confidently following His lead are marks of a champion—a champion who is focused firmly upon Him.

Prayer: Lord, please help me to stay focused on You at every moment today.

Let us fix our eyes on Jesus, the author and perfecter of our faith, who for the joy set before him endured the cross, scorning its shame, and sat down at the right hand of the throne of God (Hebrews 12:2).

August 10

The Daily Way

Champions Pray in the Dark

The true test of our character is not measured when we are on stage with the spotlight shining upon us—the true test is when no one is watching but God. Many people make the mistake of wearing their spiritual maturity on their sleeves. But God is not impressed with how many Bible verses we know or how many Sunday school lessons we teach. In fact, nothing we do can impress God.

What God desires from us more than anything is a relationship. He designed us for this. We function best when we have others around us supporting us and challenging us in our relationship with God. No relationship can thrive without communication.

In 1 Samuel chapter 22, we find David tucked away in a cave in the mountains, hiding from King Saul and his army. Day after day, he scampered through the mountains to avoid Saul's sword. And after days of running, David also discovered an important truth: Only God could save him. No matter how clever he was in escaping Saul's clutches, he began to understand that true salvation comes only from God.

As a result of David's understanding of this principle, he spent those dark nights in mountain caves praying to God. He understood that in order to be used by God in the light, true champions prayed in the dark.

It is in the dark that God brings to light His promises. It also is in the dark that He gives us the peace and assurance we need to endure difficulty and heartache. If we desire to be true champions, we must boldly pray to God, no matter how dire our situation appears. It is what He wants us to do.

Prayer: Lord, instill in me the truth that You desire a personal relationship with me and that You are always willing to help me no matter how discouraging my situation seems.

I call on you, O God, for you will answer me; give ear to me and hear my prayer (Psalm 17:6).

The Daily Way — August 11

God Is Our Guide

When we find ourselves in one of life's darker moments, we often forget that Jesus is the Light of the World. We grope in the dark for something that will shed light on our situation and lead us to hope. Sometimes we trip and fall numerous times before the truth in our heads makes its way to our lips.

Stuck in a cave while hiding from King Saul, David quickly learned where to turn when groping got him nowhere: he cried out to God. Throughout the book of Psalms, we read David's heartfelt cries to the Lord.

David yearned for God to reach down and bring him salvation from the looming disaster. And time and time again, God answered David's prayers by delivering him from his enemies.

When trouble struck, David turned to God almost immediately because he realized one important fact: He was helpless without Him. Understanding our depravity is a key step for us in turning to the Lord in prayer.

When we think we can solve all our problems on our own, we make a huge mistake. Failure to consult the Lord on which direction we should take only leads to more trouble. Plotting and trying to determine our own course leaves us exhausted and confused.

However, when we realize that we, like David, are helpless without God, we quickly turn to Him in prayer. Groping around in the dark only results in scars and rough tumbles. There are no light switches in caves, only passageways to the surface—and God is the best guide we could ever have.

Prayer: Lord, help me to understand that I cannot solve all of life's problems on my own. I need Your help more than anything else.

Praise be to God, who has not rejected my prayer or withheld his love (Psalm 66:20).

August 12 — The Daily Way

Our True Colors

We tend to learn more about ourselves in the difficult times than we do in other periods in our lives. When everything in life just seems to glide along effortlessly, we appear as people who have everything together, sufficient unto ourselves. Yet when life hurls an unexpected curve our way, our true colors are revealed.

However, this is how God shapes and molds us. He adds pressure to our lives, and just as a diamond undergoes intense heat and pressure before it emerges as a sparkling jewel, we must do the same.

Where do you turn when adversity comes and the walls of life begin to close in around you? To whom do you cry out—a loved one? Do you rely upon your own ingenuity? Or do you turn to the Lord—calling upon Him to rescue you in your time of need?

True champions always pray during the dark times. This is a real indicator of where their loyalty rests—with God. Life can feel relentless at times, yet nothing is impossible for God. He can pluck us from the doldrums of circumstance, placing us on the mountaintop far from the troubles nipping at our feet.

As you turn to God in the midst of trying circumstances, remember He is faithful to hear your cries and will answer your prayers. Although He may not answer in the way you expect, He will always do what is best.

When we cry out to Him to save us, our hearts are revealed. He alone is our salvation. True champions turn to God in dark times and trust Him to bring them to the light.

Prayer: Lord, give me the faith to trust You with each and every circumstance in my life.

Blessed is the man who trusts in the Lord, whose confidence is in him (Jeremiah 17:7).

The Daily Way — August 13

Champions Don't Lose Their Confidence

To walk truly in confidence, we must realize its source. If we place our full confidence in our human abilities, we will be sorely let down time and again. No matter how accomplished we are, no matter how much intelligence we have acquired, no matter how talented we may be—God alone is our deliverer, and He must be the One upon whom we rely.

Though David was being run ragged through the mountains, fleeing a mad king, he never lost confidence that God was going to deliver him. However, David ventured into new situations with extreme caution, consulting the Lord before acting. "[David] inquired of the Lord, saying, 'Shall I go and attack these Philistines?'" (1 Samuel 23:2).

True champions do not lose their confidence because they know they alone are not the sole source of victory. They understand that their confidence rests in a loving heavenly Father, who has hopes and dreams for their lives far beyond what they could ever imagine.

David knew that while he was fleeing King Saul, he was under the protection of God's wing. During our journey with Christ, we can probably mark with ease the days, months, and years when we were seeking direction from Him. And with the same ease, we can tell when we were not.

When we inquire of the Lord, asking Him to prepare the way for us to walk in His calling, He is faithful to do so. When prayer becomes a discipline in our lives, we will never lose confidence, and we will walk boldly with God into what He has called us to do.

Prayer: Lord, instill in me the discipline to seek Your direction at every decision-making point in my life.

In him and through faith in him we may approach God with freedom and confidence (Ephesians 3:12).

August 14 — The Daily Way

Victory through God

It happens quite often in the world of sports: a player or a team once atop the heap comes crashing down amidst intense pressure. Instead of dominating their sport like they once did, they suddenly begin making mistakes they have never made before. Rather than winning championships, they hope just to be respectable. And somewhere buried beneath the rubble is their confidence.

In today's media-hungry world, it only takes a few people to begin denouncing the reign of a team or player before everyone joins in, including the players and teams. What once seemed invincible now seems average. Climbing out of such a devastating place is a difficult task.

We, too, face public opinion each day in our lives. Though we may firmly espouse the doctrines of our faith, when life turns dark and we become gloomy, the people we interact with on a daily basis begin to question our faith. Whenever we experience tragedy, our tendency is to shake an angry fist at God rather than turning to Him for comfort.

Many people begin to drift away from their faith because events occur in their lives that make them doubt God's sovereignty.

Whether it is a broken relationship or the death of a loved one, God does not abandon us; rather, He takes those situations and begins to weave His love into our lives in unexpected ways.

We see His hand at work and realize He has never left us. As believers dedicated to following God, we must not let public opinion sway our faith in Him, holding fast to our confidence that He alone is our Savior.

Prayer: Lord, help me to recall Your victories in my life in the past and trust You no matter what.

You give me your shield of victory, and your right hand sustains me; you stoop down to make me great (Psalm 18:35).

The Daily Way

August 15

Champions Play by the Rules

Cheating produces hollow victories, yet people cheat every day in some form or another. They cheat in their jobs, taking shortcuts to get desired results instead of doing their work the longer, more tedious way. People cheat on their families, robbing them of quality time for other selfish ambitions. People cheat in school, foregoing time and energy spent in study in exchange for a quick and easy answer.

And even if a person cheats and wins, does he really win? How satisfying is it to reach a goal that is obtained only because of cheating? What an empty accomplishment!

Playing by the rules is the only way to play. As believers in the middle of God's script for our lives, there are no shortcuts to the end. We cannot opt to skip life's difficulties in favor of a quick road to God's blessings. We cannot be molded into His image without having our feet held to the fire. It is during these character-building moments we define what kind of believers we are going to be: those who run when life gets tough or those who are faithful to God no matter how difficult the situation appears.

When the prophet Samuel came to David's home and anointed him as the next king of Israel, David probably did not know what was ahead for him. Yet even when King Saul pursued him in an effort to kill him, David never attempted to circumvent God's plan for his life. With a quick stroke of his sword, David could have ended Saul's life and reign as king of Israel. But David wanted God to be the One who placed him in power.

Prayer: Lord, give me the patience to wait upon Your timing for my life.

The end of a matter is better than its beginning, and patience is better than pride (Ecclesiastes 7:8).

August 16

The Daily Way

Champions Play with Integrity

If we desire to have true integrity of heart, we must not be shy about checking our motives with regularity. No matter how much we love God and desire to serve Him, we must be on guard against selfish ambitions that tend to creep into our hearts on occasion.

We have the tendency to compare our own journey with the journeys of others—and when it does not look like we are getting a fair shake, we begin to plot and to scheme. Whenever our selfish ambitions begin to take over, we say things and do things that grieve God's heart. Instead of acting lovingly, we act selfishly. Our goal slowly switches from serving God to serving ourselves. If we are not careful, our purpose in life will become to fulfill our wants, regardless of the cost.

This scenario arises in many different facets of life. In relationships, in work environments, in churches, in families—we begin to seek to satisfy ourselves rather than serve others. When we suspect this attitude in our lives, we can ask ourselves some questions to shed light on our hearts. Are our actions revengeful? Are our hearts covetous and ambitious? Are we impatient with God's timing?

Loving others begins to squelch such attitudes. Instead of trying to exact our revenge, we begin to show mercy and love. The ambitions in our hearts begin to fade as we turn our focus back to our loving Savior. James reminds us: "Mercy triumphs over judgment!" (James 2:13).

Playing by the rules means we choose to live God's way over our own. We choose to live by His rules, which include putting others before ourselves.

Prayer: Lord, place in me an attitude that puts others ahead of me.

Before his downfall a man's heart is proud, but humility comes before honor (Proverbs 18:12).

The Daily Way

August 17

The Right Perspective

As we face discouraging events in our lives, there is a danger lurking—self-pity, which can quickly become a source of deadly comfort. The gloomy clouds hanging over our lives should never be permitted to remain, especially in light of God's hope and truth.

Pressing through any disappointment means being careful not to linger long in a place of discouragement. Discouragement is like a piece of clothing—it can be worn for the world to see or it can be placed in the closet. While each of us will face times of discouragement, we must also realize that discouragement has the ability to rob us of something very important—our godly perspective.

As David entered into a place of discouragement, he found himself grasping for hope. He needed to gain the right perspective on his situation, but it was difficult. No matter how hopeless or how discouraging our situations might be, God has the ability to bring eternal hope and peace to our lives when we need them the most.

Discouragement wars against the very trait that faith and hope in God brings—courage. In order to stand up to the trials and tribulations of a fallen world, we must turn to God for courage and make a commitment to stand strong in our faith through Jesus Christ.

God's best for your life does not include remaining in a place devoid of hope, faith, and courage. Therefore, when facing discouragement, turn to God. He will bring the hope and courage you need to live victoriously over life's hardships.

Prayer: Lord, give me the right perspective in every situation so that I can go through each one trusting You for wisdom to live a godly life.

Guide me in your truth and teach me, for you are God my Savior, and my hope is in you all day long (Psalm 25:5).

August 18 — The Daily Way

Champions Stand Strong

One of our initial and natural responses to difficulty is to look for an immediate solution. We do not like tension and pressure in relationships. We despise disunity and spend enormous amounts of time trying to repair such problems. But when attempts to bring about resolution fail, often run, abandoning the problem and situation altogether.

Our reaction to difficulty is a proving ground for our faith. Does our faith rest in our ability to resolve situations on our own? If we run, the answer is there for the world to see, no matter how adamantly we proclaim our faith in God with our mouths. Does our faith rest in God alone? If we determine to stand strong and face whatever the world brings in our direction, the answer is there for the world to see as well.

While God may not cause the difficulty in our lives, He certainly uses it to mature us. He shapes and fashions us more into His image as we learn to trust Him more. And it is in these times of testing that God begins to refine our hearts in new ways.

Running from the trials and tribulations in our lives in an attempt to escape the difficulty carries some harsh consequences: We may escape the testing, but we will also escape God's blessing.

God enjoys rewarding His children with blessings from heaven. But no reward comes without personal sacrifice. His wondrous blessings await those courageous enough to face each challenge. Are you willing to take the challenge?

Prayer: Lord, give me the strength to face every challenge You send my way today.

The eyes of the Lord are on those who fear him, on those whose hope is in his unfailing love (Psalm 33:18).

The Daily Way — August 19

Champions Learn from Their Mistakes

On the tennis court, a young woman flashed a smile of admiration at her opponent after he hit a winning shot. His floating backhand carried so much spin on it that the moment it hit the court, it bounced back over the net before the woman had a chance to hit it.

Sensing that he had spotted a weakness in the woman's game, he attempted the same shot again. But this time, the woman never let the ball hit the court. Instead, she smashed it back over the net and at her opponent's feet for a winning shot.

A lesson learned? Most of us would hope so. However, many people fail to learn from their mistakes and are doomed to repeat them over again. Chances are, in an effort to impress his court companion, this fellow tried the shot yet again and was met with the same result. God wants us to learn from our mistakes.

Whenever we feel that we have already conquered a certain problem, we must take time for some serious reflection and ask ourselves why we have to repeat the process over again. When we pray, God will answer.

True champions do not spend their lives trying to get it right—they spend their time getting better. If we desire to be all God has called us to be, we must be a people who are willing to do it over until we get it right and then go on to get it even better!

God wants you to learn all you can from life's difficulties. As you go through each one, ask Him to help you grow in your faith and show you ways you can honor Him with your life.

Prayer: Lord, please help me discern what lesson You want to teach me in each situation in my life.

The righteous will flourish like a palm tree, they will grow like a cedar of Lebanon (Psalm 92:12).

August 20   The Daily Way

To Be First, We Must Be Last

Throughout the Bible, we learn how the wisdom of God confounds the wisdom of man. And as we look at some of the teachings of Christ, the principles He taught seem contradictory to conventional knowledge. To be first, we must be last? How much sense does that make, especially today in our ego-driven society?

Biblical principles contain tremendous truth. David personally discovered that brokenness leads to godly wholeness. Brokenness can come to the life of the believer in many ways—disappointment, sorrow, and sin.

Maybe God instructs us to go one way, but we are determined to go another. The result is frustration and brokenness. Sometimes, brokenness comes not because we have done anything wrong, but because God wants to test and strengthen our faith. This was true in David's life.

He had not sinned against the Lord. Instead, God used the fires of affliction in David's life to shape and mold him for greater service. The Lord also knew that when future difficulty came or disappointment struck, David would be prepared and his faith would not waver or fail.

Brokenness has a way of revealing our level of faith better than anything else. When it continues over months and even years, we truly learn where the focus of our faith lies. When we begin to identify with the words of David, as he fled from a jealous and enraged King Saul, then we will know that brokenness is accomplishing its greatest work in our lives.

Remember, if God has chosen you to face a time of brokenness, it will be followed by a season of tremendous blessing.

Prayer: Lord, I surrender my life to You.

Those who know your name will trust in you, for you, Lord, have never forsaken those who seek you (Psalm 9:10).

Champions Know When to Lean on God

In today's society, people desperately try to avoid accepting blame. There is always some excuse to explain away the actions of people who need to be held accountable. While our society loves to bestow grace, it struggles to see how grace and consequences for our actions can live together. Adopting this type of attitude can stunt our relationships with God.

God is a God of grace and redemption, so much so that He sacrificed His only Son for the forgiveness of our sins. Yet, Jesus' death was the consequence of our sin. The consequences of sin are not dismissed simply because grace is endowed upon us.

Confessing our sins to God and taking full responsibility for our actions tests our belief in this kingdom principle. Do we really think we need to confess our sins? And if so, do we think it is our fault that we sinned?

If we intend to experience wholeness, we must confess our sins to God and ask for His forgiveness. Whenever we turn to Christ—even in the midst of our brokenness—He is there for us, putting back together for us the shattered pieces.

A true champion knows when to lean on God—and that time is always. We cannot conquer the sin in our lives on our own. We need to put on the altar those attitudes and habits that produce sin in our lives and invite God to bring about the cleansing that purifies us. When we are diligent to confess our sins and accept responsibility for our actions, God is faithful to respond and lovingly restore us to wholeness.

Prayer: Lord, help me to be more aware of my sin and more faithful to confess it to You.

He who conceals his sins does not prosper, but whoever confesses and renounces them finds mercy (Proverbs 28:13).

August 22 — The Daily Way

Champions Victoriously Honor God

In the New Testament, Jesus made it clear that we have to make a choice: Either we will serve God or we will serve something else.

You can dedicate your life to living for the Lord, or you can spend your life living for yourself. However, to truly honor God in a way that places Him in high esteem over everything else, He must be at the center of your affections.

Many people do good works. Some non-believers even do more good works than Christians. Yet, a look at the heart reveals their true motivation—whether their deeds are truly done for themselves or for the people they are serving. Some Christians are doing good works out of guilt or obligation, as opposed to the purest reason—love for God.

To honor God is to serve Him out of our strong desire to see His name exalted, not our own. If we are doing something in order to earn recognition, is God at the center of our motivation? If no one would ever know what we did, would we still do it? Do we serve others because we love God so much that we want to be the hands and feet of Christ to our dying world? Or do we serve others because it will get us noticed and recognized as great humanitarians by our friends and communities? Is our service self-serving?

God knows our hearts, and He knows if our lives are honoring Him or honoring ourselves. As believers who desire to honor Him, we must endeavor to put Him at the center of all we do. All our decisions, all our thoughts, all our actions—they must be centered on God.

When you do this, you honor Him more than you ever imagined.

Prayer: Lord, help me to place You at the center of my life in everything that I do.

My salvation and my honor depend on God; he is my mighty rock, my refuge (Psalm 62:7).

The Daily Way — August 23

Champions Do Things God's Way

In an effort to please his boss, the young man devised a plan that would ultimately bring praise to the company. He made the contacts and connections, carrying through on his plan.

When he revealed the plan to his boss, the reaction the young worker received was not what he had anticipated. His actions were met with furrowed brows and a stiff reprimand. His plan was not what the company wanted.

Sometimes even the best of intentions can be wrong, and we find ourselves waltzing down the road of folly when it comes to serving God. With the purest of hearts, we seek to bring praise and honor to God's name, but we fail to ask God what He wants us to do. We assume we know His plan and begin to carry it out promptly, without prayer or wise counsel.

In order to live a life that honors God, we must not only put God at the center of our lives, we also must be committed to doing things God's way. Too often, we make the mistake of trying to get God to go along with our plans instead of taking the time to find out His plan for our lives.

Do you desire to honor God with your life? If so, begin by asking God to show you how to do things His way. No matter how many needs you may see in your community or how much you know about how to meet them, take time to seek His guidance and plan. Don't be quick to rush ahead. Make sure that you have clear guidance for the future. You will honor Him through your desire to serve only Him.

Prayer: Lord, I want to honor You with my life, and I want to commit to doing things Your way.

The fear of the Lord teaches a man wisdom, and humility comes before honor (Proverbs 15:33).

August 24 — The Daily Way

Champions Seek God's Will

Even after we pray and seek God, there may be a time of waiting for His answer to come. This waiting period is a crucial time in our lives as believers. If we jump ahead of God, we could miss His blessing. If we lag behind, we also could miss the joy of knowing that we have followed His leading. Take a moment to ask yourself if the Lord is the center of your life. Are you doing things His way?

If so, then you are probably encountering resistance from the enemy. Satan wants to do all that he can to cause you to feel disappointed and deflated.

David, in his pure intentions to bring the Ark of the Covenant back to the temple, put the ark on a cart to transport it. And while that may seem trivial, God specifically outlined how the ark was to be transported: It was to be carried with poles (2 Samuel 6).

But David failed to do this. When the ark began to slide off the cart, one of the workers reached out to grab it and died instantly. David quickly developed a godly fear of the Lord. This fear was not a fear that God would kill him if he made a mistake.

Instead, his fear of God was based on the desire to serve and honor God with purity and integrity of heart. This included doing things God's way.

A healthy fear of God motivates us to change the way we live our lives so that we honor Him all the more. When we realize that we are doing God's work, but not the way He wants us to do it, we should immediately stop and seek His will for our lives.

Be willing to change your path if necessary in order to please the Lord.

Prayer: Father, show me what it means to have a healthy fear of You.

The fear of the Lord is pure, enduring forever. The ordinances of the Lord are sure and altogether righteous (Psalm 19:9).

The Daily Way — August 25

Champions Have Humility

Becoming a champion challenges our faith in more ways than we think. When we experience a great deal of success and numerous victories in our lives, human nature begins to enjoy the praises that are given to us.

Before we know it, the excitement that people have for us changes the way we view life and we start believing our own press. Instead of dwelling on who got us to this point, we begin dreaming about where we are going to take ourselves in the future.

Humility is the mark of a true champion. Godly love is emblazoned on his or her heart. Most people can sniff out false humility miles before they get to it. They hear the clichés about how we had nothing to do with it—and they know we do not believe a word we are saying.

Sincere humility, however, is not making ourselves doormats or denying, ignoring, and undermining the gifts and talents God has given us. When we put God first, we begin to understand what true humility is. It is recognizing God as the reason for our success, the mastermind behind the plan that has brought success to our lives. Humility also means we are quick to acknowledge—and to believe wholeheartedly that God is the One who has designed this plan, and equipped us with the tools to accomplish it.

When our focus in life is to honor God, we naturally put Him first in everything we do. There is no tension in our hearts over who belongs on the pedestal. We know we would be nothing without God. He is our everything, and for that we must give Him our hearts and our sincere devotion.

Prayer: Lord, help me to walk in sincere humility, honoring You with everything I do.

Humility and the fear of the Lord bring wealth and honor and life (Proverbs 22:4).

August 26

The Daily Way

Champions Put God First

From the first moment we step into church we are taught to put God first in our lives. Yet, are we really doing this? Does He own first place in our hearts all the time or simply when it is convenient?

It is easy to proclaim that we have placed the Lord first; however, the true test comes when life throws us an unexpected curve. This is when we discover if what we say with our mouths is really true in our hearts.

Authentic humility and love aspire to put God before everything else no matter what the price may be. It might cost us our dreams. It might cost us our jobs. It might cost us status in society. But the cost of failing to put God first is far more astronomical.

David's heart was one finely tuned to God's love and affection. When he received the disappointing answer to his request to build the temple, David's love did not collapse. Instead, he was inspired to a deeper sense of worship and love for God.

In 1 Chronicles 17:16, we learn of David's response: "King David went in and sat before the Lord." David was a man of war. Therefore, God had chosen not to use him as the principle architect of His temple, but David would have input in its design and construction.

For David, building the temple was all about honoring God, not going down in history as the king who built it. As believers with the amazing privilege of getting to participate in advancing God's kingdom, we must make sure our motives are solely to see His kingdom advanced and His name glorified. That is how we put Him first.

Prayer: Lord, help me to put You first today in everything I do.

As God's chosen people, holy and dearly loved, clothe yourselves with compassion, kindness, humility, gentleness and patience (Colossians 3:12).

The Daily Way — August 27

Champions Show Grace and Kindness

Inside each of us there is a hunger and a thirst for justice. We want to see the guilty person get his just due. Yet, when it comes ourselves, we want mercy and grace extended in our direction. We may be deserving of the worst kind of punishment, but we long for someone to give us a second chance before harshly condemning us.

Although God is just in His ways, He also is merciful. In fact, God's Word makes it simple: "Mercy triumphs over judgment" (James 2:13). God would rather extend mercy toward us than the harsh consequences of judgment. That is why Jesus gave His life for us—so we would not have to suffer the consequences of sin. Jesus paid the debt we owe for our sin.

As believers pursuing the heart of God, we must realize that if this trait of grace and kindness is at the heartbeat of God, we, too, should emulate this. When someone sins against us, we should not judge him for his actions and sever our relationship with him; rather, we should lovingly approach him and seek reconciliation.

Instead of carrying around in our hearts a thirst for vengeance against someone who has wronged us, we should bestow upon him an abundance of grace and kindness, knowing that such an act can soften even the hardest of hearts. If we are living for Christ, we are living proof that His grace and kindness can transform a heart of sin into a heart that loves God.

Set a goal to demonstrate God's grace and kindness to everyone, for all men and women are in need of His life-changing compassion.

Prayer: Lord, fill my heart with grace and kindness for the world around me.

You gave me life and showed me kindness, and in your providence watched over my spirit (Job 10:12).

August 28

The Daily Way

Champions Have Hearts of Love

There is something contagious about a heart of love. People who are selfless with their love can make giant waves in this world where those who cling to selfish desires cause only ripples. In fact, those who have hearts of love view the people around them as being most important. A heart that bears the marks of God's intimate love is not a selfish heart.

The truth is that when we look directly into God's heart of love, we are transformed forever. The selfish desires that once dominated our hearts' landscapes vanish in an instant—replaced by a desire to lavish love on others.

As God begins to transform our hearts through His grace and kindness, we become vessels willing to reciprocate this type of love. Something happens inside of us. We begin to realize the twofold effect of loving God and loving others—not just friends and family, but others who cross our paths every day.

Hardened hearts begin to melt beneath the warmth of Christ's love overflowing from our lives. People who we never thought would let the name of Jesus roll off their lips suddenly praise Him because we have taken the time to love them the way God has commanded us to love. Once we learn how to abide in His love, our feelings of jealousy, greed, and anger die a quick death.

A true champion extends grace and kindness because he knows the transformation that has taken place in his own heart, and he realizes those who receive God's love and grace have no other course of action but to give God's love away.

Prayer: Lord, help me to be a conduit of love through which You flow.

By the grace of God I am what I am, and his grace to me was not without effect. No, I worked harder than all of them—yet not I, but the grace of God that was with me
(1 Corinthians 15:10).

The Daily Way — August 29

Champions Loathe Sin

It is easy, especially when we are living in a world riddled with sin, to become repulsed by sinful behavior. On the radio, disc jockeys make crude remarks. On television, we see an array of acts that break God's heart. And as these ideas and new cultural shifts become more and more commonplace, we grow numb to their presence.

While it might be difficult for us to imagine God becoming outraged, He does. Sin stirs His anger because He knows its evil potential. In Jeremiah 44:4, God says, "Again and again I sent my servants the prophets, who said, 'Do not do this detestable thing that I hate!'" God is not merely disturbed by sin—He loathes it.

Sin is diametrically opposed to loving God. Sin breeds on the credence that says, "I don't believe that God knows what is best for my life, so I'm going to do it my way. Whatever I feel, I'm going to do it because that will make me happier than obeying God."

At the root of sin is a defiance to live life any way other than God's way. And God hates this. He knows that when people enter into this pattern of thinking, they are venturing down a dangerous road. In His infinite wisdom and love for us, He knows what is best—and it is not sin.

To walk in the light of God's love, we must understand how He feels about sin, and we too must feel the same way. Sin should not simply annoy us. It should stir us to action, to repentance, and to prayer—motivating us to pray for ourselves and others. When we see sin, it should make us defiant toward the enemy and more determined to live holy lives.

Prayer: Lord, help me to realize the gravity of sin in my own life and the lives of those around me.

Great is [God's] love, reaching to the heavens; your faithfulness reaches to the skies (Psalm 57:10).

August 30 — The Daily Way

Champions Are on the Lookout

The longer we walk down the road with God, the more self-aware we must become. To go the distance, we cannot wander aimlessly toward God, oblivious to our surroundings. It takes focus and determination, as well as a heart bent on serving Him and putting Him above everything else in our lives.

As we pause to analyze our hearts, we must be on the lookout for anything that would open the door to sin in our lives. As David faced trial after trial, he tried to stay focused on the Lord. Yet in times when he lost his focus, he found disaster waiting around the next bend.

By keeping your mind and heart set on God, you can be on the lookout for the very things that can trip you up spiritually, emotionally, and mentally. If you are feeling bored, lonely, tired, or rejected, beware. These feelings can betray you and lead you to sin. If you slip into laziness and refuse to hear God's truth, you may also be strolling down a dangerous path.

When we choose to be led by our flesh—which is what happens when we allow our feelings to tempt us into acting contrary to God's Word—we are destined to sin. God loves us dearly and He desires the best for our lives.

To serve and honor Him at every turn in life, we must follow the voice of the Holy Spirit and not our flesh. In our desire to live holy and righteous lives, we must determine to rely upon Him for guidance and direction. When we do, we will avoid potential pitfalls and heartache.

Prayer: Lord, allow Your Holy Spirit to be the voice of direction for my life today.

Give me understanding, and I will keep your law and obey it with all my heart (Psalm 119:34).

The Daily Way

August 31

Champions Know How to Repent

As believers, we should know that God hates sin. We also should recognize many of sin's warning signs. Yet despite all of this, we can still fall into Satan's handy trap of sin and disillusionment. When this happens, how should we respond to our failure so that God is honored and we are able to break free of sin's grasp?

All too often, we simply want to be pardoned from our sin. The thought of repenting is almost foreign to us. To repent means to stop what we are doing and to go in the opposite direction. However, most of the time we want a simple dismissal of our actions and a warning not to commit them again.

Yet when we recognize that we have sinned and offended the heart of God, we must come clean and desire wholeness again. David discovered that grieving God's heart was painful. Therefore, a simple "I'm sorry" would not do.

He approached God with all humility and a brokenness which showed that his heart was in the right place. Later, David wrote, "The sacrifices of God are a broken spirit; a broken and contrite heart, O God, you will not despise" (Psalm 51:17).

Whenever we come before God with a heart that is contrite—sincerely sorry for what we did wrong and longing to change our ways—God is moved. He sees that we recognize what we did was wrong and that we want to be pure again.

True repentance means we love God more than we love our sin. When He sees this type of devotion, He opens up His arms and welcomes us with His unending grace.

Prayer: Lord, instill in me a heart of repentance that returns to You when I realize I have sinned.

Godly sorrow brings repentance that leads to salvation and leaves no regret, but worldly sorrow brings death (2 Corinthians 7:10).

Becoming a Hero to Others

The Daily Way — September 1

Answer God's Call

To be an effective hero for God, you must remember the source of your power. Never confuse your human ability with God's ability. Never place so much emphasis on what God is doing through you that you think you are better than others. There is great danger in taking pride in what you have done. Give the glory to the Lord!

Moses was called to do a certain task. God empowered him for the work and gave him the ability he needed. There was no confusion about who was at work in Moses' life—it was God.

When Moses and Aaron went to Pharaoh, the Lord was the One guiding them. They heard God's call and responded in obedience. They knew God had called them, and they were going to answer the call by doing His will, regardless of the obstacles along the way.

Meeting with Pharaoh simply was a step in the process—a difficult step, but a necessary step. Both men knew there was no room for compromise. Therefore, when Moses instructed Aaron to touch the Nile River with the staff God had given him, Aaron did what Moses said, and the river flowed with blood.

The Egyptians worshipped this river. To them, it was a vital source of life. Without its waters, the Egyptians would die. God always knows how to get the enemy's attention. Pharaoh was furious and frightened. He realized God's power rested on Moses, but he was not willing to listen to the Lord. He was not ready to let God's people go.

Moses' obedience and devotion was evidence that the Lord was with him and the nation of Israel. Is God's presence evident in your life? Do others see you and long to know Christ?

Pharaoh summoned Moses ... "This time I have sinned," he said ... "The Lord is in the right, and I and my people are in the wrong" (Exodus 9:27).

September 2 — The Daily Way

Me, Myself, and I

I have heard of an unusual place of worship called The Temple of the Thousand Buddhas. There are more than 1,000 likenesses of Buddha inside the shrine—each one is a little different than the others. They were created so that a worshiper could come, find one that looks something like himself, and worship it.

The concept of self-worship is not confined to Buddhism. Today, we see this taking place throughout life. It is a marketing technique used over and over again to sell everything from makeup to home decorations. The packaging may vary but the message is the same: me, myself, and I.

We do not have to travel to a foreign land to practice self-worship; we simply can go to the shopping mall or, sadly, visit any sports arena where athletes are paid salaries way beyond sensible and reasonable amounts. Self-worship is all around us, and if we are not careful, we will turn our allegiance away from God and to things that glorify the flesh.

Once the people of Israel left Egypt, the temptation to worship other gods was far from over. What they had learned in captivity they carried to the base of Mount Sinai where it spilled over into the image of a golden calf.

Satan never comes to us announcing his deception and evil folly. Instead, he creeps in through areas of weakness in our lives. One of Israel's weak points, pride, led to their failure to worship the Lord and eventually to sin and idolatry. Even after God had displayed His power and infinite love for His people, they continued in their quest to worship other gods.

Today, we have a High Priest who lives in the life of every believer. We do not need to go any further than our knees to receive His forgiveness and cleansing for our sins. If you find that you have drifted away from God, know that He is available to show you a better way, but you must make the choice to follow Him and not another god.

You shall have no other gods before me (Exodus 20:3).

The Daily Way — September 3

Trust God's Plan

At the Red Sea, Moses and the nation of Israel were faced with a demoralizing dead end. Pharaoh had released God's people, but he certainly was not happy about what he had done. He immediately gathered his soldiers and led the pursuit to recapture God's people.

The Israelites, in the meantime, felt amazingly free. They temporarily forgot the sorrows of Egyptian bondage. However, with Pharaoh's army suddenly breathing down their necks, they realized their only avenue of escape was blocked. They were unarmed and had no way of defending themselves. Death seemed imminent.

Have you ever felt this way? You may have tried to do what was right and even sensed some release from your problems. However, the moment you drew in a deep breath, you felt the pursuit was on again, and there was no way to outrun the problem pursuing you. When your back is against a wall and there appears to be no way of escape, remember, God will make a way of escape for you.

At the first sight of the Egyptian soldiers, the people of Israel cried out and turned on Moses:

> "What have you done to us by bringing us out of Egypt? ... It would have been better for us to serve the Egyptians than to die in the desert!" Then the Lord said to Moses, "Why are you crying out to me? Tell the Israelites to move on. Raise your staff and stretch out your hand over the sea to divide the water so that the Israelites can go through the sea on dry ground" (Exodus 14: 11-12, 15-16).

All the time Israel was crying and fretting, God had a plan. Trials and troubles are opportunities for God to display His power in your life. Trust Him to rescue you from the hand of your enemy.

The Israelites went through the sea on dry ground, with a wall of water on their right and on their left (Exodus 14:22).

September 4

The Daily Way

Accept God's Counsel

Moses was tired. He was trying to do it all—be the leader of Israel along with countless other duties. One of his responsibilities was to be the nation's judge over personal disputes.

When Jethro, Moses' father-in-law, caught up with him at Mount Sinai, he could not believe what he was seeing. To say that Moses' time was spread thin is a gross understatement. In fact, he was one step away from mental and emotional burnout. We read that Jethro wasted no time in talking to Moses about this:

> When his father-in-law saw all that Moses was doing for the people, he said, "What is this you are doing for the people? Why do you alone sit as judge, while all these people stand around you from morning till evening?" Moses answered him, "Because the people come to me to seek God's will. Whenever they have a dispute, it is brought to me, and I decide between the parties and inform them of God's decrees and laws" (Exodus 18:14-16).

Jethro quickly discerned the truth—Moses had taken on more than God intended. Therefore, he encouraged Moses to appoint judges to handle lesser disputes. He also admonished Moses to "teach [the people God's] decrees and laws, and show them the way to live and the duties they are to perform" (Exodus 18:20). In other words, Moses needed to teach the people what God desired and how to take responsibility for their own actions before the Lord.

Are you willing to accept godly counsel? The moment Moses heard Jethro's words, he knew his father-in-law was right, and he was not too proud to accept his advice. Always be sure that what you hear from others is in line with the Word of God. Listen, pray, and ask God to confirm what has been suggested. The Lord will guide you when you seek His wisdom.

Moses listened to his father-in-law and did everything he said (Exodus 18:24).

The Daily Way — September 5

Follow God's Leading

Not only did God save Israel from the Egyptians, He also destroyed the enemy of His people. Over the years, many people have tried to explain what happened at the Red Sea. They have tried to lessen God's involvement by saying the horses of Pharaoh's army got stuck in the mud of a shallow body of water and could not catch the fleeing Israelites.

But the truth is this: Pharaoh's army was washed away. The hand of God defeated them—not thick mud or a drifting waterspout.

> [God] made the wheels of their chariots come off so that they had difficulty driving. And the Egyptians said, "Let's get away from the Israelites! The Lord is fighting for them against Egypt." Moses stretched out his hand over the sea, and at daybreak the sea went back to its place. The Egyptians were fleeing toward it, and the Lord swept them into the sea. The water flowed back and covered the chariots and horsemen—the entire army of Pharaoh that had followed the Israelites into the sea. Not one of them survived (Exodus 14:25, 27-28).

When we place our trust in God, He will fight our battles for us. Remember that Pharaoh made a choice not to listen to the Word of the Lord. The nation of Egypt suffered through a list of plagues without making a heart choice to obey the Lord. Any one of us can have a touch of Pharaoh in our lives. This is why it is crucial to our spiritual growth to keep our hearts set on God and not on man.

If you sense the Lord leading you, be sure that you follow. Do not harden your heart, but freely give yourself to God and He will guide you into a broad place of ministry and service. His power is yours to experience when you surrender your life to Him.

The Lord is a warrior; the Lord is his name (Exodus 15:3).

September 6   The Daily Way

Claim God's Love

God's redemptive love for us is beyond anything this world offers us. There is nothing we can do to earn it. It is a free gift that God has chosen to give us. It is, however, our responsibility to accept His gift by faith. Paul admonishes us to "fight the good fight of the faith. Take hold of the eternal life to which you were called when you made your good confession in the presence of many witnesses" (1 Timothy 6:12).

E. Stanley Jones writes:

> I am inwardly fashioned for faith and not for fear. Fear is not my native land. Faith is. I am so made that worry and anxiety are like sand in the machinery of life and faith is the oil. I live better by faith and confidence than by fear, doubt, and anxiety.

We have been redeemed from eternal death through Jesus Christ. We no longer have an occasion to fear. Our fate has been sealed, and we have every reason to have hope for the future. Many people, however, do not realize the power of God's redemption. They cower in fear and worry about tomorrow.

Each one of us can think back to a time when we felt fearful and wanted to retreat. God, however, calls us to move forward in victory.

- Fear stifles creativity.
- Fear destroys our dreams.
- Fear blocks God's love.
- Fear prevents us from telling others about the saving grace of Jesus Christ.
- Fear is one of Satan's favorite weapons against the believer.

The apostle Paul reminds us that we are more than conquerors through Christ who loves us and gave Himself for us (Romans 8:37). Refuse to allow fear to rob you of God's blessings.

God is our refuge and strength, an ever-present help in trouble (Psalm 46:1).

The Daily Way — September 7

Trust in God's Protection

History books are filled with evidence of how fear can paralyze and defeat even the strongest person, while faith and courage give victory to the weakest individual.

One of the most dramatic examples of fear leading to defeat happened in 1588. Spain was posed to attack England's small and, compared to the Spanish navy, insignificant fleet. The Spanish had huge ships, which contained massive cannons, while the British navy was no match for the Spaniards.

However, Vice Admiral Sir Francis Drake was not about to give in to fear or defeat. He made a crucial decision that not only turned the war around, it led to the British defeat of Spain and the ultimate decline of Spanish domination.

Drake set eight British battleships on fire and floated them out into the midst of the Spanish fleet. When the Spanish saw the ships coming toward them, they became fearful and began to retreat.

In their haste to get away from the British floating arsenal, they were caught in the middle of a crosswind and were blown out into the North Sea. The storm was so great that the Spanish fleet was beached on the coast of Ireland. No one understands exactly why the Spanish became so fearful. Regardless, fear cost Spain a great battle and eventually an empire.

What has sailed into your life that is tempting you to become fearful? Remember, God never slumbers or sleeps. He is sovereign, and He is in perfect control of every situation you face. You can trust Him to protect you and to do what is best. Learn to rest in His redemptive love, and you will find an abundance of hope and joy.

The Lord Almighty is with us; the God of Jacob is our fortress (Psalm 46:7).

September 8 — The Daily Way

Celebrate God's Promises

God allowed the Israelites to leave Egypt. He had heard their cries for help and sent Moses to lead them out of bondage and to the Promised Land. More than likely, when Israel left captivity, they thought that they were free and would not have to face fear again.

None of us should face difficulty with the idea that it will all begin again within weeks. Instead, when trouble comes we need to celebrate God's deliverance, provision, and blessing. However, many times we forget that God uses life's difficulties to train us for even greater blessing.

The people of Israel left Egypt, but they had to face the Red Sea, Pharaoh's army, and 40 years in the desert before they were ready to enter the land God had promised Abraham. Thus, their freedom from Egyptian slavery was their first step toward blessing, but it also was a step toward another faith experience. Would they trust God or cry out in fear? They cried out—even with the Angel of the Lord going before them and a pillar of cloud behind them.

The cloud later represented the presence of God's Spirit, and the Angel of the Lord was the pre-incarnate Christ. Yet Israel was not tuned into God's provision. As they approached the Red Sea and saw that Pharaoh's army was pursuing them, they became fearful. The physical evidence of God's presence was not enough, and they missed a tremendous blessing.

God has never failed to keep His promises. He was faithful to Israel then, and He will be faithful to us today. We may not see a pillar of fire or a cloud in front of us, but we have the Spirit of God living within us. The same Person who was with the Israelites at the crossing of the Red Sea is with you today.

The angel of God, who had been traveling in front of Israel's army, withdrew and went behind them (Exodus 14:19).

The Daily Way — September 9

Rest in God's Shelter

We do not have to feel lonely. Jesus has promised to be with us. There are people, however, who struggle with feelings of loneliness and sorrow. Jesus told His disciples that He would not leave them comfortless. He would send a counselor—someone who would come along beside them and help them bear their sorrows (John 14:16).

At the time when Christ said these words, the disciples did not know what they were about to face. Within hours, their Lord would be arrested, tried, and sentenced to death. The impact of these events sent them into hiding. They were sure the Romans would hunt them down and do the same to them.

The disciples did what we do sometimes: they forgot Christ's promises, and the result was fear. They allowed their minds to wander to places of defeat, instead of recalling the words that the Lord had said to them.

Fear always sends its victims running for shelter, but none of us who know the Savior have a reason to be comfortless, vulnerable, isolated, or unprotected. God, Himself, stands guard over our lives. Those who know Christ as their Savior have a unique opportunity to rest in the protective cover of God's wings. Rest does not mean being unconcerned about the problems of the day.

The disciples should have been concerned, not fearful, that Jesus was no longer with them. Maybe you are experiencing a form of God's protection over your life. You want to move forward, but something is preventing you from taking this step. You feel as though your life is going unnoticed and unrewarded. God has not forgotten you. His Spirit lives in you, and He will not abandon the works of His hands. Trust Him to shelter you and to guide you to a broad place of ministry and blessing.

I am the Lord your God, who brought you out of Egypt, out of the land of slavery (Exodus 20:2).

September 10

The Daily Way

Choose God's Strength

Imagine being asked to do a job and then not being given the support you need to get the work done. In fact, instead of hearing words of encouragement, you only hear one discouraging report after another.

The Israelites longed to be free from Egyptian bondage. They had prayed for this. In fact, Scripture indicates that they had cried out to God for years, seeking freedom from Egyptian enslavement.

Moses was a willing candidate for the job of deliverer. His resume was almost impeccable. But from the beginning, things did not go well for Moses. Even before the plagues began, his approval ratings took a nosedive. After being told they would be forced to make bricks without straw, the Israelite women met Moses with these words, "May the Lord look upon you and judge you! You have made us a stench to Pharaoh and his officials and have put a sword in their hand to kill us" (Exodus 5:21).

Pharaoh's anger frightened the people, and they turned on Moses. Even after they were released from bondage, their criticism of God's leader continued. By the time they reached the shoreline of the Red Sea, the Israelites were furious with Moses and Aaron and shouted, "Was it because there were no graves in Egypt that you brought us to the desert to die?" (Exodus 14:11).

While the words of the Israelites may have given occasion for weariness, Moses refused to give up—choosing instead to trust God. If you are the target of someone's criticism, take heart—you are in good company. Jesus endured the cruelty of others, too. Guard your heart and take care that you do not become critical in the process. Allow God to protect you and to give you the strength you need each day to face your accusers victoriously.

Then the Lord said to Moses, "Now you will see what I will do to Pharaoh" (Exodus 6:1).

The Daily Way

September 11

Respond in God's Love

The person who reacts to life based on sheer human nature is often fickle. When the Israelites were waist deep in Egyptian mud with the whips of the slave masters on their backs, they wanted to be free. They cried out to God, and He heard their plea.

Then, the moment they faced the slightest problem, they criticized Moses, whom God had used to deliver them from slavery. The people complained and grumbled to Moses even though he did everything for their own good. When they would get in trouble, he would intercede before God on their behalf.

Do you ever feel like Moses? You know you are doing the right thing—but, for certain people, it is not good enough. Is there someone in your life who is critical of you no matter what?

Constructive criticism can be helpful. When someone tells you in sincerity something that is beneficial to you, accept it in the spirit in which it is given. However, do not accept or dwell on the unjust criticism of those who seek to tear you down for their own edification.

Moses was patient with those who criticized him. He did not respond in anger or hate. He did not stop interceding for them. Some would say he kept his Christ-like attitude.

Learn to be someone who recognizes the differences between right and wrong criticism. With God's help, you can respond with an attitude of grace and forgiveness to those who may unjustly criticize you. Be careful not to fall into the act of criticizing others. The Bible instructs us to treat others as we would like to be treated (Mark 12:31).

Prayer: Lord, please help me to be a person who understands who I am in You. Help me to recognize unjust criticism and respond in Your love.

So the people grumbled against Moses, saying, "What are we to drink?" (Exodus 15:24).

September 12 — The Daily Way

Bear with One Another in Love

Some people are cheerful by nature. Nothing seems to get them down. When they receive bad news or when something doesn't turn out the way they thought it would, they do not lose their pleasant attitudes.

The opposite of cheerfulness is constant criticism. No matter what happens, there is always something to complain about. For those who have a critical nature, there is no satisfaction—even if they get what they want.

Aside from complaining and whining, criticism can come in the form of a false accusation. It may be slandering or speaking evil of someone. It can even be gossip. James warns us to watch the words of our mouths: "We all stumble in many ways. If anyone is never at fault in what he says, he is a perfect man, able to keep his whole body in check" (James 3:2).

If they are not careful, Christians can fall into the trap of discontentment and envy, which left unchecked, can lead to criticism of others. But we can overcome the criticism that rises up within us—through the power of God! When we submit ourselves to Christ, He transforms our lives. He gives us a spirit of contentment when we look to Him as the source of our happiness.

As God's servant, Moses endured much criticism throughout Israel's journey in the wilderness. Despite God's amazing provisions, the reluctant travelers were not satisfied. Instead, the words of their mouths were set on hurting Moses.

How do you respond when things don't happen as you desire? Do you keep your joy or do you become critical? As children of God we are to "be completely humble and gentle; be patient, bearing with one another in love" (Ephesians 4:2). If we make this our motto in dealing with other people, there will be little room for criticism in any form.

Set a guard over my mouth, O Lord; keep watch over the door of my lips (Psalm 141:3).

The Daily Way — September 13

Achieve God's Goal

Have you ever wondered how Moses handled discouragement? Or how Paul maintained a positive attitude when he faced the criticism and threats of others?

Surely Paul fought with discouragement when he faced the threat of death. However, he kept his focus set on Christ, who was his infinite strength and eternal hope. We can do the same.

Life may have many challenges—especially when you are doing what God has given you to do. But you don't have to be overwhelmed by disappointment. We should long to be heroes of the faith—people who seek to win the race set before us and to achieve the goal that God has given.

When trouble comes, don't give up. Don't lose heart, and don't listen to harassment. God has a plan for your life. When you feel like quitting, think about Paul's life and all he did for the Lord. He was not called to be famous or to have a vast sum of money. He was called by God to preach His Word to the lost. Paul did exactly what he was given to do. He obeyed God and surrendered his life to Christ. He went from being a man of position in the Jewish faith to an outcast and traitor. What may have appeared to be failure from a human standpoint was actually the mark of true victory.

God does not ask you to cross a finish line with the goal of reaching worldly success. He does not hand out trophies that look good in a case or sitting on a shelf. The trophies of our faith come at a price. Just as Christ gave His life, are you willing to give your life to Him? Forsaking all else, will you follow Christ and proclaim His love and forgiveness to a dying world?

Who is it that overcomes the world? Only he who believes that Jesus is the Son of God (1 John 5:5).

September 14 — The Daily Way

Carry Each Other's Burdens

Moses sent Joshua to fight against the Amalekites. Then he, along with Aaron and Hur, went to stand on top of a hill overlooking the battlefield. As long as Moses prayed with his hands held up, the Israelites would gain ground and win. However, whenever he lowered his hands, they began to lose.

Have you ever stood with your hands lifted up for any extended time? It is tiring. Your arms become heavy and your hands begin to feel tingly. Imagine Moses standing with his hands held high and then lowering them as he struggled under their weight. He couldn't do it. He needed help, so Aaron and Hur placed a stone for Moses to sit on. Then they held up his hands—holding them steady until the sun set and God granted the nation of Israel victory.

How many times have you tried to fight a battle by yourself? You think you are strong. You pray and seek God, but the battle becomes fierce and you grow weary. Before you lose hope and give up, remember you are not alone. God is with you.

Galatians 6:2 commands, "Carry each other's burdens." James tells us to pray for each other (Galatians 5:16). We need to support others in prayer and with words of encouragement. Sometimes just being near a friend speaks volumes of concern and care. Jesus said, "I tell you that if two of you on earth agree about anything you ask for, it will be done for you by my Father in heaven" (Matthew 18:19).

There can be no victory without prayer. Whatever you are dealing with in your life, remember you don't have to fight on your own. Seek the Lord, ask others to pray with you, and the victory will be yours.

As long as Moses held up his hands, the Israelites were winning, but whenever he lowered his hands, the Amalekites were winning (Exodus 17:11).

The Daily Way — September 15

Lead without Compromise

Have you ever caught yourself wondering what others think about you? All of us have done this from time to time, and most of us quickly find that our impressions are not true. Even in the Old Testament, image was important. In fact, this concern with image caused Aaron a lot of trouble.

God's chosen people were in mutiny against Him. While Moses was on Mount Sinai with the Lord, the people gathered around Aaron and said, "Come, make us gods who will go before us. As for this fellow Moses who brought us up out of Egypt, we don't know what has happened to him" (Exodus 32:1).

Aaron did not stand against popular opinion or demand. He could have and the rebellion would have ended, but he didn't. Instead, because he wanted to be liked and accepted, he compromised.

How often do we do the same? As parents we may give our children more than is necessary because we want them to like us. A wife may see her husband doing the wrong thing and not speak the truth to him in love. Or though we know a friend is in a wrong relationship, we choose to say nothing because we don't want to risk losing the friendship.

Many times we are concerned about our images simply because we want to be liked. Margaret Thatcher wisely said, "If you just set out to be liked, you would be prepared to compromise on anything and at any time, and you would achieve nothing."

Through His earthly life, Jesus demonstrated how we should follow Him. He was often disliked because He took a stand for what was right and true. Make sure that you are not so concerned about your image that you lose sight of the principles in God's Word.

Am I now trying to win the approval of men, or of God? (Galatians 1:10).

September 16

The Daily Way

Rely on God's Wisdom

The Israelites wanted Aaron to build an idol for them to worship. They were impatient, restless, and tired of waiting for Moses to come down from the mountain where he was receiving God's commandments.

Aaron thought he had a clever way out—to demand something they would not be willing to give. So he asked the people to give up their gold and jewelry. Surely they would not agree to this and would retreat from their insatiable desire to worship idols.

Not a chance! In relying on his wisdom instead of God's, Aaron attempted to appeal to the people's materialistic desires instead of the fear of the Lord. Be careful in relying on your wisdom when you are faced with pressure from other people or the temptation to take the easy way out. Don't trust your own cleverness when dealing with your weaknesses. Your wisdom, strength, and ability will always backfire.

Aaron did not think the people would part with their possessions. He did not understand that people by nature are willing to spend their fortunes, whether large or small, on their pleasures. He did not understand that human behavior generally gives up everything to support an addiction, whatever it may be.

When the Israelites put their jewels at his feet, Aaron was caught in his own clever snare. Now he was compelled to make them a golden calf and when they saw it, they were delighted—even though God forbade what they were doing.

Aaron knew, like many compromising Christians, that his decision and actions were wrong. We are all accountable for what we do. Remember, no matter how hard we try, human cleverness can lead to compromise and sin.

He took what they handed him and made it into an idol cast in the shape of a calf, fashioning it with a tool (Exodus 32:4).

The Daily Way — September 17

Confess and Repent

We all have done something that we knew we should not have done. When confronted with our action, how do we respond? Aaron's reaction, when Moses confronted him about making the golden calf, was one of rationalization.

He did not deny his wrong, but merely explained it away. It is a classic example of our own tendency toward self-deception and dishonesty. But making excuses will not absolve us from the consequences of compromise and bad judgment.

Aaron said to Moses:

> "You know how prone these people are to evil. They said to me, 'Make us gods who will go before us. As for this fellow Moses who brought us up out of Egypt, we don't know what has happened to him.' So I told them, 'Whoever has any gold jewelry, take it off.' Then they gave me the gold, and I threw it into the fire, and out came this calf" (Exodus 32:22-24).

How many times have we had our backs against the wall and come up with a ridiculous reason for our actions? It would be so much better to confess our wrongdoing and repent. The Bible is full of examples of those who denied their wrongdoing, and those who confessed and repented. Adam, after eating the forbidden fruit, tried to pass the blame onto Eve.

In contrast, David repented when confronted with his sin with Bathsheba and God forgave him. However, his action was not without consequences. Repentance restores our relationship with the Lord but does not remove the consequences of our actions.

God wants us to honor and obey Him. When we do the wrong thing, we should confess our sin, and seek His forgiveness.

The next day Moses said to the people, "You have committed a great sin. But now I will go up to the Lord; perhaps I can make atonement for your sin" (Exodus 32:30).

September 18 — The Daily Way

Give Back to God

Once the Israelites were set free from bondage in Egypt, through the miraculous escape provided by the Lord, they traveled across the desert. During these Old Testament days, the tents where God's people dwelt were near the large tent of the Lord.

Every time the people looked outside, they were reminded of the presence of Jehovah and His constant care and provision. God supplied their every need, just as He does for us.

Through Moses, the Lord communicated His laws and decrees for the people to live by, including specific instructions for the sacrifices, burnt offerings, special gifts, and tithes God desired of His people.

Tithing is a starting point in our giving back to the Lord, but it should never be done with an ungrateful heart or wrong motive. Jesus revealed the heart of the issue when He said, "For where your treasure is, there your heart will be also" (Matthew 6:21).

There is no more certain way for us to demonstrate our obedience and loyalty to the Lord than through our giving. What kind of Christians would we be if we did not present anything to the Lord, while we received His blessings and provisions over and over? Giving to God is a demonstration of His Lordship in our lives and of our surrender to His will. It is a way of showing that we place our trust and faith in Him.

Whether we have much or little, God is interested in the attitudes of our hearts. He wants more than an act of giving born of obligation. He desires us—our talents, abilities, time, energy, and devotion. Take a moment to ask, "What am I giving to the Lord?"

A tithe of everything from the land, whether grain from the soil or fruit from the trees, belongs to the Lord; it is holy to the Lord (Leviticus 27:30).

The Daily Way — September 19

Give Thanks for His Blessings

Moses told the Israelites they were to give from what they had as an offering to the Lord. This freewill offering, would provide for building the tabernacle of the Lord. The people responded:

> And everyone who was willing and whose heart moved him came and brought an offering to the Lord for the work on the Tent of Meeting, for all its service, and for the sacred garments (Exodus 35:21).

The flood of generosity from the people was so great that Moses gave an order to restrain the people from bringing more! Their participation in the freewill offering was a joyful demonstration of love and thanksgiving to the Lord.

The result was similar when the people responded to David's challenge to give freely for the building of the temple. David prayed:

> But who am I, and who are my people, that we should be able to give as generously as this? Everything comes from you, and we have given you only what comes from your hand (1 Chronicles 29:14).

Whether we realize it or not, we have nothing without the Lord. When we give back to God, we are expressing the thankfulness and joy we have for all He has blessed us with—forgiveness, salvation, hope, new life, and so much more.

So how can we continually receive without ever giving in return? God wants more than our biblical tithe. He wants our love and devotion, our faithfulness and trust, and our commitment to follow His Word and obey His commands. Don't hold back; give freely to God, and you will be blessed.

All the Israelite men and women who were willing brought to the Lord freewill offerings for all the work the Lord through Moses had commanded them to do (Exodus 35:29).

September 20 — The Daily Way

Unjust Criticism

Have you ever worked as diligently as you know how, only to have somebody criticize you for something irrelevant to what you have accomplished? People who are critical often focus on unimportant things. They are motivated by envy and jealousy. Miriam and Aaron were jealous of their brother, Moses. They were envious of his godly anointing and the leadership role he had among God's chosen people. However, instead of expressing their true feelings, they criticized Moses for marrying a non-Israelite.

Personal criticism, even when justified, is painful. Unjust and irrelevant criticism hurts deeply, especially when it comes from someone you love and trust. The criticism Moses was getting from his siblings was unjustified. Moses had interceded for them to the Lord for their idolatry, immorality, and continual murmuring. Miriam and Aaron knew that Moses was not motivated by personal gain. Numbers 12:3 states, "Now Moses was a very humble man, more humble than anyone else on the face of the earth."

Often, people strike out at someone whom they perceive is more important, more successful, or more popular than they. Even Jesus suffered the pain of criticism and misunderstanding. The chief priests and elders questioned His authority over the things of God (Luke 20:1-2).

Maybe you are experiencing unjust criticism. Are you quietly doing what the Lord has called you to do, but keep getting ridiculed from those who know you best? Don't despair or give in.

The Lord knows. He will be your source of strength and determination. Allow Him to take care of criticism and the critics by keeping your eyes focused on Christ.

Miriam and Aaron began to talk against Moses because of his Cushite wife, for he had married a Cushite (Numbers 12:1).

The Daily Way — September 21

A Forgiving Spirit

How did Moses respond to the criticism of Aaron and Miriam? He exhibited a forgiving spirit. He could have lashed out and said things that would have been justified. He could have accused them of hypocrisy. He could have defended himself.

Sometimes it is necessary to defend ourselves, but in this case Moses did not. He remembered that Miriam was part of God's plan in saving him from a watery grave as a child. He did not forget that Miriam sang the song of praise after they crossed the Red Sea. He thought of Aaron standing with him against Pharaoh.

Do you know the reason why people try to tear someone else down? To build themselves up. If we remember that God has a purpose and a plan for each of us, then we do not need to be negative and critical toward others. In His eyes we are all equal.

Not only does God choose to use us for His purpose, He also stands between us and those who would seek to slander and harm. While it may seem like a long time before God acts, He will.

How do you respond to criticism born out of jealousy and envy? Pray for opportunities to minister to the person. Instead of being glad that Miriam was punished with leprosy, Moses cried out to God to heal her. God responded to Moses' prayer even though He did not heal Miriam instantly. God taught Israel that you could not make false accusations without consequences.

Are you a critical person? Or are you suffering from unjust criticism? Take your requests to the Lord today. Let Him deal with the one criticizing you, or your own critical spirit.

"Has the Lord spoken only through Moses?" they asked. "Hasn't he also spoken through us?" (Numbers 12:2).

September 22   The Daily Way

The Price of Disobedience

The chosen people of God were, once again, complaining to Moses. Since their escape from Egypt, they had grumbled and whined. They missed the rich food of Egypt. They wanted the comfort they had known, all the while forgetting they had been slaves.

Finally, they were on the edge of the land God promised them. They brought their latest grief to Moses—no water. Moses once again cried out to the Lord who said, "Take the staff, and you and your brother Aaron gather the assembly together. Speak to that rock before their eyes and it will pour out its water" (Numbers 20:8). Moses lifted his hand and struck the rock. Not once, but twice. In his anger, he did not obey the Lord's command.

How many times do we know what we are supposed to do, but we choose to do things our own way? Then, we try to justify our actions because we were tired, upset, or even angry.

No doubt Moses was frustrated with the people and tired of their complaining. He had a choice of whether or not to obey God—just as we do. He blatantly disobeyed. Disobedience is costly and dangerous. When we disobey, we deviate from God's plan.

Did God deny Moses water, even though he didn't obey His command? No. God, in His mercy and grace, forgave Moses. However, Moses' disobedience cost him entrance into the Promised Land.

Have you disobeyed God's commands? Are you willing to pay the price of disobedience? Remember, God does not ask more than we can do. Instead, He seeks our obedience so we can walk with Him and do His will.

Then Moses raised his arm and struck the rock twice with his staff. Water gushed out, and the community and their livestock drank (Numbers 20:11).

The Daily Way — September 23

The Choice of Obedience

Charles Spurgeon writes, "The first thing God requires of His child is obedience." But human nature often rebels against obedience.

The Bible is full of examples of individuals who disobeyed God. Adam and Eve ate the forbidden fruit. Lot's wife blatantly looked back to see the destruction of Sodom. Jonah refused to go to Nineveh. Moses struck the rock, instead of speaking to it as God commanded.

We all can remember incidents when we have disobeyed—whether it was against an authority figure, a law of the land, or a biblical principle. Most likely we even remember our punishment or the consequences we suffered. The act of disobedience brings guilt, sadness, and shame.

There is no long-lasting pleasure in getting our own way. It brings grief to our heavenly Father because He longs for us to walk with Him. Our disobedience separates us from Him. Yet God extends His grace toward us even when we disobey His Word. Therefore, our response should be to seek His forgiveness with a repentant heart and to learn from the consequences of our disobedience.

What about when we face a hard decision—do we do what we know is right or what we want? The choice of obedience is blessed with a heart filled with joy and peace. No matter how you may be ridiculed or how hard it may be to follow God's guidance, obedience is its own reward.

Jesus lived a life of obedience. His earthly ministry was to do the will of His Father. However, He did have a choice and He said, "Not my will, but yours" (Luke 22:42). The Lord desires our obedience, but He never demands it. The choice is ours. Commit your life to Christ. He will enable you to walk in obedience.

This is love: that we walk in obedience to his commands (2 John 1:6).

September 24 — The Daily Way

The School of Obedience

True, genuine obedience is not an act born out of defiance. It is born out of love. It is a desire to show our Lord and Savior our respect and worship by submitting our lives to Him.

As children of God, we should be constantly learning more about the Lord. This will happen as long as we seek Him and desire to know Him better each day. From a young age, Moses learned of God's hand on his life—how he was saved from certain death and adopted into Pharaoh's home.

Moses, like us, had to learn the lessons of obedience. And like us, often he did not pass with flying colors the first time. Because of uncontrolled anger, he had to flee Egypt. But God would later ask Moses to return to deliver the Israelites from bondage. At first Moses did not want to obey. He had all kinds of excuses, such as not being qualified for the task and not being a good speaker. In the wilderness, Moses continued his education in the school of obedience. Some lessons he passed right away; others he failed and had to repeat.

Sound familiar? Do you feel like you are learning the same lesson over and over because you've not quite grasped it? Are you still holding on to your insecurities, fears, and uncertainties? Are you obedient in some areas and rebellious in others?

You can't rely on your own strength to graduate from the school of obedience. Instead, place your trust in the great Teacher. If you are willing to surrender your will, God will change your life. Your submission to Him will be a demonstration of your love and devotion. The most precarious thing is to try to live without being obedient to the Lord.

If anyone obeys his word, God's love is truly made complete in him. This is how we know we are in him (1 John 2:5).

The Daily Way — September 25

All Things Are Possible in God

Visionaries are people who see the big picture and are not afraid of change. They don't hold back by refusing to leave their comfort zones.

Those who have the "show me" mentality will move only if they see proof that the change is good. They will embrace the vision if they see evidence and proof that it is the right direction. Then there are those who refuse to change or adapt at all. They often disagree simply for the sake of disagreeing.

The Israelites arrived at the edge of the land the Lord had promised to them after a long journey from Egypt. The journey was a process of learning lessons of obedience and faith. Now they were ready to enter the land.

> The Lord said to Moses, "Send some men to explore the land of Canaan, which I am giving to the Israelites. From each ancestral tribe send one of its leaders" (Numbers 13:1-2).

The mission was simple—"See what the land is like and whether the people who live there are strong or weak, few or many" (Numbers 13:18). After 40 days of looking around, the 12 men returned and reported incredible prosperity and fertile land.

However, 10 of them gave a bad report because of the fortified cities. Only two, Joshua and Caleb, had a different opinion. What seems impossible to us is possible to God—no matter how daunting. Do you fall into the "show me" category like the majority of Moses' scouts? Do you want complete proof of success before you will participate in change? It is better to be like Joshua and Caleb—visionaries who could see that with God on their side they could not fail.

If the Lord is pleased with us, he will lead us into that land, a land flowing with milk and honey, and will give it to us (Numbers 14:8).

September 26   The **Daily** Way

Giants and Grasshoppers

God had promised to give the Israelites the land of Canaan. They simply had to believe His promise and take the land, but when they heard the scouts' report of fortified cities and people of great size, fear gripped their hearts.

The majority is always wrong when God is not at its focus. When we look at our circumstances from a human perspective, we often see impossibilities instead of God's provision. Then we miss out on the blessings of God. Doubt, unbelief, and negativity can lead us to question God's Word.

Obedience, and not opinions, will bring you blessings. God promised His people the Promised Land. He had delivered and sustained them. He had guided them day and night through the wilderness. But the moment they faced an obstacle, they questioned, "Where is God?"

Giants become grasshoppers in the eyes of faith. Ten scouts saw the Canaanites as giants and themselves as grasshoppers. But two saw themselves as giants because of God's promise. Only someone who is strong in his faith can challenge unbelief. When you take a stand for Him, the Lord will never let you down.

Obedience has its own reward. Two of the 12 men Moses sent to explore the Promised Land knew that if the Lord was with them, He would defend, protect, and lead them. Worry, anxiety, and fear may no longer keep us from entering our promised land, but these emotions can prevent us from enjoying God's many blessings.

Do you wake up in the morning worrying about the future? Do you go to bed at night thinking about the same miserable giants in your life? Place your faith in God, be obedient, and trust His Word, and you will experience God's blessing for your life.

We seemed like grasshoppers in our own eyes, and we looked the same to them (Numbers 13:33).

The Daily Way — September 27

The Perfect Model

When buying a new car, you can purchase a model with standard features or order one that has been custom built. In this instance, choosing particular features over others is a great benefit. However, when it comes to our obedience to the Lord, we cannot pick and choose what we will and will not do.

Sadly, many believers approach their faith in this way. They refuse to believe there is a level of accountability to which all are held. Instead, they opt for "custom-built" faith, the kind of faith that chooses what tenets of the faith are appealing while discarding the others.

While God allows us to make our own choices, He clearly spells out in His Word what a godly lifestyle entails: a life that models Jesus Christ. Jesus lived without sin. He honored God with every breath He took. One such way He honored God was through giving all He had for those who had nothing.

Jesus' life, death, and resurrection paved the way for mankind to have an intimate relationship with God. In fact, Christ's life is a perfect model of what it means to have intimacy with God. Throughout every trial and tribulation, throughout every victory and valley, Jesus was in perfect communion with God. He listened for the voice of His Father and responded appropriately.

As we determine to follow the model of Jesus, we must remember that every facet of His life expressed communion with God, including the act of giving. Jesus gave and gave until He could give no more. We, too, must be willing to give and give until we cannot give another breath. It is with grace that Jesus gave—and it is with grace that we should give also, being complete Christians who seek to follow every example Christ gave us.

Prayer: Lord, show me places in my life where I have held back from giving so I can give them to You.

For you know the grace of our Lord Jesus Christ, that though he was rich, yet for your sakes he became poor, so that you through his poverty might become rich (2 Corinthians 8:9).

September 28   The Daily Way

Play by His Rules

One of the best ways to test your Christian identity is to see how willing you are to tell others what God has done for you through Jesus Christ.

Another way to check your true identity is to measure your level of dedication. Dedicated soldiers in God's army:

- Don't expect a safe or easy time.
- Take hardships as a matter of everyday experience.
- Are willing to take risks.
- Fight to win.

In a spiritual battle, there are only two people: the defeated and the victor! We are conquerors for Christ, and we have been given the victory!

A third way to test your true identity is by asking yourself if you are an athlete who is willing to play by the rules. In ancient Greece, winning athletes were crowned with an evergreen wreath. But no athlete, no matter how brilliant or successful, received a crown if he did not compete according to the rules.

In 2 Timothy, Paul admonishes us to remain faithful to God. We are to play according to His rules, not by the rules of the world's morality. We are not to operate by rules of a rewritten Bible, which tell us to do whatever feels right to us. Rules like these offer no standards. In order to live a victorious life, we need a solid, unshakeable framework, and this is what God provides through His Word.

Set a goal for your life: Be committed to learning more about God—His truth, His Word, His love, and His forgiveness. Then share His love with someone who is lost and in need of eternal hope. When you play by His rules, you will discover a lasting peace that satisfies your soul.

Endure hardship with us like a good soldier of Christ Jesus (2 Timothy 2:3).

The Daily Way — September 29

Conquering Fear

Do you live in fear? Do you feel like your life is an emotional prison? If you are constantly afraid, then you may be living behind bars more powerful than steel. If you live each day immobilized by fear, you may feel as if you are literally trapped or imprisoned.

Fear will destroy your joy. It hinders your potential for God. It will ruin your family, friendships, and relationship with God. It always masquerades as something else—as super caution, as timidity, as insecurity, as lack of confidence, or procrastination.

You don't have to fear the unknown because Jesus is the Alpha and the Omega, the beginning and the end (Revelation 21:6). He says, "I am the way and the truth and the life. Because I live, you also will live" (John 14:6, 19).

Paul—along with many other biblical heroes—discovered the antidote to fear: faith in Christ! In other words, when you realize that God is in total control of your life, fear will be banished.

Is fear stopping your effectiveness for God? What excuse has the devil given you for not serving Christ? Is it fear of failure? It is better to try to do something and fail, than to succeed at nothing. You cannot be defeated unless you accept defeat in your heart. Falling down does not make you a failure. But staying down does.

Failure is never a dead-end street with God. Remember, He buried your sins in the deepest sea. They are removed by His grace and mercy. Do you fear the unknown? Isaiah 54:17 states, "No weapon forged against you will prevail." The Lord is your light and salvation. Fear not. God loves you. He is in control, and no matter how the devil may try to defeat you, you have the victory in Christ. God has given you power over fear.

There is no fear in love. But perfect love drives out fear, because fear has to do with punishment. The one who fears is not made perfect in love (1 John 4:18).

September 30

The Spirit of Power, Not Fear

If you visit Rome, you can see the dungeon that once housed the apostle Paul. You can stand within the same four solid walls that once formed his cell. You can look up through the hole in the center of the ceiling from which he received food and water.

There are no windows, no doors, and no way of escape; and yet, for Paul, it was not a place of defeat or fear. It was a place of both victory and hope. Though Paul was confined physically, he was free spiritually.

We don't know how long Paul was in this environment. However, we do know that from here he was taken to a place of execution. But even in death, Paul did not face defeat. The moment after he drew his last earthly breath, he was embraced by the Lord.

There are times when we view our circumstances from the wrong perspective. We face difficulty and wonder how God can be glorified. We suffer through loss and heartache and can't imagine how He will turn our circumstances around.

When we set our focus on the problem instead of on Christ, we miss the infusion of God's power. Paul's spiritual gaze was set on an eternal goal, not his earthly problems.

In times of sorrow and hopelessness, there is a spiritual power available to each one of us through Jesus Christ. Therefore, there is never an occasion to give up. We have an eternal hope that will never abandon us.

What are you facing today that has the potential to cause you to quit, throw in the towel, and walk away? Remember, Jesus Christ is your strength. He has the power you need to live in victory. When you place your trust in Him, He lifts you up and gives you the strength you need to endure the trials of life.

God has not given us a spirit of fear, but of power and of love and of a sound mind (2 Timothy 1:7, NKJV).

Cultivating Relationships That Please God

The Daily Way

October 1

Add to Your Faith

Can you imagine a group of carpenters gathering to build a skyscraper without architectural blueprints? The results would be horrendous! Have you ever heard of a medical student failing his medical exams numerous times and still having a successful career as a physician? This would be impossible!

You would never trust your health to someone who has not passed his medical exams, and you would never live in a home that was built without a plan. Just as we need structure for buildings, we also need structure in our relationships.

On any level, this can prove to be challenging. Whether dealing with a spouse, sibling, parent, child, co-worker, boss, or friend, the key to building solid relationships is learning how to interact successfully with one another.

When it comes to the subject of relationships, what is your greatest fear? Rejection? Or do you struggle with the thought of not meeting someone's expectations? Don't despair; God has given His Word to you as a guide.

God knows how to deal with all types of people. When you develop Christ-like characteristics in your own life, you begin to view others as God views them. 2 Peter 1:5-7 tells us to:

> Make every effort to add to your faith, goodness; and to goodness, knowledge; and to knowledge, self-control; and to self-control, perseverance; and to perseverance, godliness; and to godliness, brotherly kindness; and to brotherly kindness, love.

Ask God today to impart to you His love and acceptance of others. When you choose to become more like Christ in your relationships, God gives you the ability to love and live in harmony with those around you.

Live in harmony with one another; be sympathetic, love as brothers, be compassionate and humble (1 Peter 3:8).

October 2

The Daily Way

Contentment Designed by God

Have you ever played the comparison game? The rules are simple: Look at what other people have or do, and then desire those things or accomplishments for yourself.

This so-called "game" brings discontentment and envy. The Bible teaches that we are to be content with the life God has given us (Philippians 4:11-12). This does not mean that we settle for less or stop trying to reach our goals.

Contentment is something God has designed for us. Whether we are single or married, we can achieve contentment and peace within our hearts. In order to do this, we must first discover who we are in Christ and realize what He has done for us. He has saved us from an eternal death and chosen us as His beloved children.

During the apostle Paul's time, some Jews were not content being Jews. It was fashionable to act as Gentiles. On the other hand, some Gentiles didn't think they were spiritual enough as Christians unless they became like the Jews. They each thought the other had something more.

Do you ever compare yourself to someone you think is more spiritual? Do you think less of your prayer life when you compare it to that of a prayer warrior you admire? Do you feel inadequate to share your testimony after hearing someone else share his? God does not measure your life against the life of another.

Therefore, don't allow people to pressure you into doing what is popular. Don't long for their possessions and personal achievements. Don't let someone else's unhappiness infect you. Seek God and learn to be content with what He has provided. He is your greatest source of contentment and satisfaction.

Each one should remain in the situation which he was in when God called him (1 Corinthians 7:20).

The Daily Way — October 3

Dejection and Rejection

When on trial for her life, Joan of Arc said she felt abandoned, even by her own family. In the midst of her trial she cried out, "It is better to be alone with God."

Have you ever felt abandoned? The apostle Paul did. If there was one thing that caused Paul sorrow, it was the lack of courage of some of his closest friends.

This doesn't mean that all of his friends and colleagues abandoned him. Luke was with him, but many of the others were scattered throughout Asia Minor. Near the end of his life, he expressed his feelings of loneliness when he recalled his former companion and colleague in the ministry—Demas. Paul wrote, "Demas, because he loved this world, has deserted me" (2 Timothy 4:10).

Few things break the heart of a servant of God more than to witness people who have every reason to succeed in their Christian faith choose to take another road. It causes despair for a parent to watch his child walk away from God. It also is heart-wrenching for a godly man or woman to watch as a spouse lives with spiritual rebellion.

The next time someone hurts you, remember what Philip Brooks said: "In Christian life, the deeper depth of sorrow and higher heights of joy often come together."

Is there a Demas in your life who is breaking your heart? Are you experiencing the hard, cool hand of rejection from someone you love? Paul experienced the same thing. If you are feeling dejected because of another's rejection, consider Paul's life and words. He did not give up or lose faith. He continued on with the work of God—remaining faithful regardless of his personal disappointments. You can, too.

I have fought the good fight, I have finished the race, I have kept the faith (2 Timothy 4:7).

October 4 — The Daily Way

The Power of Forgiveness

Perhaps you feel as though another person has treated you unfairly. Your best friend or a loved one has betrayed you, and now your sorrow is turning into anger and bitterness.

You know that forgiveness is something God has commanded you to do, but you can't let go of the hurt you feel inside. It seems that you now have one goal and that is to find a way to make the person who has harmed you pay for his or her actions.

Unforgiveness can leave us drowning in a sea of frustration, rage, and resentment. If left unchecked, it also can cause physical problems. Without repentance, it can tempt us to question our own forgiveness by God. When we add up all the problems that accompany unforgiveness, we quickly see why Jesus was so firm in His command to forgive.

Clinical studies show the number one cause of depression is anger, which often results from a lack of forgiveness and an inability to let go of feelings of resentment. What we fail to realize is that it takes less energy to forgive and to forget than it does to maintain our anger and unforgiveness. Jesus told his disciples, "Forgive, and you will be forgiven" (Luke 6:37). Peter wanted to get technical by asking how many times he should forgive someone who has harmed him, but Jesus saw through his legalistic plot. "Seventy times seven," was the Lord's answer—in other words, an indefinite number.

God does not keep a running record of our sin. Instead, He forgives when we pray and seek His righteousness. Never lose sight of the fact that our eternal forgiveness cost Him His very life. Therefore, it is not too much for God to request that we forgive as He has forgiven us.

Prayer: Lord, teach me how to forgive others the way You have forgiven me.

Father, forgive them, for they know not what they are doing (Luke 23:34).

The Daily Way

Forgiveness God's Way

The first of the seven statements Jesus spoke from the cross is crucial to God's eternal plan of salvation. Most of the people present for the crucifixion probably expected Jesus to curse His executioners, but He didn't. Instead, He forgave them!

"Father, forgive them, for they do no know what they are doing" (Luke 23:34). In Christ's day, forgiveness was not viewed as a mark of strength. Even today, many people refuse to forgive others, thinking that to do so would mean they have become weak.

What we fail to realize about unforgiveness is that it has a remarkable ability to hold us captive and bound to the one whom we refuse to forgive. While the Jews had laws concerning forgiveness, the greater emphasis was placed on the actual act and not on the motive of one's heart. Forgiveness done God's way, on the other hand, frees us to live victoriously—the way Christ lived. It gives us an opportunity to be like Him to others—forgiving.

We also need to remember that God knows the motives of our hearts. Quick prayers lifted to Him in an effort to avoid feelings of guilt or the consequences of sin are easily discerned. We can't mislead an all-knowing God.

If you are struggling with feelings of anger toward another, tell God. He knows what you are facing, and He will show you how to tackle your greatest regrets and sorrows. Let Him be the One who deals with your offender. You may not know how He chooses to do it, but He has promised to punish those who have acted unjustly.

Prayer: Father, I don't want to be held captive any longer by resentment or bitterness. I forgive (the person's name) and ask that You would free me from the bondage of unforgiveness.

For if you forgive men when they sin against you, your heavenly Father will also forgive you (Matthew 6:14).

October 6

The Daily Way

God's Perfect Plan

While many legal and financial forms ask for your marital status, God does not judge or rate you based on whether you are married, single, divorced, or widowed. No matter what box you check on the form, God loves you without condition and He has a plan and purpose for your life.

A particular marital status does not make one spiritually superior. Being married will not solve all your problems. While marriage can provide a basis for our feeling secure, it can also reveal our many weaknesses.

You can be married and still be lonely. You can be married and feel unfulfilled. Marriage does not change your state of happiness. You can be married and still be insecure. Likewise, if you feel constrained in marriage, being single will not make you feel free.

Instead of focusing on your marital status, take time to pray and focus on God. He alone is the source of security, peace, happiness, joy, freedom, love, and contentment. When you feel discouraged, disappointed, left out, or sad—remember that God's grace is sufficient (2 Corinthians 12:9).

Each person has a choice. Either you can accomplish God's plan for your life or you can reject it. You can choose to live in joy and faith, or you can become paralyzed by unsatisfied desire and want. Philippians 4:6-7 urges:

> Do not be anxious about anything, but in everything, by prayer and petition, with thanksgiving, present your requests to God. And the peace of God, which transcends all understanding, will guard your hearts and your minds in Christ Jesus.

Don't let sorrow or discouragement overwhelm you. God is faithful. Therefore, trust Him with the future.

The fear of the Lord leads to life: Then one rests content, untouched by trouble (Proverbs 19:23).

The Daily Way

October 7

Broken Relationships

Many who have had to sign divorce papers know the huge weight of guilt that can linger for a long time. Others may feel as though they have let God down. Jesus was firm about the subject of divorce because He knew the reckless hearts of the people:

> Moses permitted you to divorce your wives because your hearts were hard. But it was not this way from the beginning. I tell you that anyone who divorces his wife, except for marital unfaithfulness, and marries another woman commits adultery (Matthew 19:8-9).

Even though God's plan did not include divorce, we know that broken relationships happen. Circumstances that go beyond our control can lead to separation and divorce. Other times, divorce comes as a result of irresponsibility.

Our love for our spouse is precious in God's sight, and He has given specific guidelines for us to follow to ensure we will never have to face the sorrow of divorce.

But if a person is faced with a divorce, he or she must remember that God's love continues. The Lord will never withdraw His care. While there are consequences to any broken relationship, God has the ability to heal and restore.

If you are divorced, never allow the enemy to tempt you into thinking that you will never be the person God wants you to be. This is just not true. God does have a plan for your life, and it begins the moment you place your trust in Him. The brokenness that comes with divorce can be painful, but God will ease the pain and show you how to begin again.

Prayer: Lord, I never thought that life would turn out like this. Please help me to begin again and learn how to trust others without being fearful.

With God all things are possible (Matthew 19:26).

October 8

The Daily Way

Single and Focused on God

After reading Paul's words in 1 Corinthians, a single person may wonder, "Should I get married or remain single?" Paul writes, "Now to the unmarried and the widows I say: It is good for them to stay unmarried, as I am" (1 Corinthians 7:8).

Sometimes we may think God's Word contradicts itself, but it doesn't. Paul is not saying that it is better for men and women to be single, nor is he suggesting that it is God's will for everyone to be married. Instead, Paul is admonishing us to be content. Whether we are married or single, we can have a tremendous sense of peace and joy, but only if the focus of our lives is set on Jesus Christ.

People who are single often get off course by comparing their lives to others. They watch as their friends fall in love and get married. Before they know it, they are wondering if they have missed God's plan for their lives, but they haven't.

If we will seek the Lord above the things of this world, He will provide just what we need for every area of our lives (Matthew 6:33). Does this mean that we will find the right person to marry at the "right time?" God certainly gives good things to His children but His first desire is for us to know His love.

It is all a matter of focus, and if we are majoring on the right things, we will be blessed in every way. Never allow the mindset of popular culture to squeeze you into its mold. Instead, ask God to be your guide through life. When you do, you will be surprised at the opportunities He will bring your way.

Prayer: Lord, thank You that You are with me and You provide much more than I could ever imagine possible.

I am saying this for your own good ... that you may live in a right way in undivided devotion to the Lord (1 Corinthians 7:35).

The Daily Way

Waiting for His Best

At times, life will seem uncertain. Things we once held as familiar will change. This is when it helps to remember that God never changes. Throughout our trials and struggles, He remains the same—faithful and sure.

You may be going through a difficult time. No one seeks out adversity. However, when it comes, you can find hope by taking time to see your circumstances as opportunities for God's glory to be displayed.

Self-sufficiency and pride are revealed when we are at our weakest point. God wants us to learn to depend on Him alone. Hard times provide the right opportunity for us to learn God-dependence instead of self-reliance.

When it comes to relationships, this is especially true. A temporary setback in a close relationship can become an open door for a fresh commitment and blessing. Remember, each season has a purpose. In times of stress and pressure, one of the most common mistakes is to make permanent decisions based on temporary circumstances.

God, however, wants us to be willing to wait for His best. If you have been praying for that "right" person to come into your life, be willing to trust Him to bring to pass all His promises in His good timing. The answers to your prayers may not come in the way you imagine.

However, God will never waver in His goodness toward you. He will keep His appointment. He always honors His Word and will accomplish His purpose in your life. God is a matchmaker—working to bring things about for your good and His glory. If you will trust Him, He will match you with blessings, people, opportunities, healing, joy, and peace.

"For I know the plans I have for you," declares the Lord, "...plans to give you hope and a future" (Jeremiah 29:11).

October 10

The Daily Way

The Heavenly Matchmaker

You may remember the song in the movie Fiddler on the Roof, "Matchmaker, matchmaker, make me a match…"?

The book of Ruth is about another matchmaker. In the midst of trouble and pain after the death of her husband and sons, Naomi set out to return to her homeland. When she began her journey, she quickly discovered that Ruth, her daughter-in-law, insisted on going with her. All the while, God was working to match His plan with their lives. God's grace sustained them through their difficulties and gave them hope and provision beyond their need and expectation.

What need do you have? Are you overwhelmed with your circumstances? Remember, God is your heavenly matchmaker. He knows you and what is best for you. When you place your trust in Jesus Christ, He will match you with His divine intention and strategy.

God provided a kinsman redeemer for Ruth through the love and commitment of Boaz. What appeared to be an impossible situation was really an opportunity for God to fulfill His promise of salvation to each one of us. Take a moment to look over the genealogy of Jesus Christ and you will find the names of Ruth and Boaz.

You do not have to worry about how you will face tomorrow. God has provided a Kinsman Redeemer for you through the life, death, and resurrection of His Son. God's forgiveness, mercy, and grace are the very elements that lead to your redemption.

He has promised to provide for every need you have. At each turn in life, He is the One who holds you securely in the hollow of His omnipotent hand. How comforting it is to know that your heavenly matchmaker knows what is best for you.

My God will meet all your needs according to his glorious riches in Jesus Christ (Philippians 4:19).

The Daily Way

October 11

Created for Relationships

For the past several decades, the roles of men and women have been compared, debated, and challenged. If the numerous books and articles about the roles of men and women confuse you, you are not alone. In our society, there are conflicting ideas on the position of men and women in the workplace, the church, and in relationships, particularly marriage.

While these countless philosophies attempt to capture our attention, there is one reliable source we can turn to for answers and assurance—the inspired and infallible Word of God.

Some people see the biblical duty of a husband and wife as outmoded and obsolete. However, when we study God's Word we gain a far greater perspective on the subject of marriage. Marriage is a complex and wonderful relationship ordained by God. In fact, He created us for relationships. God knew that it was not good for man to remain alone (Genesis 2:18). From its beginning, the institution of marriage was designed as a partnership, with the husband as the head of his household.

Perhaps you have not yet married. Paul reminds us that Christ is the head of every man and woman (1 Corinthians 11:3). He is the One who loves us with an everlasting love. This is the same love He requires us to have for one another, and especially for our spouses.

Just as He loves His Church, which is the body of Christ, God commands husbands to love their wives. This means loving your wife more than you love yourself.

For the husband is the head of the wife as Christ is the head of the church, his body, of which he is the Savior (Ephesians 5:23).

October 12

The Daily Way

Leadership in the Home

What comes to mind when you think of leadership? Do you immediately think of unquestioned authority? Or do your thoughts turn to protection and nurturing?

For too long, leadership has been a misunderstood subject, especially within our homes. The role of leadership within our families was never meant to lead to a form of dictatorship.

Those who are true leaders know that leadership does not include one person always getting his or her way over the other. Nor does it mean that the leader's views are always right and others are wrong.

However, with any God-given leadership there must be a desire to submit to the one in charge. While leadership involves teamwork, self-sacrifice, and an open heart, it also involves obedience. There is no place where this is truer than within our families. Husbands are called by God to be leaders. But God's design for leadership is based on His eternal love. Just as He willingly sacrificed for us, we must be willing to sacrifice our desires for those we love.

Scripture reminds us that just as Christ is the head of the Church, He also is our Leader, Savior, and Lord. He always leads us with love. Is this the same principle that you practice within your home? God's love for you is an example of how you should love those around you—your family, co-workers, and especially your husband or wife.

God is full of grace and mercy. When He becomes the head of our lives and hearts, then our homes will reflect His transforming love and mercy to all.

Husbands, love your wives, just as Christ loved the church and gave himself up for her (Ephesians 5:25).

The Daily Way

October 13

Freedom through Submission

William F. Buckley, modern-day thinker and author, writes, "The most important intellectual enterprise is the distinction between right and wrong." Often our thoughts about right and wrong get blurred. We allow the world's view of sin to change our perspective of God's truth. One moment's worth of compromise can dull our senses to God's truth.

Our emotions are notoriously undependable. If you rely solely on your feelings, you will find yourself becoming both miserable and confused. This is true for every relationship, but it is especially true of husbands and wives. In intimate relationships, we need to be sure that we live life from a perspective of what is true and right according to God.

We also need to make sure that we willingly submit to one another. This means we value one another as God values each of us. For example, we listen in kindness to the views of our spouse or our friends because we love them and not because we are forced to be in their presence. James writes:

> What causes fights and quarrels among you? Don't they come from your desires that battle within you? You want something but don't get it. ... When you ask, you do not receive, because you ask with wrong motives (James 4:1-3).

Genuine happiness does not come from getting your own way or by avoiding God's plan. Happiness comes from obeying His Word and His will. It comes from obedience and submission.

Obedience is not meant to be a chore or a duty. When God is involved, submission and surrender are both liberating and fulfilling. In fact, when your life is submitted to Jesus, you will experience His lasting freedom and joy each day.

I run in the path of your commands, for you have set my heart free (Psalm 119:32).

October 14 — The Daily Way

United in God's Love

When you think of the word submission, what images come to mind? Do you think of the relationship between parent and child, an employer and employee, or do you immediately think of the marriage relationship?

In the area of marriage, God's Word is very clear. From His point of view, the husband is to be the head of his wife. He is the one who stands accountable for his family. To his wife, he is a representative of the glory of God. Just as Christ is the head of the Church, a husband is the head of his wife.

However, we must understand that God commands a husband to love his wife with the same love that Jesus has for the church—unconditional and full of grace and mercy. This love is an eternal love and does not fade with time, nor is it marred by stormy trials.

In fact, a man is required to love his wife as he loves himself. Few women or men would ever turn away from this type of love. God's plan for marriage was designed to enable a husband and wife to grow together in God's love.

Almost every year a new book appears on the bookshelves declaring the age-old truth that men and women are different. While this is true in many areas, we must not forget that marriage is a union—not a competition. There should not be a struggle over who is weak and who is strong.

When both husband and wife are submitting to God in their devotion to one another and to Him, there will be a wonderful sense of freedom that emerges from their lives and from the lives of everyone in their family.

If you are struggling with the thought of submission, ask God to help you view it from His perspective. The first step to true love and unity within the family begins with love through submission.

Submit to one another out of reverence for Christ (Ephesians 5:21).

The Daily Way — October 15

Honor with Love

The subject of roles within a marriage can be a topic for strong debate. However, God has a clear design for us to follow. There are specific roles for a husband and a wife.

The reason many couples struggle with their marriages is because they fail to apply God's principles to their lives and to their relationships. When they do this, they miss a blessing.

The word submission has become a very emotional word for many people. Often we resist submitting our lives to one another because we fear we will be hurt.

However, when we follow God's plan for submission, the result is not a low self-esteem, as some would have us believe. Instead, it is an increased sense of love for our partner and for the Lord.

Without a doubt, Jesus Christ is our model for godly submission. He submitted His life to God's plan to the point of enduring death on the cross. When we obey God's commands and base our plan for marriage on His Word, our lives are changed and our marriages are strengthened. We learn to love one another the way Jesus loves us. Submission no longer is an issue to be debated; it is the natural thing to do. Paul writes:

> As God's chosen people, holy and dearly loved, clothe yourselves with compassion, kindness, humility, gentleness and patience. Bear with each other and forgive whatever grievances you may have against one another. Forgive as the Lord forgave you (Colossians 3:12-13).

Do you honor your spouse above yourself? Is your desire to give love and support rather than tear down? When you honor one another with your love, you really are honoring the Lord.

Be completely humble and gentle; be patient, bearing with one another in love (Ephesians 4:2).

October 16 — The Daily Way

Crisis in the Family

The unity of the family is under attack in a serious way in our society today. Divorce rates for first-time marriages in America are at 50 percent. Families are constantly ripped apart due to the relative ease by which a couple can terminate the covenant they made before God. Children do not know the security of having a healthy, stable upbringing but live in a constant state of flux. This is not how God designed families!

You may have experienced the pain of divorce as a child or adult. And changing the world's ideas about what a good family system is might be difficult. However, doing something about your own family and changing it from the inside out is an attainable goal God can help you accomplish.

One of the places to begin is the prioritization of your time. We can say that family is important. We can tell our wives or husbands or children they are the most important people in our lives. Yet, when we act differently, they get another message loud and clear.

To make someone a priority, you must make time for that person. Another way to show your family members they are important to you is by speaking words of affirmation over their lives. When your husband, wife, or children hear your words of approval, they get excited inside. We all know what it is like to hear that we did a good job, but it is even better to hear it from the people who are closest to you.

If you want to avert your own family crisis, begin to place the highest priority upon your relationship with your family. Not only will your family be blessed, but you will enjoy the rich fruits of having deep, meaningful relationships with those you love the most.

Prayer: Lord, help me to be one who strengthens my family and brings everyone together in a new way.

They are no longer two, but one (Matthew 19:6).

The Daily Way

October 17

Make Your Time Count

God has wonderful plans for our lives. However, in order to experience these, we must learn to obey Him and not be drawn off course by the enemy's schemes. For example, not only are we to be good stewards of our money, but we also need to be good stewards of the time we spend on earth.

It is amazing how much time we waste by filling our minds with thoughts that are far from what God wants us to think. Before we know it, we can become entranced by various media—radio, television, and movies—and begin to think that these have greater moral value than the truth of God's Word.

The world's ways are diametrically opposed to God's way. The world screams, "Look out for yourself!" God says, "Put others first."

It should come as no surprise that God's principles are in direct opposition to those of the world. Nor should it surprise us that the enemy is at work constantly seeking to destroy us and our families.

Therefore, we must be careful how we live, what we allow to come into our minds, and what we say with our mouths. Patterns of sin quickly take root and soon a stronghold for the enemy is established. As believers, we must set up spiritual safeguards against anything that would prevent us from living for Christ.

In your family, take a role in encouraging family members to embrace worthwhile pursuits rather than wasting away, idly watching television or surfing the internet. Make your time count for positive change in this world by embracing God's values. Take time to study His Word and seek His wisdom for the lives of your family members.

Prayer: Lord, make me sensitive to philosophies that are contrary to Your Word in my life today.

May they be brought to complete unity to let the world know that you sent me and have loved them even as you have loved me (John 17:23).

October 18 — The Daily Way

Leadership Is the Husband's Role

Our society today does not embrace many of God's edicts with open arms. And when it comes to the subject of men and their role in the family, the world usually turns up its collective nose at what the Bible says and pronounces it antiquated and old-fashioned.

However, there is nothing out of date about what the Bible says. There are times when people misunderstand or misinterpret God's Word. Yet, when God calls men to be the leaders of their families, He does so unapologetically. The trouble begins when others mistakenly determine what it means to be a leader.

When the Bible says men are to love their wives as Christ loved the Church, we must look at this relationship carefully. Jesus clearly led His disciples with love, stemming from a heart of servanthood.

To lead anyone truly, we must first understand what it means to be a servant. God did not call men to lord over women; rather, He called men to be humble servants who put their wives first in all decisions.

In fulfilling God's calling to lead their wives, men must view this position with high regard. It takes strength and wisdom, both of which come in ample supply to a heart that is yielded to the Holy Spirit. It takes tenderness and kindness, both of which are crucial to developing a servant's heart.

Being called the leader of the home is an awesome privilege, but so is being a servant. As you serve those you love, ask God to teach you how to love your wife the way Christ loved the Church, and to be the kind of leader who honors God in the way you live.

Prayer: Lord, help me to be the leader and the man You have called me to be.

Husbands, in the same way be considerate as you live with your wives, and treat them with respect as the weaker partner and as heirs with you of the gracious gift of life, so that nothing will hinder your prayers (1 Peter 3:7).

The Daily Way — October 19

Lead with Love

In understanding the man's role as leader of the home, we must grasp what it means to love. Without God's love—the kind of love that drives you to do everything you can to put the other person first and to enable her to reach her full potential—the voice of the leader is hollow and empty. Would you follow a leader if you knew he did not care about you?

As our society has ripped apart the notion that the man should be the leader of the home, we must return to the basics of what the Bible says, delving into the study of what it means to lead. And we discover that God says the heartbeat of leadership is love.

God's love does not give us the right to demand our way. When we study God's Word, we quickly see that love is not selfish or concerned with getting our desires met first. His love does not give us the right to control others. Instead, the love of God calls us to be faithful and true. God's love calls us to sacrifice and to nourish, to cherish, and to honor others above ourselves. So often, we associate leadership with power and authority. We forget that God's definition of leadership never omits love.

When God calls people to lead His church, He also calls them to love His church. Some of the most endearing Christian leaders of today are so loved because they love God's people.

As a man, if you love your wife like Christ loved the church, you will never have to affirm yourself as the leader of the home—she will do it for you. Be faithful to God's call on your life as a man: Lead with love.

Prayer: Lord, enable me to lead today with the same kind of love and compassion that flowed from Jesus as He walked on earth.

This is a profound mystery—but I am talking about Christ and the church. However, each one of you also must love his wife as he loves himself, and the wife must respect her husband (Ephesians 5:32-33).

October 20 — The Daily Way

Always Holding Somebody Up

Our society has slyly attached negative connotations to the word submission. Instead of finding joy in serving others, our minds often run to thoughts of service under a ruthless taskmaster.

However, when the apostle Paul wrote about wives submitting to their spouses, he was giving an edict of love and not a directive for one to control the other. In fact, he was issuing an invitation for husbands and wives to pursue godliness in lifting up one another. This principle applies to all of us.

Dawson Trotman, founder of the world-wide discipleship ministry called The Navigators, was a man who truly modeled his life after the Lord Jesus Christ. He died in Schroonlake, New York, of, all things, drowning—for Trotman was an experienced swimmer.

A speedboat accident left two women in serious trouble. During Trotman's last few moments in the water, he saved both of them. He lifted the first one out and then swam toward the other one, grabbed her, and lifted her up before he submerged and drowned. The next week, TIME Magazine ran an article on Trotman's life. The caption that ran beneath his name read, "Always holding somebody up." In one phrase, that was Trotman's life—holding people up.

Perhaps this is what the apostle Paul was writing about when he instructed husbands and wives to love one another and be willing to sacrifice for each other. Men must park their egos and women must serve with humility. Submission can be a difficult task but with God's direction, you will reach your goal.

Prayer: Lord, help me uphold those around me in this day.

Submit yourselves for the Lord's sake to every authority instituted among men...to the king, as the supreme authority (1 Peter 2:13).

The Daily Way

October 21

A Godly Household

It's odd how we sometimes attempt to improve upon the perfect model God has given us. In the Bible, God makes it clear that men are to be the head of the household. Yet our "society of equality" mentality storms back at the philosophy of God's Word.

God's directives do not need a fresh revision to fit within our "forward-thinking" society. When God laid out what a godly household should look like, He never intended for it to change.

While God sees men and women as being equal, they certainly have different roles. Is one more important than the other? Of course not! Yet, many in our secular society would say differently. There are those who oppose God's Word to such a great degree that they would want us to believe that He is far more interested in the role of a man than that of a woman.

The woman at the well was one of the first people in the New Testament to learn that Jesus was the Son of God—the One who could satisfy her deepest longing. The Lord elevated women and was not ashamed to be seen talking with them and teaching them the truth of God's Word.

Being obedient to God and fulfilling the role He has given you leads to tremendous blessing. His call to you is one of submission to Him first and then to one another as husband or wife. When you are living out the role God has given you, you are going to be more fulfilled than at any other time in your life.

Prayer: Lord, show me how to walk more in Your ways today.

Now the Lord is the Spirit, and where the Spirit of the Lord is, there is freedom (2 Corinthians 3:17).

October 22

The Marriage Partnership

As we discover what God's Word says about our lives, we discover the roles He gives husbands and wives. And they are distinctly different. At the same time, they are both incredibly transforming when the husband and wife take their roles seriously.

To our modern-day ears, submission may sound like a word related to suppression. It does not sound exciting to serve someone who is in charge of your life, but it can be. God wants us to learn first how to submit to Him through faith and then to submit to one another.

A deep, abiding sense of love develops when we open our lives and hearts to others—especially our spouses. Submission within the context of the marriage relationship is a partnership—where we lay down our wants and desires and live as one before God.

The more we grow in our relationships with the Lord, the more we begin to see submission as a position of freedom and security. We have purpose because we are living for Christ, who died and gave Himself for us. He submitted to the Father's will, and today, we are saved through our faith in Him. His submission overthrew Satan's dark plan to control the hearts and minds of men and women.

God, however, did not create men or women to control one another; rather, He created them to complement each other. So those who are united in marriage will be powerful together as husband and wife. When we understand our roles within the family unit and how to carry them out in a godly manner, God will begin to do a mighty work in our lives.

Prayer: Lord, show me how to meet my potential in living out the role You have for me.

Live as free men, but do not use your freedom as a cover-up for evil; live as servants of God (1 Peter 2:16).

The Daily Way

October 23

Inner Beauty

Whether you are married or not, Peter has some good advice: The beauty of your character is your greatest asset. No matter what people say about you or do to you, your character says the most about who you are. The decisions you make when no one is watching determine the depth of character you possess.

In speaking directly to wives with unbelieving husbands, Peter reminds these women of the importance of letting their inner beauty shine brightly. He writes:

> Your beauty should not come from outward adornment. ... Instead, it should be that of your inner self, the unfading beauty of a gentle and quiet spirit, which is of great worth in God's sight (1 Peter 3:3-4).

As we respond to the call God places on our lives as believers, we cannot ignore the importance of living a life beyond reproach. The world can strip away all our worldly possessions, but it cannot take our names, what our names represent, and the character associated with them.

The more genuine you are with those around you, the more God will be able to use you as an encourager. Your credibility will rise. People will acknowledge you as a person of authority because you not only talk about it, you live it. As we spread the Gospel to a world desperate for the truth, we must make sure our words align with our actions.

For the wife of an unbeliever, this passage in 1 Peter 3 is heavy, yet full of hope. It is possible to see the hardest of hearts softened and dramatically transformed through the power of God's love.

Prayer: Lord, help me live a life honoring and pleasing to You today—and let the world know it is real.

Finally, all of you, live in harmony with one another; be sympathetic, love as brothers, be compassionate and humble (1 Peter 3:8).

October 24

The Daily Way

Our Life Stories

When we know and understand people better, we are more empowered to relate to them. We know their biggest delights in life as well as their biggest disappointments. We know what brings them joy along with what brings them sadness. Knowing more about individuals allows us to speak directly into their lives where they need it most, when they need it most.

Whether you are in a marital relationship or not, taking time to get to know someone will help you bring out the best in that person. In 1 Peter 3:7, husbands are given the charge to honor their wives. This is a powerful life principle that we should apply to all relationships.

People respond to different acts of love in different ways. However, everyone responds in a positive manner when someone takes interest in his life. We all enjoy sharing our life stories. And when you take an interest in someone that goes beyond the courteous "How are you doing?" question, people come alive and open up their lives.

During Jesus' time on earth He had a large following, but He did not act like a superstar. He spent time with people and ate in their homes. When Zacchaeus was struggling to get a glimpse of Jesus from atop a sycamore tree, Jesus looked up at him and took more than a passing interest in his life. He suggested they eat dinner together.

After one meal with Jesus, Zacchaeus, the once-hated tax collector, experienced a changed life. He returned the money to those he had taxed unfairly. In fact, he was so moved by the Savior's love that he returned much more than was taken.

Prayer: Lord, show me how to invest in people today and allow You to flow through me into their lives.

Therefore encourage one another and build each other up, just as in fact you are doing (1 Thessalonians 5:11).

The Daily Way

October 25

Children Are a Heritage from the Lord

Some parents who are knee-deep in diapers and family deadlines may wonder if there will ever be a time when they can just relax and enjoy their children. The truth is children can be a great comfort from the Lord. In them we can learn to see life from a different perspective—one of wonder and freshness.

When we get older, our children will be the hope of our heritage. Abraham understood this principle. He longed for a son but remained childless. God had promised him that Sarah would have a son. As the years moved on, Abraham wondered if this promise would be fulfilled. Then when Sarah was past childbearing age, she gave birth to Isaac. Scripture says:

> Now the Lord was gracious to Sarah as he had said, and the Lord did for Sarah what he had promised. Sarah became pregnant and bore a son to Abraham in his old age, at the very time God had promised him (Genesis 21:1-2).

Isaac's birth was a cause for celebration but not just because of his birth. We rejoice over the fact that God did exactly what He promised He would do.

Like Sarah, you may have waited for years to have a child. Or there may be another promise you have from the Lord that has up until this point gone unanswered. When you think all hope is gone, God will step into your situation with an answer to your deepest prayer. There is no higher calling than to be a person who helps to mold and shape the life of a child. And there is no greater experience than to trust in Jesus Christ.

Prayer: Father, thank You for the gift of my children. Teach me to be a parent whose life is guided by Your truth and wisdom.

God is the strength of my heart and my portion forever (Psalm 73:26).

October 26   The Daily Way

Teach Your Children Well

Training children to love and to serve the Lord, to be compassionate toward others, and to have consistent walks of faith is the most noble and important work any parent can do. Therefore, we should find great joy in the fact that the Lord has called us and entrusted us to be parents!

Never lose sight of the fact that you are training your child not only to take a role in God's kingdom on this earth, but also to assume a place and an inheritance in heaven.

Many parents wonder what the most important lesson is that they can teach their children. The answer is simple. Nothing can take the place of teaching your child about the forgiveness and love of God. Telling him or her about the saving grace of Jesus Christ is the most important thing you will ever do.

Too often, mothers and fathers become weary in the process and say, "I am raising children" or "I am supporting a family." However, we need to view our parental roles as being a privilege. We are training heirs to the kingdom of God—children who will make a difference in this world for God, children who will love others in Christ and lead others to salvation, children who will live together with you in eternity, children who will know the fullness of God's blessings, guidance, and favor!

As you pursue the challenge of being a godly parent, you can be assured that God is on your team. He will provide the wisdom you need for every situation. He also will protect you and bless you as you walk in His ways and bring glory to His name.

Prayer: Lord, I realize that as a parent I have a tremendous task. I know I cannot do it on my own. I need Your wisdom to guide me each day.

Unless the Lord builds the house, its builders labor in vain (Psalm 127:1).

The Daily Way — October 27

Believing God for Your Family

The very first step to becoming a godly parent is to accept Christ as your Savior. If you have never asked Him to come into your heart and forgive your sins, then you will not know how to meet your children's needs effectively. The Lord is the One who has given us the ability to have children, and in order to tap into His mind, you have to have a personal relationship with Him.

The second step to becoming a godly parent is dependence on God. Children are great imitators. If we have a sincere walk of faith, they will follow our lead. Let your love for your children be rooted in your love for God. It is only to the degree that you love the Lord that you will be able to show your love to your children and other family members.

The third step is one of humility. Your children need to recognize the fact that you are the head of the household. However, they also need to know you can make mistakes, and when you do, you are not slow in seeking God's forgiveness. When your child hears you praying, his or her life is changed. Suddenly, he realizes Mom or Dad's faith is in God and nothing else.

Make sure you find time to praise God for your salvation, His provision for your family, and the wisdom He gives each day. Thank Him for His blessings and protection. Pray for a spirit of gratitude so your children will learn to have grateful hearts instead of being consumed with their personal wants and desires.

Prayer: Lord, I know there are times when I forget to say thank You for all You have done. Forgive my ingratitude and teach me to be grateful for the love You have shown to my family and me.

Do what is right and good in the Lord's sight, so that it may go well with you (Deuteronomy 6:18).

October 28   The Daily Way

Unconditional Love

Another role of the godly parent is to cultivate compassion for others. Job trained his children to be generous, hospitable, responsible, kind, and considerate, and to be leaders when it came to building up others, building up the family, and building unity and harmony in the community.

This did not mean Job taught his children to compromise for the sake of agreement, but rather to hold strong principles and demonstrate genuine love.

How do we develop compassion for others? We first must experience God's love—and then be challenged to pass on that love. Children first experience God's love by experiencing the love of their own parents. The more their parents express love to them, the quicker they are to show compassion.

Assure your children repeatedly of God's love, even when they disobey. Be affectionate with them—hugging and kissing them and putting your hand on their shoulders as a sign of encouragement.

Also, don't link your love to any behavioral trait in your child. Let your children know you love them just as God loves them—unconditionally. God loves us solely because we are His beloved, uniquely created children. Learn to love your children in the same way.

When you demonstrate love to your children, they gain a proper perspective of God. They learn to view the Lord as being a God of love and not wrath.

Prayer: Lord, teach me how to communicate Your love better to my family. I know when I learn to love You better, I can then pass this love on to others. Thank You for Your faithfulness in my life.

These commandments that I give you today are to be upon your hearts. Impress them on your children (Deuteronomy 6:6-7).

The Daily Way — October 29

Walk the Walk

As a godly parent, one of the things you will want to do is to cultivate consistency in your family's "walk of faith." Job valued spending time with his family and communicating with them—not only speaking to them but listening closely as they voiced their concerns, needs, and opinions.

Being consistent in our faith is not the same thing as perfection, nor does it mean we are always right. Rather, consistency means we make our families a priority when it comes to our time and our schedules.

Consistency also means "walking the walk" and not just "talking the talk" of your faith. It means going with your children to church every Sunday, including attendance at Sunday school. It means praying with your family daily, memorizing Scripture, and talking about the things of the Lord and the principles of the Bible in a natural, ongoing way.

Use every moment of your relationship with your children to establish the reality of both God's love and your love in their lives. Keep His love and the Bible's teachings at the heart of your discussions with your children—about what they see on television, learn in school, or hear from other children. Make God your number one resource to consult any time they face problems, are sick, or have specific needs.

It is in this daily walking-and-talking, dawn-to-dusk way that we train our children to have the right attitudes and to express the right behavior to others. It is a daily challenge to teach our children compassion and to lead them into a consistent pattern of godly living.

Prayer: Lord, I know when the focus of my life is set on You, then the focus of my family will be the same.

Lay hold of my words with all your heart; keep my commands and you will live (Proverbs 4:4).

October 30 — The Daily Way

A Father's Sacrifice

For decades, Sam Rayburn was recognized as one of the most powerful politicians in America. When asked by a reporter to recount the most important moment of his life, his thoughts went back to his father as he began to tell about the day he left his East Texas home. He was 18 years old and on his way to college. His father was a man of few words but full of wisdom.

Standing on the train platform, both men looked down at Sam's suitcase that was nothing more than a bundle of clothes tied together with a rope. It was obvious the family did not have much money. Sam's presence was really needed at home but the elder Rayburn knew the opportunities awaiting his son were many and could only be experienced by his willingness to allow his son to leave.

As the train arrived and Sam prepared to get on board, his father reached deep into his pocket and pulled out a fist full of dollars and placed them in Sam's hand. There were 25 single dollar bills.

"Only God knows how he saved this money." Sam later said. "We never had any extra. He barely earned enough for the family to live on. It broke me up, and I often wondered what he did without—what sacrifices he and Mother made—so I could go to school."

Fathers have an immeasurable impact on the lives of their children. Always believe in your children. Help them to understand the cost of sacrifice and how it is given as an act of love—the greatest being God's sacrifice to us through His Son.

Prayer: Father, help me to be a person who reflects Your love and sacrifice to others, especially to those in my family.

Parents are the pride of their children (Proverbs 17:6).

The Daily Way — October 31

The Priesthood of the Father

Job is an excellent example of a man who loved his family and wanted God's best for each one of them. He also understood the role of the priesthood of the father and never hesitated to take responsibility for his loved ones.

He was up early in the morning, not so he could check the weather report or the stock market predictions. His first concern was not whether he could beat the traffic rush into work. He didn't turn on his computer to check his e-mail or "log on" to read the Wall Street Journal. Instead, Job was up early in order to spend time with God. He worshiped the Lord and offered sacrifices for his wife and children. He was aware of their personal needs and he was a committed provider.

There are three things a man should do as a family priest:

- He needs to cultivate a strong commitment to the Lord. God must be first in our lives. If we have allowed anything to come before Him, then we will not have the godly wisdom we need to provide for those we love.

- He should cultivate compassion and be sensitive to his family's needs.

- He needs to cultivate consistency. Job never swayed in his devotion, commitment, and love for the Lord, and you can have the same type of lifestyle.

If you are a single parent, God understands the challenges you are facing. If you simply cry out to the Him in difficult times, He will turn your trials into moments of blessing and praise. When you seek Him with your whole heart, He will come to your rescue as your faithful provider and living Lord, and give you a double portion of His strength.

Prayer: Lord, show me how to pray for those I love and teach me more about You each day.

Have you considered my servant Job? There is no one on earth like him (Job 1:8).

The Names and Character of God

The Daily Way — November 1

Elohim: The Most High

Who or what do you worship in your life? Your first instinct may be to answer "God," but what other idols are lurking in your heart? Is it your ambition and career? Maybe it is a hobby or sport that you pursue to the exclusion of most everything else. It could be a relationship that is not submitted to God. Think about it. Is God truly first and foremost in your life?

The first name God uses to reveal Himself is "Elohim." This name occurs in the book of Genesis more than 200 times and 2,570 times in the whole of the Old Testament. When the people of God heard God's name, they knew exactly what it meant. It meant "the highest," "the most high," or "the exalted above all creation."

This name is particularly significant in the Old Testament, when many people were worshipping gods they had created. To declare that there was only one God and that He reigned supreme over the entire universe was a radically different concept. Even today we battle false gods and idols. Satan uses every possible selfish desire and activity to distract us from the one true God.

Elohim refers to the "Most High" God or the "highest" God—the God above all creation, the God who initiated and created all of life. God created the universe and every living thing in it from nothing. "By faith we understand that the universe was formed at God's command, so that what is seen was not made out of what was visible" (Hebrews 11:3).

Do you worship God as the Most High?

Prayer: Lord, reveal your Almighty nature in my life and reveal any areas where I am not honoring you as the Most High.

Let them know that you, whose name is the Lord—that you alone are the Most High over all the earth (Psalm 83:18).

November 2 — The Daily Way

The God of all Creation

Elohim, the God of all creation, includes all three persons of the Trinity. We know that Jesus was present at Creation. John writes: "In the beginning was the Word, and the Word was with God, and the Word was God. He was with God in the beginning. Through him all things were made; without him nothing was made that has been made" (John 1:1-3).

We also know that the Holy Spirit was present at creation: "The Spirit of God was hovering over the waters" (Genesis 1:2). God the Holy Spirit has been "moving" and "hovering" over life ever since. He is the Creator of all "newness of life" that we experience in Christ Jesus.

Praise God—Father, Son, and Holy Spirit—for His vast and glorious creation; for His unfathomable power to create everything out of nothing. Praise Elohim for being the one true and living God. He alone is God. He is the Creator of each new day in our life, each new experience we encounter, and each new spiritual work in us. He is the Author and Finisher of our faith.

When was the last time you slowed down and treasured God's creation? Take some time today to discover His exquisite handiwork.

Prayer: Thank you, Elohim, for Your magnificent creation that declares Your glory and majesty.

For since the creation of the world God's invisible qualities—his eternal power and divine nature—have been clearly seen, being understood from what has been made, so that men are without excuse (Romans 1:20).

The Daily Way — November 3

God Almighty

Do you ever feel as if your life is out of control? Although you may sometimes feel that life is full of chaos, God is in complete control of everything around us. God is El-Shaddai, which means "God of power and might." El-Shaddai is the all-powerful, all-sufficient God. El-Shaddai is God Almighty.

The name El-Shaddai is a close complement to Elohim. If Elohim reveals the God who created and sustains nature, El-Shaddai reveals a God who constrains nature, controls nature, and subdues nature. El-Shaddai is the God to whom all nature listens and obeys.

Psalm 89:8-9 says, "O Lord God Almighty, who is like you? You are mighty, O Lord, and your faithfulness surrounds you. You rule over the surging sea; when its waves mount up, you still them." More than 300 times in the Old Testament, God calls Himself El-Shaddai. God wants there to be no misunderstanding—as El-Shaddai, He is the Ruler and Owner of all things. He is the controlling force of all nature and all history.

Do you need God to calm a storm in your life? Do you need healing that He alone can give? Then cry out to El-Shaddai. Begin to praise God Almighty! He alone can hold you up when all seems to be crumbling around you. He alone can sustain you. He alone can protect you. He alone can redeem you. The God who is in control of the entire universe wants to work on your behalf.

Prayer: Lord, thank You for Your power, strength, and love. Help me to remember that You are in control no matter what is happening around me.

Great is our Lord and mighty in power; his understanding has no limit (Psalm 147:5).

November 4

The Daily Way

Letting God Change Me

Because all things fall under God's rule, God has the power to intervene in the course of nature and change circumstances to conform to His purposes. Nearly every time God expresses Himself to someone as El-Shaddai in the Old Testament, He indicates a change that will occur in that person's life, a change that will involve a miraculous intervention.

We make a great mistake when we attempt to do things in our own strength. El-Shaddai desires to manifest Himself as God Almighty on our behalf. "Come and see what God has done, his awesome deeds for mankind!" (Psalm 66:5). He is at work inside your heart. He desires to change you, to change conditions around you, and ultimately to change the entire world.

If we understood this name alone, it would radically change our lives. It would radically revolutionize the way we think. It would change our life habits. We would no longer need to worry about our circumstances because we would embrace the fact that God is in control and is concerned over all the details of our lives.

What change does El-Shaddai want to do in your life today? Will you let Him?

Prayer: Lord, show me how You want to work through me and what You want to change in me.

He changes times and seasons; he deposes kings and raises up others. He gives wisdom to the wise and knowledge to the discerning (Daniel 2:21).

The Daily Way

November 5

Our Provider

Are you grateful to God or do you take His blessings for granted? Do you look around at your home, your family, your opportunities and thank God for providing those to you? Do you thank God every time He helps you out of a difficult or painful situation? God provides for us everything we need—not only our material possessions but also His help in times of trouble. God is Jehovah-Jireh, which means "the Lord will provide."

Jehovah-Jireh even helps us when we are tempted. The Bible tells us that, "No temptation has seized you except what is common to man. And God is faithful; he will not let you be tempted beyond what you can bear. But when you are tempted, he will also provide a way out so that you can stand up under it" (1 Corinthians 10:13). God has already foreseen everything you will face today and in the future, and He has arranged everything you will need. There is no troublesome circumstance or difficulty for which He has not already provided your victory or a way of escape.

Praise Jehovah-Jireh! God is our Provider today, tomorrow, and for eternity. He knows precisely what we need, and He already has a plan for meeting our needs.

Prayer: Jehovah-Jireh, thank You for providing help in times of trouble and a way out when I am tempted.

The LORD is gracious and righteous; our God is full of compassion. The LORD protects the unwary; when I was brought low, he saved me. Return to your rest, my soul, for the LORD has been good to you (Psalm 116:5-7).

November 6

The Daily Way

He Sees Ahead

One of the greatest examples of God's provision is when He provides the ram for Abraham's sacrifice. Read Genesis 22:1-14. Jehovah-Jireh is the name that Abraham used for the place on the mountain where God had sent him to sacrifice his beloved son, Isaac, as a burnt offering. On the way up the mountain, Isaac asked his father where the lamb was for the burnt offering. Abraham replied, "God himself will provide the lamb" (Genesis 22:8).

After Abraham bound his son, laid him on the altar, and raised his knife to slay him, an angel of the Lord called to him: "Do not lay a hand on the boy. ... Now I know that you fear God, because you have not withheld from me your son, your only son" (Genesis 22:12). Then Abraham saw a ram caught by its horns in a nearby thicket. He took the ram and sacrificed it in place of his son. And he called that place Jehovah-Jireh, "The Lord Will Provide" (Genesis 22:14).

The word "jireh" literally means "he sees ahead." God sees what you need before you need it—even before you know you need it. For every task that God gives you, you can be assured that He has already made full provision for all you will need to complete that task. Just as God had placed the ram in the right place at the right time for Abraham, so will He provide for you whatever is needed to fulfill His will. There is no problem for which Jehovah-Jireh has not already prepared a solution. We can take comfort in knowing that even when a situation looks hopeless, God already has everything resolved for us. He is our great Provider. Praise our God who sees ahead to provide everything we will ever need!

Prayer: Lord, thank You for seeing ahead and knowing just what I need for every situation.

And my God will meet all your needs according to the riches of his glory in Christ Jesus (Philippians 4:19).

The Daily Way — November 7

He Is Healing

Are you hurting today? Maybe you are struggling with physical pain or emotional pain. Perhaps you are hurting spiritually from bitterness, unconfessed sin, or a broken spirit. If you are hurting today, then seek the help of Jehovah-Rapha, the Great Physician.

In Exodus 15:26, God introduces His name Jehovah-Rapha, "the Lord who heals." The word "rapha" means "to heal, to cure, to restore." God does not promise to heal us only in an isolated instance of illness or need. Rather, God says He is healing. By calling Himself Jehovah-Rapha, He is saying, "Healing is what I am."

Jehovah-Rapha is our wholeness. We see this truth echoed in the New Testament every time Jesus says to a person, "Be made whole." Wholeness is God's desire for us. No disease—nothing that causes us pain or suffering—can withstand the healing touch of Jesus. As Christians, we experience wholeness even in death as we spend eternity with Him.

Jehovah-Rapha is what we ultimately need, no matter what area of weakness, sickness, disease, or trouble we encounter. This doesn't mean we will never get sick or that we are immune to death. But God will be with us through every pain we experience. If you are suffering, you can be assured that God desires to use your suffering to bring an even greater reward to you, and to bring an even greater awareness of His presence to others who may witness your steadfastness.

Prayer: Jehovah-Rapha, thank You for being my Healer, for being with me in my suffering, and for the promise of an eternity with You.

And the God of all grace, who called you to his eternal glory in Christ, after you have suffered a little while, will himself restore you and make you strong, firm and steadfast (1 Peter 5:10).

November 8

The Daily Way

Our Restorer

Jehovah-Rapha is our Restorer. He is our healer of not only physical illness, but of the hurts in our heart and soul. When we are emotionally overwhelmed, depressed, anxious, grieving, or distressed, God is there for us. Only God can repair a broken heart. Only God can purify an unclean soul. Only God can set us free from addictions.

Only God can heal us of sin. The Scriptures tell us that, "He [Jesus] himself bore our sins in his body on the tree, so that we might die to sins and live for righteousness; by his wounds you have been healed" (1 Peter 2:24).

What a tremendous encouragement it is to know that God is healing us day by day, week by week, year by year. He takes all of those broken bits of our lives—even those which we aren't aware of—and mends them with His tender love and great healing power. One day we will stand perfectly whole in Christ Jesus before His throne.

The ongoing work of the Holy Spirit in our world is the work of Jehovah-Rapha. It is the Holy Spirit who mends broken hearts, renews degenerate minds, and restores shattered relationships. It is the work of the Holy Spirit to conform us to the likeness of the perfect, complete Christ Jesus. Jehovah-Rapha is the God who heals us and makes us whole.

If you are suffering from emotional or spiritual hurts today, cry out to Jehovah-Rapha. He wants to restore you. He wants to make you whole.

Prayer: Father, thank You for healing my broken heart and restoring my relationship with You through Your death on the cross.

Surely he took up our pain and bore our suffering ... he was pierced for our transgressions, he was crushed for our iniquities; the punishment that brought us peace was on him, and by his wounds we are healed (Isaiah 53:4-5).

The Daily Way

November 9

The Lord Is My Banner

Are you fighting a battle today? Whether it is a difficult relationship, a struggle with a particular sin, or a debilitating illness, we all face battles. There are even times when the battle is with ourselves. But we can take comfort in knowing that we have God fighting for us.

In Exodus, God reveals His name to Moses as Jehovah-Nissi, which means "the Lord is My Banner." Think of a battlefield. In our war with whatever is opposing us, God is our flag of victory. When spiritual battles are waged against us, there is only one banner under which we can gather to gain the victory, and His name is Jehovah Nissi.

The book of Exodus tells us that the Amalekites, a tribe descended from one of the giants who had occupied Canaan, wanted to prevent the Israelites from continuing their journey toward the Promised Land. So Moses called Joshua, the commander of the Israelite army, and said, "Choose some of our men and go out to fight the Amalekites. Tomorrow I will stand on top of the hill with the staff of God in my hands" (Exodus 17:9).

The "staff of God" was no ordinary rod. This was the rod that turned into a serpent before Pharaoh, that parted the Red Sea, and that brought forth water from a rock. The staff of God that Moses raised during the battle was synonymous with God's miracle-working power on behalf of the Israelites.

As Jehovah-Nissi, God raises His miracle-working power over our lives to bring us victory against the enemy of our souls. His staff, or His "banner" over us, is the assurance that we will move forward to achieve all that God has planned and purposed for us.

Your giants may be great, but they are nothing when you lift your hands in praise to God and trust Him to be a strong staff of victory over your life.

Prayer: God, thank You for fighting the battle for me and for Your power over the giants in my life.

No, in all these things we are more than conquerors through him who loved us (Romans 8:37).

November 10

The Daily Way

A Temple of the Holy Spirit

Mekaddish is the Hebrew word for holy or sanctified. The term mekaddish is also used to describe people who are set apart for divine callings. In Leviticus 20:7-8, God says, "Consecrate yourselves and be holy, because I am the Lord your God. Keep my decrees and follow them. I am the Lord, who makes you holy." And this last phrase is the name Jehovah-Mekaddish.

Ultimately, it is God Himself who is the Holy Temple in which all of us live and move and have our being. John wrote in his revelation of heaven, "I did not see a temple in the city, because the Lord God Almighty and the Lamb are its temple" (Revelation 21:22).

We are made holy not only by being in God's presence, but also by having His presence in us. The apostle Paul wrote about our being temples of the Holy Spirit on this earth: "Don't you know that you yourselves are God's temples and that God's Spirit lives in you? If anyone destroys God's temple, God will destroy him; for God's temple is sacred, and you are that temple" (1 Corinthians 3:16-17).

And later in 1 Corinthians 6:19-20, Paul says, "Do you not know that your body is a temple of the Holy Spirit, who is in you, whom you have received from God? You are not your own; you were bought at a price. Therefore honor God with your body."

Are you honoring God with your body, His temple, today?

Prayer: God, forgive me for not treating my body as Your temple. Help me to honor You with my body.

Let us purify ourselves from everything that contaminates body and spirit, perfecting holiness out of reverence for God (2 Corinthians 7:1).

The Daily Way — November 11

Holiness

What does holiness mean to you? Many people are uncomfortable with the word holy—they think it refers to unreasonable restrictions on their behavior or appearance. The word holy, however, means to be cleansed and separated for God's purposes. All Christians are called to be holy. We are called to be cleansed of our sins by the shed blood of Christ, sealed for God's purposes by the power of the Holy Spirit, and to live righteous lives for God.

Holiness is a great responsibility for the Christian, and yet we can take comfort in knowing that our holy God will help us in the process. God does not expect us to be holy in our own strength or virtue.

Instead, we have the Holy Spirit who lives within us and sanctifies us. If it were up to us to live a holy life in our own strength, or to cleanse our lives by our own efforts, we would have failed long ago. It is not our own efforts, but God's work within us that makes us holy. We are holy because He says we are holy.

What a tremendous and awesome mystery that we can be made and called holy by a holy God. Praise God today that He is Jehovah-Mekaddish. He is our holiness.

What are the ways in which you have neglected God's holiness in your life?

Prayer: God, thank You for Your holiness and for making me holy.

My mouth will speak in praise of the Lord. Let every creature praise his holy name for ever and ever (Psalm 145:21).

November 12

The Daily Way

God Is Peace

Where do you seek peace in your life? Do you try to establish peace in your relationships by avoiding conflict? Do you seek peace through popularity, status, or being well-liked? Only the peace that comes from God will satisfy us. Our own attempts at creating peace will leave us disappointed.

Our God is peace. His name, Jehovah-Shalom, tells us so. When you yield your life to Him, repent of your sins and make Christ your Lord, only then can you experience the peace of God. When Jesus died on the cross, He enabled us to enter into a spiritual rest where there is no longer agitation in our souls caused by guilt, shame, or a fear of eternity. We are released from the bonds of sin and have peace knowing that Jesus is living within us.

The peace of God is not merely a contented feeling. The Hebrew word for peace, shalom, far transcends our modern-day meaning of the word "peace." Shalom describes a perfect and comprehensive peace. It is a peace that surpasses our understanding.

We will still face spiritual battles in our lives. We will still experience trouble, difficulties, and pain in our relationships. A shalom-filled life is not one of complete ease and a carefree attitude. But when you have Jesus in your heart, you know that your battles are only temporary. You know that you will spend eternity in heaven and the troubles of today will never reach you there. You have peace in knowing that the God who created and controls the universe has a personal interest in you, and no matter what you are facing, He will be there with you.

When you face conflict and pain in life, remember Jesus' words to his disciples: "In this world you will have trouble. But take heart! I have overcome the world." Nothing you will face is bigger than the power of God.

Prayer: God, thank You for giving me peace that can only come from You and that can't be taken away.

Peace I leave with you; my peace I give you. I do not give to you as the world gives. Do not let your hearts be troubled and do not be afraid (John 14:27).

The Daily Way

November 13

The Good Shepherd

One of the most familiar passages in the Bible is Psalm 23, which begins with "The Lord is my shepherd." There is no more tender image to describe the relationship between God and His people than this. Rohi is the Hebrew word for shepherd, and Jehovah-Rohi is the Shepherd who cares for us, guides us, and restores us.

Our Jehovah-Rohi surpasses the definition of a shepherd who herds sheep. Our Shepherd's guidance is perfect. His patience is enduring. His leading is thoughtful. His comfort is superior. His companionship continues even in the dark valleys. His assurance banishes all fears. His provision makes the enemy squirm.

The Lord leads us into places of abundant nourishment and rest, and into times of spiritual refreshment and retreat. He provides for all of our needs so that we are never in want. He guides us into right choices, decisions, beliefs, words, and actions, so that all of our life brings glory to His name. He protects us during times of danger. He is always present with us.

Our Shepherd made the ultimate sacrifice for His sheep by dying on the cross. And His care for us transcends any human understanding of love and sacrifice. Jesus said, "I am the good shepherd. The good shepherd lays down his life for the sheep … I know my sheep and my sheep know me—just as the Father knows me and I know the Father—and I lay down my life for the sheep" (John 10:11, 14-15).

No caretaker we have known in our lifetime can compare to the care that God gives us. When you feel that you are wandering in unknown territory, Jehovah-Rohi will show you the way out. When you fear the storms that come or the wolves circling around you, Jehovah-Rohi will protect you. When you are tired and worn out, Jehovah-Rohi will give you soft, green pastures to rest in.

Prayer: Lord, thank You for being my Shepherd, protecting and guiding me, and for providing places of rest.

He tends his flock like a shepherd: He gathers the lambs in his arms and carries them close to his heart; he gently leads those that have young (Isaiah 40:11).

November 14

The Daily Way

The Lord Our Righteousness

Righteousness is a term that has lost some of its meaning over the years. Today we associate the word with being morally acceptable or conforming to rules of conduct. But the biblical usage has a far deeper meaning and implies a covenant relationship with God. One of God's names is Jehovah-Tsidkenu, "The Lord Our Righteousness."

Righteousness goes beyond being a character trait of God. The people of the Old Testament saw righteousness as being what God does in fulfillment of His covenant. God tells us, "I am the Lord, who exercises kindness, justice and righteousness on earth, for in these I delight" (Jeremiah 9:24). We are not simply to know that God is righteous, but we are meant to experience His righteousness.

One of the first examples we see of God's righteousness is in the book of Jeremiah. During that time, God's people were living in sin and idolatry, and their land was oppressed on all sides by violence and crime. King Josiah attempted to bring some reform, but the corruption of the society was too entrenched. The spiritual leaders were confused and scattered. The prophets were lying to the people rather than proclaiming God's truth. Righteousness was a distant concept.

But to one prophet, Jeremiah, God promised a coming day when a righteous King would reign wisely and "… do what is just and right in the land. …This is the name by which he will be called: The Lord Our Righteousness" (Jeremiah 23:5-6).

Prayer: God, thank You for fulfilling Your covenant, for being our Righteousness, and for allowing us to experience Your Righteousness.

It is because of [God] that you are in Christ Jesus, who has become for us wisdom from God—that is, our righteousness, holiness and redemption (1 Corinthians 1:30).

The Daily Way

November 15

Living a Righteous Life

The word Tsidkenu, the Hebrew term for righteousness in "The Lord Our Righteousness," means upright, straight, and narrow. The righteousness of God is the root of all integrity. It is the definition of all that is genuinely good in this life.

Many people worry about trying to achieve righteousness on their own. They think church involvement or following the rules will make them a righteous person. But Paul clearly says, "… if righteousness could be gained through the law, Christ died for nothing!" (Galatians 2:21). Romans 5:17 describes our righteousness as a gift from God.

We cannot earn righteousness, but because Jesus Christ became our righteousness, it is ours through Him. Romans 3:22-24 explains, "This righteousness from God comes through faith in Jesus Christ to all who believe. There is no difference between Jew and Gentile, for all have sinned and fall short of the glory of God and are justified freely by his grace through the redemption that came by Christ Jesus."

Once we receive righteousness through our commitment to Christ, God continues to work His righteousness in us. We are not alone in this struggle between our flesh and spirit. In our daily lives, the Holy Spirit will guide us and convict us of what is right and wrong. God gives us the strength to turn from temptation if we seek His help (1 Corinthians 10:13).

God has also blessed us with a manual on righteousness—the Word of God: "All Scripture is God-breathed and is useful for teaching, rebuking, correcting and training in righteousness" (2 Timothy 3:16).

Prayer: Jehovah-Tsidkenu, help me to have a heart that is open to the guidance of the Holy Spirit that I may live a righteous life, applying the truths of righteousness from Your Word to my daily life.

Blessed are those who hunger and thirst for righteousness, for they will be filled (Matthew 5:6).

November 16 — The Daily Way

Our Ever-Present God

How many times have we heard the cry, "Where is God?" in the midst of suffering and tragedy? Some people think that God has abandoned them, but God is always there. His name, Jehovah-Shammah, means "God Is There," or "God Is Always Present."

The Lord shared with Ezekiel a vision about the future of Jerusalem and said, "And the name of the city from that time on will be: the Lord is there" (Ezekiel 48:35). God's presence is with His people. God is ever-present among us. As Christians, God dwells inside of us. "For we are the temple of the living God. As God has said: 'I will live with them and walk among them, and I will be their God, and they will be my people'" (2 Corinthians 6:16).

As a believer, you are a temple of God. Live your life knowing that God is present with you and within you at all times. "Don't you know that you yourselves are God's temple and that God's Spirit dwells in your midst?" (1 Corinthians 3:16). You are not only the Holy Spirit's dwelling place but also a living testimony for Christ.

You can trust in God's presence, both now and in the future. His love is unconditional, and His faithfulness is unwavering.

Prayer: God, thank You for being ever-present, dwelling within me.

No one will be able to stand up against you all the days of your life. As I was with Moses, so I will be with you; I will never leave you nor forsake you (Joshua 1:5).

The Daily Way — November 17

Never Alone

No matter what obstacles or heartaches you face, God is with you. The Lord says, "When you pass through the waters, I will be with you; and when you pass through the rivers, they will not sweep over you. When you walk through the fire, you will not be burned; the flames will not set you ablaze" (Isaiah 43:2). God always keeps His promises. We can take confidence because God tells us His presence is always with us.

Jehovah-Shammah truly will never leave us—even when we don't feel Him near. While in the depths of depression, David would cry out to God. But at times even David did not feel God's presence. "How long, O Lord? Will you forget me forever? How long will you hide your face from me?" (Psalm 13:1).

Does this mean God abandoned David in his despair? No. But sometimes we let negative emotions and fears consume our thoughts, and we think we have been abandoned. We may feel that God is distant, but God is walking next to us through our darkest valleys.

Later, David proclaims, "The Lord is close to the brokenhearted and saves those who are crushed in spirit" (Psalm 34:18). Sometimes we can look back and see how God worked on our behalf in a situation. If you are facing a struggle today and do not feel close to God, seek comfort in knowing that He is still at your side. Keep seeking His face, and pray using the names of God.

God is there for His children through every moment of every day. He will never turn away from you, and will remain present with you always. What crisis are you facing today? What need is consuming you? Share your heart with Jehovah-Shammah. He is there for you and wants to hear your concerns, fears, and anxieties.

Prayer: Jehovah-Shammah, help me to remember Your promise that You will never leave me.

And surely I am with you always, to the very end of the age (Matthew 28:20).

November 18 — The Daily Way

My Lord

Who is in charge of your life? Is it God—or you? Adonai means "lord, master, owner," and is used over 400 times in the Old Testament as one of God's names. The Bible tells us that, "You are not your own; you were bought at a price" (1 Corinthians 6:19-20). That price was not cheap—Jesus Christ died so that we may enter into God's kingdom. We need to submit to God's authority as Lord and Creator of everything. "If we live, we live to the Lord; and if we die, we die to the Lord. So, whether we live or die, we belong to the Lord" (Romans 14:8).

Adonai is our Lord, and we can trust in His lordship. He is not a cruel master, but a just and loving God. He protects us from harm and wants to bless us. Yet He is a jealous master and demands our full commitment to Him. To be a faithful servant to Adonai, we must live in obedience to Him. We must yield our own ambitions and agendas to Him. We must surrender our lives in service to our Master.

And even though this total submission to God may seem frightening at first, the more you submit to God, the clearer your understanding of His lordship. "What is more, I consider everything a loss compared to the surpassing greatness of knowing Christ Jesus my Lord, for whose sake I have lost all things. I consider them rubbish, that I may gain Christ" (Philippians 3:8).

Prayer: Adonai, help me to totally submit to Your lordship that I may know You more.

The earth is the Lord's, and everything in it, the world, and all who live in it; for he founded it upon the seas and established it upon the waters (Psalm 24:1-2).

The Daily Way — November 19

Making Him Lord

When you say that Jesus is Lord of your life, are you living a life of submission to His lordship—or do you still try to manipulate events to your own advantage?

God's lordship provides for His servants. God knows the limits of our abilities, and He provides the strength and power to do His work. Trying to step into God's role as the Lord of your life will lead to frustration and exhaustion. Let God be the Lord of your life. You may be hesitant about relinquishing control, but you will quickly find that true freedom is in submitting fully to Adonai.

As our Lord's servants, we are also stewards of His resources which He has entrusted to us. Part of recognizing Adonai as Lord is realizing that nothing we have is our own. We can be faithful stewards by giving a tithe, making the most of our time for God's work, and managing our spiritual gifts and talents.

Sometimes we give our resources more control over our lives than God, but Jesus tells us, "No one can serve two masters. Either he will hate the one and love the other, or he will be devoted to the one and despise the other. You cannot serve both God and money" (Matthew 6:24).

Be honest with yourself today. Is God truly the one and only Lord of your life? Does God make the decisions in your life and influence your every word and action? Do you see God as your leader and Lord or simply as a wish-granter for your desires? Making God the Lord of your life transcends church attendance or reading the Bible—it requires a complete surrender of your life to God.

Prayer: Thank you, Lord, for being the Perfect Master. Help me to trust and obey You in all things.

Trust in the LORD with all your heart and lean not on your own understanding; in all your ways submit to him, and he will make your paths straight (Proverbs 3:5-6).

November 20 — The Daily Way

God the Father and God the Holy Spirit

When God shared His self-appointed names with His people, He revealed major insights into His nature. Throughout the Bible, however, we also see many descriptive names, titles, and word pictures for God—all revealing His character and His relationship with us.

In these descriptions, we discover how God provides leadership to us: He is our judge, our ruler, and our commander-in-chief. We learn of His almighty power: He is the Holy One, the King of kings, and the Lord of lords. We are reminded that God provides safety: He is our rock, our stronghold, our refuge, our shield, and our warrior. We gain insight into His personality: He is jealous and avenging, yet loving, faithful and comforting.

Through studying these word pictures of God, we also learn the specific roles taken by God the Father, God the Son, and God the Holy Spirit.

In the Bible, God the Father is called our heavenly Father; Abba ("Daddy"); Holy Father; Everlasting Father; and the God of Abraham, Isaac, and Jacob. He is the maker and author of life, our keeper, the Father of glory, and the lifter of our heads. God the Father created us, He sustains our existence, and He seeks to protect us. "Praise be to the God and Father of our Lord Jesus Christ, the Father of compassion and the God of all comfort, who comforts us in all our troubles" (2 Corinthians 1:3-4).

Consider the Holy Spirit. He is called the breath of the Almighty and the power of the Highest. He is the Spirit of might, glory, holiness, judgment, grace, and life. He is the Spirit of comfort, counsel, understanding, knowledge, and truth.

Prayer: God, thank You for being my protecting, compassionate, comforting Father. Thank You for Your Spirit who guides me in truth.

May the grace of the Lord Jesus Christ, and the love of God, and the fellowship of the Holy Spirit be with you all (2 Corinthians 13:14).

The Daily Way — November 21

God the Son

As we continue to look at the word pictures of God and the Trinity, let's focus on God the Son.

God the Son is revealed to us throughout the Bible, from Genesis to Revelation. In the Old Testament, Jesus Christ is called the commander of the Lord's army, the refiner's fire, and the arm of the Lord; yet He also is a man of sorrows and a servant. "And he will be called Wonderful Counselor, Mighty God, Everlasting Father, Prince of Peace" (Isaiah 9:6).

In the New Testament, Jesus is called Messiah, Teacher, Master, and Advocate. He is the head of the Church, heir of all things, chief cornerstone, and a horn of salvation. In the book of John, Jesus describes Himself as the bread of life; the light of the world; the gate for the sheep; the good shepherd; the resurrection and the life; the way, the truth, and the life; and the true vine.

In Revelation, Jesus is identified as the Living One, the Alpha and the Omega, the Amen, the Lamb of God, the Word of God, the Lion of the tribe of Judah, and the bright Morning Star.

Thank Jesus for leaving His heavenly throne to become man and suffer the crucifixion to redeem you from your sins. Praise Him for His almighty nature. "The Word became flesh and made his dwelling among us. We have seen his glory, the glory of the One and Only, who came from the Father, full of grace and truth" (John 1:14).

Isn't God amazing? He is more than everything we need.

Prayer: God, thank You for leaving Your throne to come to us as a man that You might redeem us from our sins. Thank You for all that You are.

In the beginning was the Word, and the Word was with God, and the Word was God (John 1:1).

November 22

The Daily Way

Why Do You Seek Him?

What matters most to you in this life? We can easily become preoccupied by the concerns around us: our finances, our family's well-being, our success at the office, or our popularity in the community. But Jesus tells us that what matters more than any earthly concern is where we will spend eternity.

Read John 6:1-15, 25-59. In this passage we see Jesus performing the miracle of feeding the crowd of five thousand by supernaturally multiplying the fish and loaves of bread. The next day the crowd went out in search of Jesus. Yet Jesus knew the crowd had not chased after Him in order to hear about the kingdom of God. Instead, they were hoping for another meal. Jesus rebuked them by saying, "I tell you the truth, you are looking for me, not because you saw miraculous signs but because you ate the loaves and had your fill. Do not work for food that spoils, but for food that endures to eternal life, which the Son of Man will give you" (John 6:26-27).

The crowd was not focusing on the supernatural power of Christ. They were not focusing on the miracle He performed or the manifestation of the glory of God that they witnessed. They did not realize the One who fed them fish and bread was their Creator God. They were not seeking the Messiah, they were looking for a chef.

How many Christians do the same thing today? We chase after Jesus in prayer, not to glorify His kingdom, but to see what gifts He has for us. We want our free meals. We want God to provide for our every physical needs and wants, without realizing that we are starving spiritually. God is seeking a relationship with us and He should be at the center of our entire lives.

Prayer: God, forgive me for the times I come to You only for selfish reasons. Help me to come to you focused on the eternal things.

But seek first his kingdom and his righteousness, and all these things will be given to you as well (Matthew 6:33).

The Daily Way — November 23

The Bread of Life

After the feeding of the five thousand, when the crowd continued to chase after Jesus with misguided motivations, He points them to a better way of life. "Then Jesus declared, 'I am the bread of life. He who comes to me will never go hungry, and he who believes in me will never be thirsty'" (John 6:35). The most important thing in our lives should not be about the bread on our dinner plates, but the Bread of Life, which is Jesus Christ. A loaf of bread may temporarily satisfy our stomachs, but the Bread of Life can eternally satisfy our emotions, our intellects, and our souls.

Too often we focus on our problems. We worry about our bills. We fret about our dwindling bank accounts. We are anxious about our job security. But Jesus wants us to stop fixating on these earthly concerns. God knows our needs and He will provide for us. The most desperate need we have is Jesus Christ. Our focus should be on loving Him, obeying Him, and following Him in all things.

The crowd understood that bread represents a necessity of life. Jesus used this opportunity to explain that just as bread is a necessity for our physical lives, Jesus is a necessity of our spiritual lives. We cannot live spiritually without Christ. He is the only One who can give us eternal life in heaven. Jesus calls Himself the Bread of Life—the basic, absolute necessity for living. He is not one of many options to fill our spiritual hunger. He is the only bread that will fill us spiritually. He is the only thing that can save us from eternal damnation.

Prayer: God, thank You for being the Bread of Life. I know that You are the only one who can truly satisfy me.

I was young and now I am old, yet I have never seen the righteous forsaken or their children begging bread (Psalm 37:25).

November 24

The Daily Way

Give Thanks

Have you ever experienced ingratitude from someone? Perhaps you gave a thoughtful gift that received no thanks; or maybe you invested yourself in helping a friend who took it for granted. How did you feel, knowing your efforts weren't appreciated?

But what about the times when you did something small for someone, yet they couldn't stop thanking you for it? How were you blessed through that experience?

Read Luke 17:11-19. Out of the 10 lepers Jesus healed, only one expressed gratitude. Jesus did not simply cure them, He transformed them from being unclean to clean. As lepers, they were socially isolated and considered outcasts. By healing them, Jesus completely turned their world around. Yet only one of them thanked Him.

Only the Samaritan came back to show His gratitude. "One of them, when he saw he was healed, came back, praising God in a loud voice. He threw himself at Jesus' feet and thanked him—and he was a Samaritan" (Luke 17:15-16). This man didn't simply say "thank you" but fell at Jesus' feet in appreciation. In this situation, there were two different responses, but only one of them honored God.

Think about this passage in modern terms. How many times has God rescued us from suffering and shame, yet we took it for granted? Do we thank God every day for our salvation? When God blesses us, are we satisfied or do we immediately ask for more? How often do we fall at the feet of Jesus to worship Him for His blessings? When was the last time you were excited to thank God?

Prayer: God, help me to develop a grateful heart and a lifestyle of thanksgiving.

Rejoice always; pray continually; give thanks in all circumstances, for this is God's will for you in Christ Jesus (1 Thessalonians 5:16-18).

The Daily Way

November 25

The Light of the World

Light serves many purposes. The light of a single candle illuminates a darkened room, making us aware of obstacles. The great light of the sun gives us warmth, makes plants grow, and takes away the night. Headlights on our vehicles show us our path. Spotlights focus our attention to what is important on stage. Motion-sensor lights alert us when an intruder is present. Without light we would stumble around in darkness, and that is why Jesus said, "I am the light of the world. Whoever follows me will never walk in darkness, but will have the light of life" (John 8:12).

Read John 8:12-30. When Jesus told the crowd He is the Light of the World, He was saying that He is not only the light, but He is the only One who can give us that light. Only Christ can show us the way to the Father. Only Christ's light can cut through the darkness of evil around us. Jesus said, "I have come into the world as a light, so that no one who believes in me should stay in darkness" (John 12:46).

When God's people were slaves in Egypt, God sent plagues upon the land. In Exodus 10, God sent a plague of great darkness. "Then the LORD said to Moses, 'Stretch out your hand toward the sky so that darkness will spread over Egypt—darkness that can be felt.' So Moses stretched out his hand toward the sky, and total darkness covered all Egypt for three days. No one could see anyone else or leave his place for three days. Yet all the Israelites had light in the places where they lived" (Exodus 10:21-23).

Is there a dark corner in your heart that you are trying to keep away from Christ's light? Is there a sin you are trying to hide in the shadows?

Prayer: God, shine Your light on my heart. Forgive me for what I have been trying to hide from You.

For you were once darkness, but now you are light in the Lord. Live as children of light (Ephesians 5:8).

November 26

The Daily Way

Let Your Light Shine

God not only provides light for His people, but this light should be evident in our dwelling places. During the plague of great darkness in Exodus 10, the Egyptians knew that the Israelites had light and were not paralyzed by the darkness. When the light of Christ comes into our hearts, His light also shines into our dwelling places. The world can see His light surround us, whether we are at home or at work or at school. We will reflect the light of Christ that beacons to others to come and seek Him.

As followers of Jesus, we are to reflect His light to the world. We need to boldly live as testimonies for Christ and share His Gospel. Jesus said, "You are the light of the world. A town built on a hill cannot be hidden. Neither do people light a lamp and put it under a bowl. Instead they put it on its stand, and it gives light to everyone in the house. In the same way, let your light shine before men, that they may see your good deeds and praise your Father in heaven" (Matthew 5:14-16).

We live in a dark world, and people all around us are stumbling through life. Only those who have accepted Jesus as their Savior can receive His light. "This is the verdict: Light has come into the world, but men loved darkness instead of light because their deeds were evil. Everyone who does evil hates the light, and will not come into the light for fear that his deeds will be exposed. But whoever lives by the truth comes into the light, so that it may be seen plainly that what he has done has been done through God" (John 3:19-21).

We must be a light for Christ and expose the shadows around us. We must shine the light of Jesus to reveal the lies around us so that misled people may find the truth.

Prayer: God, help me to reflect Your light to the world, shining brightly for You wherever I go.

Have nothing to do with the fruitless deeds of darkness, but rather expose them (Ephesians 5:11).

The Daily Way

November 27

The Way

In John 12-13, Jesus had begun preparing His disciples for His upcoming betrayal, suffering, and death. Naturally, His disciples became troubled and confused. Noticing their anxiety, Jesus comforts them, "Do not let your hearts be troubled. You believe in God; believe also in me. In my Father's house are many rooms; if it were not so, I would have told you. I am going there to prepare a place for you. And if I go and prepare a place for you, I will come back and take you to be with me that you also may be where I am. You know the way to the place where I am going" (John 14:1-4).

Yet even in the midst of Jesus' words of comfort, Thomas still expressed discouragement and despondency. "Thomas said to him, 'Lord, we don't know where you are going, so how can we know the way?'" (John 14:5). In response to Thomas's fretting, "Jesus answered, 'I am the way and the truth and the life'" (John 14:6).

Jesus began by saying, "I am the way." Jesus is the only way to the Father. He is the revealer of the Father. Jesus said, "Anyone who has seen me has seen the Father" (John 14:9). Many people think that all roads lead to God, but Jesus—who was sent by God, and is the Son of God, and is God—said, "No one comes to the Father except through me" (John 14:6). Jesus gives us the one and only acceptable plan of salvation: through Himself. Only when we come to Jesus in repentance can we find the forgiveness and acceptance by the Father. There is no other way to the Father; only Jesus can lead us to eternity in heaven.

Prayer: God, thank You for providing a Way for us to spend eternity in heaven.

Believe me when I say that I am in the Father and the Father is in me (John 14:11).

November 28 — The Daily Way

The Truth and the Life

Jesus told Thomas and the other disciples that not only is He the way, but He is also the truth. (John 14:6) He did not simply mean that He speaks the truth or that He is an honest person. He was saying that He embodies the Truth. We may think of ourselves as truthful people, but Jeremiah said, "The heart is deceitful above all things and beyond cure. Who can understand it?" (Jeremiah 17:9). Yet Jesus is always the Truth, never wavering or misleading. To know Jesus is to know the Truth.

Jesus concluded this "I am" statement by declaring He is the life. Jesus was not just referring to an abundant life here on earth. Jesus was assuring us that through Him we can have eternal life. When Jesus is our Lord, we do not have to fear death of this physical life, because we will spend eternity in heaven.

Through Jesus we find the source of real life and a renewed spirit, even in this physical life. The more time we spend in His presence, the more our spirits are invigorated. The more time we spend worshiping Him, the more vitality we will experience. The more we seek Him, the more victories we will have because our perspectives shift from the troubles of this world to the eternal.

There is no other way to live—either in this earthly life or in our eternal future—than through Jesus. He is the only path to the Father. He is the only Truth. He is our only hope for eternal life. Have you lost your joy or peace? Are you struggling with an unconfessed sin? Are you experiencing sorrow or disappointment? Whatever you are facing, turn to Jesus in prayer today. He will show you the way, the truth, and the life.

Prayer: God, thank You that through You we can know the Truth and we can experience real, lasting life.

The Word became flesh and made his dwelling among us. We have seen his glory, the glory of the one and only Son, who came from the Father, full of grace and truth (John 1:14).

The Daily Way — November 29

He Is the Resurrection

The greatest miracle of the Bible is seen in the resurrection of Christ after His crucifixion. Jesus accomplished this amazing feat not simply to impress the crowds with another miracle. The power of the Resurrection is the same power that saves us from eternal damnation.

Read John 11:1-44. In this passage Jesus raises Lazarus from the dead. When Lazarus's sister, Martha, greeted Jesus upon His arrival, she was distraught over the death of her brother. "'Lord,' Martha said to Jesus, 'if you had been here, my brother would not have died. But I know that even now God will give you whatever you ask.' Jesus said to her, 'Your brother will rise again.' Martha answered, 'I know he will rise again in the resurrection at the last day.' Jesus said to her, 'I am the resurrection and the life. He who believes in me will live, even though he dies; and whoever lives and believes in me will never die. Do you believe this?' 'Yes, Lord,' she told him, 'I believe that you are the Christ, the Son of God, who was to come into the world'" (John 11:21-27).

Jesus holds the power of resurrection because He is the Resurrection. He alone holds the key to our future eternity. He alone holds the power over death itself. Jesus alone could command, "Lazarus, come out!" (see John 11:43-44).

Today, Jesus calls to us by name in our spiritual deadness. He is offering eternal life with Him to those who will call Him Savior and Lord. Jesus raised Lazarus, the daughter of Jairus and the son of the widow in Nain from the dead. These were great miracles, yet because these people were human, they eventually experienced death. When Jesus was resurrected, He never died again. He remained alive until He ascended directly to heaven. "For we know that since Christ was raised from the dead, he cannot die again; death no longer has mastery over him" (Romans 6:9).

Prayer: Thank You, Lord, for bringing me out of spiritual deadness into eternal life.

In the same way, count yourselves dead to sin but alive to God in Christ Jesus (Romans 6:11).

November 30 — The Daily Way

The Power of the Resurrection

Through Jesus' resurrection, we can be forgiven of our sins. No amount of good works can compensate for our sins—and we all are sinners. No amount of charitable donations or pious living or church activities will buy our entrance into heaven. Only the power of the Resurrection can overcome the punishment of sin, which is death. Without the Resurrection, we would have an empty religion without any hope. The apostle Paul said, "And if Christ has not been raised, your faith is futile; you are still in your sins" (1 Corinthians 15:17).

Through Jesus' resurrection, we can be assured of God's power. The Resurrection assures us of His power to raise our dead spirits. Jesus has the power to change us from selfish, immoral, bitter people into a new creation of selfless, self-controlled, and joyful people. The power of Jesus Christ can heal our shattered relationships, repair our broken hearts, and change our lives for eternity. The same power that resurrected Jesus from the dead is available to us to raise us from our spiritual deadness and give us victory over the enemy.

Through Jesus' resurrection, we can be assured of our ultimate victory. "But our citizenship is in heaven. And we eagerly await a Savior from there, the Lord Jesus Christ, who, by the power that enables him to bring everything under his control, will transform our lowly bodies so that they will be like his glorious body" (Philippians 3:20-21).

Have you forgotten about the power of the Resurrection in your life and allowed earthly anxieties to render you ineffective? If you are a Christian, you are never powerless, even in your darkest valleys.

Prayer: God, thank You for the forgiveness, power, and victory we have through Your resurrection. Reveal Your resurrection power to me in a new way today.

I want to know Christ—yes, to know the power of his resurrection and participation in his sufferings, becoming like him in his death (Philippians 3:10).

Preparing for the Coming Glory

The Daily Way

December 1

Whom Will You Serve?

Even in His death, Jesus was thinking of you and me. He was preparing a way for us to know the Father and for us to receive His gift of salvation. But it was not enough for the Lord merely to say, "You can be saved." He always found a way to demonstrate His Word.

It was no mistake that Jesus was crucified between two thieves. One was repentant, and the other blasphemed the Lord.

One believed, and the other denied the truth of God. One accepted God's wondrous gift of mercy and grace; the other turned his back on the offer and lost his soul.

Each one of us knows someone who is spiritually lost. We have watched this individual suffer greatly. God loves this person but because he has not made the decision to accept Christ as his Savior, he is not saved.

There is no escaping the truth. We can choose eternal life or settle for an endless death that is far worse than any torment we can imagine. The two men that hung dying beside the Savior could be any one of us.

Just like them, we must make a choice. God has chosen to save all men, but not everyone will come to Him. Those who do will immediately be with Him in paradise. Those who don't will spend an eternity separated from the love and intimate devotion of our heavenly Father.

Joshua challenged the nation of Israel with these words:

> If serving the Lord seems undesirable to you, then choose for yourselves this day whom you will serve, whether the gods your forefathers served beyond the River, or the gods of the Amorites, in whose land you are living. But as for me and my household, we will serve the Lord (Joshua 24:15).

Prayer: Lord, I want to serve You and You alone.

He who stands firm to the end will be saved (Matthew 24:13).

December 2

The Daily Way

The Assurance of Salvation

One day as the French emperor Napoleon Bonaparte was reviewing his troops, his horse bolted out of control. He was in danger of being hurled to the ground, but a young private leapt from the ranks and calmed the animal.

"Thank you, Captain," said Napoleon, thus bestowing an instant promotion on the man.

Smiling proudly, the soldier inquired, "Of what regiment, sir?"

"Of my guards," replied Bonaparte. Immediately, the soldier assumed his new rank and walked over to join a group of staff officers. "What is this insolent fellow doing here?" one questioned.

"I am Captain of the guards," the young man replied.

"You are just a private. What makes you think you are a captain?"

At that, the young man pointed to the emperor and confidently responded, "He said it!"

"I beg your pardon, Captain," the officer answered politely. "I was not aware of your promotion."

The moment we accept Christ as our Savior, we are immediately given an eternal position of authority in heaven. Our rank changes from one of no real authority to one of great reward and prominence.

With his last breath the repentant thief said, "Jesus, remember me when you come into your kingdom" (Luke 23:42). The Lord replied, "I tell you the truth, today you will be with me in paradise" (Luke 23:43). And it was immediately done. Is Jesus the Captain of your soul? If not, will you give your life to Him?

Prayer: Lord, I have sinned against You. Forgive me. I accept Your gift of salvation and know that from this day forward I am living for You, my Lord and Savior!

Everyone who calls on the name of the Lord will be saved (Acts 2:21).

The Daily Way — December 3

Run to the Lord

Even though the way before you seems dark, trust the Lord because He is faithful. When your faith is challenged, remember that Jesus never fails. He loves you and even when you drift in your devotion to Him, He will not forsake His love for you.

In Exodus 14, Israel was on the run from the Egyptians. Their escape route was blocked by the boundaries of the Red Sea, and they began to panic. But Moses called out to them:

> Do not be afraid. Stand firm and you will see the deliverance the Lord will bring you today. The Egyptians you see today you will never see again. The Lord will fight for you; you need only to be still (Exodus 14:13-14).

The King James Version of the Bible says, "Stand still, and see the salvation of the Lord."

True faith remains unshaken by the trials of life. When it seems the world has turned against you, run to the Lord. God will not allow you to be destroyed. Charles Spurgeon writes:

> Despair whispers, 'Lie down and die; give it all up.' ... But, however much Satan may urge this course upon you, you cannot follow it, if you are a child of God. His divine fiat has bid thee go from strength to strength, and so thou shalt, and neither death nor hell shall turn thee from thy course. What if for a while thou art called to stand still; yet this is but to renew thy strength for some greater advance in due time.

Prayer: Lord, in times of difficulty You are my strength. Thank You for Your gift of salvation and for Your guidance each day.

[Jesus] is able to save completely those who come to God through him, because he always lives to intercede for them (Hebrews 7:25).

December 4 — The Daily Way

Love Leads to Love

At Calvary, the cross of Christ became an eternal emblem of love. Jesus never lost sight of God's purpose for His life. Everything He learned from the Father was in preparation for this moment.

As Scripture tells us, "Greater love has no one than this, that he lay down his life for his friends" (John 15:13). Jesus not only laid down His life for those who loved Him, He laid it down for all men and women—even those who choose to reject Him. He didn't die just for those closest to Him. He died for all of us—no one is left out. But we must make a choice either to accept Him as our Savior or to turn away from Him and face the judgment of a tormenting death.

The Jews rejected Jesus. However, we know that Nicodemus and Joseph of Arimathea made a different choice. After His death, they asked for the Savior's body to be given to them. Pilate granted their request. No Jew of their social position could come in contact with the dead and remain spiritually clean. Yet, these men lovingly accepted the role they played in our Lord's burial. It is doubtful that after this event they were allowed to continue as leaders in the Jewish community. More than likely, they became followers of Jesus Christ. Love leads to love, and it is Christ's unconditional love that drew Nicodemus and Joseph to Himself, and it is that same love that draws us today.

When you find yourself being drawn away by the world's passions and temptations, remember the cross, where Christ gave His life as atonement for your sin. There is no greater love than God's love for you.

Prayer: Lord, it is hard to imagine the depth of Your love for me. Thank You for dying for me.

Carrying his own cross, he went out to the place of the Skull (which in Aramaic is called Golgotha). Here they crucified him (John 19:17-18).

The Daily Way

December 5

Mary's Son

Imagine the anguish of Mary's heart as she looked up into the face of her dying Son. Jesus had been beaten so seriously that He was probably unrecognizable. Yet, Mary would have known Him anywhere. She was His mother.

She could close her eyes and remember what it felt like to hold Him as a baby in her arms. No one has ever held the Son of God this way. She was there when He took his first steps, and she was with Him when He took His last breath.

A strong bond remained between them, and also an understanding that He must do exactly what His Father had called Him to do. She never thought His life would lead to this moment. Simeon had warned her, "This child is destined to cause the falling and rising of many ... And a sword will pierce your own soul too" (Luke 2:34-35). But no one is ever prepared for the loss of a child.

On the evening of His arrest, Jesus was with His closest followers—His disciples. Throughout the night and into the next day, John followed the Savior from mock trial to mock trial. Then Mary joined John at the cross.

There may be times when we are tempted to think Jesus does not care for us. Satan whispers that God is not interested in our sorrows or difficulties. This is not true. Even on the cross, Jesus was still saving lives and thinking of others: "Dear woman, here is your son," and to [John] "Here is your mother" (John 19:26-27). In other words, "John, My mother is now your mother; take care of her for Me."

Prayer: Lord, forgive me for doubting You and Your care for me. I know that no matter what I am facing You are beside me, giving me the strength and wisdom I need.

Cast all your anxiety on him because he cares for you (1 Peter 5:7).

December 6 — The Daily Way

Love Never Fails

In the book First and Last Things, American historian H.G. Wells wrote how Jesus Christ repelled him, "this image of virtue, this terrible and incomprehensible Galilean." Wells is not the first or the last to be repelled by the Lord.

The government of Christ's day turned its back on Him. The Jews repudiated Him. Those gathered for His crucifixion jeered Him, and His friends, who had been with Him for three years of ministry, abandoned Him—going into hiding after His arrest. Only John followed Him to the cross.

It is not surprising that Satan is still at work in our world, seeking to deceive and to draw men and women away from the only Person who can provide the hope they so desperately need.

The rejection of God's Son can be subtle. The "good" person may say, "I am a Christian because I was raised in a Christian family, but I just don't want to get too serious about church or the Bible." Another person may mistakenly believe he can live any way he chooses, and God will still save his soul. God is not the one who condemns us. Jesus told His followers that His goal was to seek and save those who are lost. We are the ones who condemn ourselves when we reject God's love and gift of salvation.

However, even when we are faithless, Jesus remains faithful. When we yield to temptation, He continues to love us, and when we seek His forgiveness, He becomes our strong advocate of mercy and grace before the throne of God.

He is your dearest friend—the One who will never abandon you. At the cross, He died for you, knowing that He was your only way to truth and eternal life.

Prayer: Lord, I confess that I don't understand the depth of love You displayed for me. I am forever indebted to You for Your selfless gift of love.

Love never fails (1 Corinthians 13:8).

The Daily Way

December 7

A Vision of Heaven

Do you ever feel frustrated that things are not going the way they should? Do you get uptight because things seem to be out of control?

Take heart, because you are not supposed to be in control. You are not on the throne—God is. His throne is the place of authority and the center of His rule for the activities of heaven. Jesus Christ, who is glorified and magnified, sits at the right hand of the throne.

Do you ever wonder what heaven is like? We can try to imagine it based on our earthly ideas. When we think of the grandest place on earth, we might imagine a palace or the sanctuary of the most architecturally elaborate cathedral ever built. We might even think of the private home of the wealthiest person on earth. No matter what we may try to compare heaven to, until we see it for ourselves we will not be able to grasp the scope of its magnificence.

When we see the splendor of heaven, we are going to fall on our faces. We are going to comprehend our complete unworthiness. We are going to regret our stubbornness, disobedience, and self-centeredness.

As you go about your daily routine and you feel tired, frustrated, and out of control, think about heaven. Remember that you are a member of God's royal priesthood, chosen by Him.

Prayer: Lord, please give me Your vision of heaven.

You have made them to be a kingdom and priests to serve our God, and they will reign on the earth (Revelation 5:10).

December 8 — The Daily Way

A Citizen of Heaven

Heaven is a real place. Even though we can't see it now, one day our eyes will take in the grandeur of God's dwelling place. We will stand before His throne, and Christ will judge all that we have or have not done.

The merciful, loving Christ of today will be the executor of judgment on the last day. He will not judge unfairly, but He will judge us perfectly. He will not trump up charges against us, but He will judge us on the basis of what we have done with Him during our lifetime.

Have you accepted Him as your Savior? Have you obeyed Him and submitted your life to Him? Have you invited Him to reign in your life? Or will your testimony prove that you were too busy, too preoccupied, too bitter, too angry, too doubting, or too full of wanting your own way to be with Him?

God wants to make us holy, pure, and righteous. However, we have to allow Him to mold us into His image. Sin is the one thing that shakes our security in Christ and our confidence in His finished work on the cross. Our old nature is at strife with our new nature in Christ—the flesh wars against the spirit.

Are you clinging to something you know God is asking you to surrender to Him? What is distracting you from growing closer to the Lord? Is it financial worries? Are you concerned about some relational problem? Are you worried about the future? These seem small in comparison to eternity in heaven.

God has a purpose for your life and a place for you with Him in eternity. When you are in heaven, you will not be a visitor with a day pass—you will be a beloved citizen of His kingdom.

Worthy is the Lamb, who was slain, to receive power and wealth and wisdom and strength and honor and glory and praise (Revelation 5:12).

The Daily Way — December 9

The Light Shining in Darkness

Even though Christ is your Savior, there will be times when you are tempted to sin. And if you yield to the temptation, you will sense a spiritual darkness around you. The closer you are to Christ in your devotion, the deeper the darkness will seem.

This is because the more we commit our lives to the Lord, the more we become like Him. Once we are saved, sin no longer reflects who we are in Christ.

One of the roles of the Holy Spirit is to draw us even closer to the Lord. He also is the One who guides us through each day. A check in your spirit may mean you are about to do something that could jeopardize your God-centered peace.

There are times when you will sense God's Spirit warning about a particular event or set of circumstances. Listen to His voice. Ask God to make His will clear to you, and never allow the enemy to twist the love and protection of God into something that yields fearful thoughts.

If you want to walk in the light of truth, having the knowledge and wisdom of God, make a commitment to read and to study His Word—which is "a lamp to our feet."

The people who gathered at the cross to witness the crucifixion were living in spiritual darkness, and God wanted to make sure they understood the choice they were making.

Beginning with the third hour of this horrendous event, a deep, all-consuming darkness fell on the land and the people were engulfed with fear. Today we do not have to walk in darkness. We have the eternal flame of God guiding our every step.

Prayer: Father, You are the light of this world, and I choose to walk in it knowing that You will give me the wisdom I need for every situation.

The light shines in the darkness, but the darkness has not understood it (John 1:5).

December 10

The Daily Way

I Thirst

With his last breath, Thomas Hobbes, the self-confessed atheist said, "I am taking a fearful leap into the dark!" On his deathbed the French agnostic Voltaire sadly spoke these words, "I am abandoned by God and man. I shall go to hell."

In contrast to these two men, who died without Christ, is Christian evangelist Dwight L. Moody, whose last words were: "This is glorious ... Earth recedes; heaven is opening, and God is calling me."

For believers, the moment we take our last breath is the first moment we will draw in the heavenly air of our new home—our abode with the Lord Jesus Christ. To be out of earth's atmosphere is to be in His holy presence.

We rarely think about the difference between life lived here on earth and the one we will have in heaven. Instead, we often focus on our temporary home—how we can make it larger, decorate it with our favorite things, and enjoy it.

At some point, our thinking has to switch from being earthbound to heavenbound. The short time we spend on this earth is not even a fraction of the time we will spend in eternity. Jesus was accustomed to setting this vision for others to reach. He never missed an opportunity to prepare His followers for His death but, more importantly, He wanted them to understand His resurrection and future blessings that would be theirs. Even

His last words, "I am thirsty" (John 19:28), remind us that nothing this world has to offer can satisfy our needs. Only Jesus has the ability to provide the "living water" that satisfies our souls.

Prayer: Lord, I realize that only You can satisfy my thirst.

Everyone who drinks this water will be thirsty again, but whoever drinks the water I give him will never thirst (John 4:13-14).

The Daily Way — December 11

The Fountain of Life

Quenching our thirst comes quite easily for most of us. Our minds tell us we need water, so we find the nearest source of water and drink. But do we apply this same principle to our spiritual lives?

Everything in life can become routine, even our relationship with God. At times, we may not feel like we are teeming with life.

We feel the thirst for God, but what are we doing about it? Sometimes, we look to sources other than God Himself—and while that may divert our attention, our thirst for Him remains.

Our bodies are designed to let us know when we need to replenish our internal water supply. Our mouths become dry and our brain quickly alerts us to the problem. The Holy Spirit also alerts us to our spiritual thirst: when we get low on our relationship with God, we need to go to Him.

But what is our response? Those who remain thirsty do so because they forget where the well is. They forget there is an unending source of refreshment and revitalization found in relationship with God.

The longer we remain numb to the problem, the larger the problem grows. We may know we are thirsty for God, but if we make no effort to pursue the fountain of life found in an intimate relationship with the Savior, we are robbing ourselves of one of the most refreshing moments in life.

No matter how long we have been away from God's presence, He welcomes us back.

Prayer: Lord, help me to be sensitive to Your Holy Spirit, and to recognize You are the only Source that quenches my thirst.

As the deer pants for streams of water, so my soul pants for you, O God (Psalm 42:1).

December 12 — The Daily Way

God Is the Source

In our daily lives, we are quick to satisfy our desires. When we are hungry, we make every attempt to eat as quickly as possible. When we are thirsty, we head for the water fountain.

When we are lonely, we call a friend or a family member. However, as Christians, sometimes we fail to recognize what our greatest needs are and who can satisfy them. The emptiness we sometimes feel can only be filled by God. Even after we come to know Christ, we may struggle to recognize that emptiness is a sign that we need to turn to Him.

The world throws so many different things in our faces that we can look at everything zipping by and mistakenly believe it will satisfy us. Maybe we seek fulfillment in our relationships with others. Maybe we are seeking fulfillment in our jobs or through financial success. So we chase after these things with reckless abandon. An intimate relationship with God is the only thing that will satisfy every need we have.

He is the One who transforms our hearts and minds, bringing us unspeakable joy even in the midst of what seems like our darkest hours. He is the One who quenches the thirst of our souls by showing us how much He loves us and cares for us.

He knows what You need, and He knows exactly how to meet you where you are. If you are thirsty, remember that God is the source that quenches. He wants you to drink in Him and fulfill your heart's desires.

Prayer: Lord, help me realize how much You love me today and that You desire to fill the deepest longing in my heart.

Jesus answered ... "Whoever drinks the water I give him will never thirst. Indeed, the water I give him will become in him a spring of water welling up to eternal life" (John 4:13-14).

The Daily Way

December 13

The Safest Deposit of All

Whom we trust with our lives says volumes about our faith. When a difficult situation arises, do we turn to others for help? Do we attempt to resolve the situation alone? Or do we ask God to give us wisdom and guidance?

The moment we give our lives to the Lord, we must sever all ties that we have with our clever minds. No matter how intelligent we are, there will be times when only God's wisdom can lead us to the perfect solution. We may not recognize it, especially if we feel trapped by our circumstances, but no problem we ever have is too great for God.

Our challenge as believers is taking this truth to heart. Sometimes, we give our hearts to God only to take them back when surrender to Him becomes inconvenient.

But when you commit your life into God's hands, you must resolve to leave it there. Just as no money market account matures with excessive withdrawals, you will struggle to grow when you continually seize control of your life after depositing it into His hands.

It is never easy to relinquish total control. We feel helpless as we sit by and watch. Yet God wants us to surrender so He can do His greatest work in us, the work of completely transforming our hearts and minds as He molds us into the image of Christ. While we may have an idea of what God wants to do with our lives, we do not know the fullness of what He desires to do; therefore, we must allow Him to have total control.

As you give God control of your life, He will shape you into the person He intends for you to be. Remember: There is no one you can trust more than the Son of God.

Prayer: Lord, I want You to be in control of my life today, leading me through Your Holy Spirit.

Jesus answered, "I am the way and the truth and the life. No one comes to the Father except through me" (John 14:6).

December 14 — The Daily Way

Give Your Life to God

The wisdom of God usually confounds man's intellect. In fact, some of the greatest truths in the Bible are paradoxical. Giving away things does not seem like the best way to receive blessing. And it does not seem right to show mercy and kindness toward those who do wrong to us. But these are actions believers are encouraged to take, as God promises blessings to those who do them.

However, one of the most difficult biblical truths to understand is this: to truly take back your life, you must surrender it to God. In order for us to live in freedom—free from bondage to sin and the enemy—we must make ourselves subject to Him.

Jesus' moment of victory came when He surrendered His life on the cross. When Jesus committed His Spirit into God's hands, He relinquished control and let God work the most amazing triumph in the history of mankind. No longer would people have to pay the appropriate penalty for their sins. Suddenly, there was forgiveness for all who would receive it through Jesus' death and resurrection.

Our moment of victory comes when we decide to give away our lives. When we make the conscious decision to quit trying to run our own lives and allow God to have control, we win. Our cry of weakness is actually our greatest moment of strength. It is the point where we stop trying to be good Christians and start allowing the Holy Spirit to finish the transforming work that remains in our hearts.

Surrendering to God does not mean you are weak. On the contrary, it means you are a person who knows where your greatest strength lies.

Prayer: Lord, make Your truths real in my life today and help me to understand the power that comes when I surrender fully to You.

Jesus Christ is the same yesterday and today and forever (Hebrews 13:8).

The Daily Way — December 15

The Satisfaction of Completion

When we take time to look at the world around us, we become aware of all the work we have to do as believers. The dying world in which we live is desperate for the Gospel. It needs to hear the truth of God's Word. Truly, we have our work cut out for us.

However, in all our striving to advance the Kingdom of God, we sometimes forget one of the biggest truths of God's Word. On the cross Jesus said, "It is finished" (John 19:30). The work which He came to do—to fulfill God's promise to mankind by making the ultimate sacrifice for the sin of the world—is finished.

In our hearts, the work of the Holy Spirit to bring us to completion is still taking place. Once we submit our lives to Jesus, the process begins and does not end until we get to heaven. Yet, we are not called to finish Jesus' work because His work is done. We are called merely to allow the Holy Spirit to complete His work in us as we share with others the Good News through both our words and actions.

It is not up to us to finish the work that only God can do in our lives. We cannot live a holy life without Him. His gift of salvation can only be received through faith in His Son. Strive as we may, eventually we will stumble. But God has promised to do what we cannot do for ourselves. He has sent His Son to save us.

While we can look forward to the day when God looks at us and pronounces a completion of His work in our hearts, we must remain faithful and allow the Holy Spirit to continue His transforming work in our lives.

Seek the Lord above all things. Desire to be a person He uses to draw others to Himself.

Prayer: Lord, thank You for the work You have started in me. Please continue shaping me into the person You want me to be.

By wisdom the Lord laid the earth's foundations, by understanding he set the heavens in place (Proverbs 3:19).

December 16

The Daily Way

Preparation for God's Work

The faster our world moves, the less patience we have. When we want something, we want it now. When presented with two equal choices, we make our selection based on availability.

Can we get it today?

Waiting on God can seem like an eternity. We have His promises, yet we wonder if He remembers us. We pace back and forth and mutter about how God never moves quickly. We wonder what is taking Him so long, and we wonder if He will keep His Word.

Just as a loving earthly father would not hand over car keys to a child who is unprepared to drive an automobile, neither would God give us something before we are truly ready. The time in which we wait upon Him often prepares us for the work He wants to do through us. He is preparing us to handle greater responsibilities.

Unfortunately, we struggle to realize this and often forget about the way He has operated in our lives in the past. God is not slow as much as He is patient. He is waiting for us to arrive at just the right place to receive His blessings. Our patience in waiting upon Him demonstrates our love and trust that He knows exactly what He is doing.

As our relationship with God grows deeper, we realize our maturity is not based on how many verses we have memorized or how many things we are doing for the church. Much of maturing in our relationship with God means we have come to a better understanding of His love for us and we trust Him fully—no matter how long it takes for Him to fulfill His promises.

Prayer: Lord, give me the patience I need to wait upon Your perfect timing for my life.

May the God who gives endurance and encouragement give you a spirit of unity among yourselves as you follow Christ Jesus (Romans 15:5).

The Daily Way — December 17

What's in a Name?

A beautiful Christmas card has these words in expressive fonts—Worthy One, Immanuel, Light of the World, Jesus, God with Us, the Risen One, the Shepherd, the Word, Prince of Peace. These are some of the names we call our Savior. They remind us of the birth of Christ, of His resurrection, of His glory, and of His power.

Saying the names of Jesus invokes reverence, awe, and amazement of our majestic Lord and Savior. While the Christmas season is a wonderful time to reflect on the names of Christ, we should express these names every day of the year.

The names of Christ hold particular significance and meaning for us as believers. His names bring us comfort and inspire us to worship Him. As Light of the World, He reminds us of God's light in the midst of whatever we might face. As God with Us, He reassures us when we feel alone or afraid. As the Risen One, we are reminded of His sacrificial death on the cross for our sins and His glorious resurrection that gives us eternal life. As Prince of Peace, He is our security and peace no matter how uncertain or how difficult our circumstances. As the Shepherd, He guides and directs our lives.

The next time you wonder what's in a name, remember that you can call upon the name that is above all names—Jesus. His name has the power to change your life. He can bring calm in the midst of any storm. He can heal the sick. He can comfort the lonely and brokenhearted. His name brings light into the darkness.

God is always with you. As you reflect upon the name of Jesus remember that God chose you, and He knows your name.

We ... testify that the Father has sent his Son to be the Savior of the world (1 John 4:14).

December 18 — The Daily Way

Follow the Star

"Where is the one who has been born king of the Jews?" asked the wise men. "We saw his star in the east and have come to worship him" (Matthew 2:2).

Imagine being an insecure king who has for years dreaded the moment these questions would be asked. Herod knew the Messiah would come. But he did not "know" in the sense that he was looking for prophecy to be fulfilled. Feeling threatened and very vulnerable, Herod demanded these wise men appear before him. Were they seeking the Savior and the one who would be known as the king of the Jews? Yes—but they were not certain of who and what they would find.

These wise men were, in actuality, astrologers—considered by many to be able to forecast future events. The sudden appearing of a new star—a very bright star—had them wondering if this was the fulfillment of a prophecy. Without really understanding their actions, they responded to the call of God.

God selected these men for a purpose: to proclaim the Savior's birth. Shepherds would never have been invited into Herod's palace, but these worldly men were invited in, and they were admonished to keep the king informed should they find the Christ. This is something they would not do. Instead, these men searched until they found the Lord, but they never disclosed his whereabouts.

You may be a person of advantage, but living without a Savior. Emptiness resides deep within your soul. Or perhaps, you know Him, but have never made a sincere commitment to follow Him. There is no better time to pledge your life and heart to Christ. Like the wise men, come and worship the King!

They saw the child with his mother Mary, and they bowed down and worshiped him (Matthew 2:11).

The Daily Way — December 19

God Revealed in Christ

Through Jesus—

God demonstrated His nature, which is to show compassion and to provide a way for us to know Him personally and intimately.

God displayed His unconditional love. He loves us without regret. However, this does not mean that He dismisses sin. We have to make the choice to turn away from everything that separates us from His love.

When we do, He goes to work in our lives, bringing heaven's convicting light to the hidden areas. His presence in us through the Holy Spirit brings freedom to our souls so we can live up to our full potential.

God disclosed His mercy. Our sinfulness is enough to condemn us and to prevent us from knowing God, but He would not allow this to happen. The birth of Jesus Christ heralded the beginning of the fulfillment of God's plan. We are no longer sinners condemned to an eternal death. We are saints—forgiven and filled with the hope of glory.

God proclaimed His justice. When a person commits a crime, there is an outcry for punishment. But through His life and death on the cross, Jesus paid the price for our sin. He lived and died so that we might know God's loving desire toward us.

There are many gifts we can give this Christmas. The greatest gift was given to us over 2,000 years ago and the greatest gift we can give today is to tell someone else about the Savior's love.

You may think you do not know the right words to say. If this is the case, pray and ask God to speak through you of the love He personally has for your lost loved one or friend.

I bring you good news of great joy that will be for all the people. Today ... a Savior has been born to you (Luke 2:10-11).

December 20

The Daily Way

The Masterpiece

Years ago, a wealthy man and his son began collecting art. Their collection of paintings grew quickly and included works by many of the world's greatest masters.

As war engulfed Europe, the son went off to fight. A few months later, the father received the news he had feared. His son had been killed in battle. Depressed and lonely, the old man viewed the upcoming Christmas holidays with anguish and sadness.

However, on Christmas morning a soldier knocked on his door. He had a package under his arm. It was a portrait of the son. The young man had commissioned an unknown artist to paint his picture as a gift for his father. A few days later, he had been killed in battle.

Later, after the father died, an auction was held. Dealers came from around the world to bid on the priceless art collection. The first painting auctioned was the one of his son, but no one was interested. "Who cares about that painting?" shouted one man. "It is just a picture of his son." But the auctioneer insisted, "We must sell it first."

Finally, with tears in his eyes, the old man's housekeeper said, "Will you take 10 dollars? That is all I have. I knew the son and would like to have his portrait." No one challenged the bid, as everyone was looking forward to bidding on the real masterpieces.

However, much to everyone's surprise, the auctioneer announced that the auction was over. "According to the will," he said, "whoever takes the son gets it all."

God's message to you is simple: "Whoever accepts My Son, gets it all—all My mercy, grace, forgiveness, and eternal love." Do you know the Savior, and have you made Him Lord over every area of your life? No greater gift has ever been given than the one God gives to us through faith in His Son.

Glory to God in the highest, and on earth peace to men on whom his favor rests (Luke 2:14).

The Daily Way — December 21

Your True Home Address

Trying to sleep in foreign quarters can be challenging. We are outside of what is familiar and comfortable to us, and there can be an irritation in our regular sleeping patterns. Regardless of whether the accommodations are better than our own home, if it is not home, it feels awkward.

As believers, our time here on earth can also feel like we are away from home. And the truth is, we are. When we choose to follow God, we discover His desire to have a personal relationship with us. Yet following God in the midst of a sinful world can be challenging.

When we go to a foreign place, we usually make an attempt to understand the culture, trying to fit in with everyone else. But the world's culture is diametrically opposed to the way God would desire for us to live. While the world encourages us to look out for ourselves first, God's Word tells us to love our neighbor. While the world says do whatever it takes to be at the top, God's Word tells us to be a servant to all.

God does not give us His Word as a mere suggestion on how to live our lives; He gives us His Word so we can truly live. He understands what we face on earth—and His Word points us toward Him.

Living on the earth should be uncomfortable for believers. The enemy goes to great extremes to distract us from loving God and loving our neighbor. We must gear up for a battle each day as we tread through life on earth, a foreign land to Christians. To experience victory over the enemy, we must firmly place our trust in God, knowing that His way is greater than any way the world can offer.

Prayer: Lord, help me to live for You today despite the many temptations of the world.

Dear friends, I urge you, as aliens and strangers in the world, to abstain from sinful desires, which war against your soul (1 Peter 2:11).

December 22 — The Daily Way

God's Ambassador

In most cases, our citizenship to the country in which we live is bestowed upon us for simply being born into that country. Receiving citizenship into God's kingdom requires us to surrender our "citizenship" to this world and devote our lives to following Christ. Becoming a citizen of God's kingdom results in some incredible benefits.

However, we must remember that wherever we go in the world, we are ambassadors for Christ. Just as your behavior in a foreign country gives others an idea of what people from your country are like, so does our behavior as believers tell the world what it means to be a Christian.

Citizens from God's kingdom carry with them the answers to some of life's most difficult questions. The dying world in which we live is desperately seeking to do something with its existence.

As believers, we are infiltrating enemy territory, armed with the truth of God's Word, which will defeat the enemy's tired, empty propaganda. And those people who are desperate for answers cannot afford for believers to live passively in their faith.

We must be wise in our approach, yet gentle in our speech. Threats of eternal condemnation will not change many lives, but the truth about how God's love washes away our sin will transform the hardest of hearts when the Holy Spirit is at work.

To live in a world that is far from our home certainly presents a number of challenges. But our citizenship in God's kingdom empowers us to live in such a manner that God will use us to radically change the world around us.

Prayer: Lord, use me to make an impact in the world around me as I passionately seek You.

Live such good lives among the pagans that, though they accuse you of doing wrong, they may see your good deeds and glorify God on the day he visits us (1 Peter 2:12).

The Daily Way — December 23

The Keys to the Kingdom

Seeing pictures of an exotic travel destination often heats our passion to get there. Instead of simply dreaming about what it would be like to visit that place, we begin making plans. We read about the country, save money to travel, and discover what it takes for us to get there. Instead of that country having a name associated with a few images we have seen, it eventually becomes a place we have visited.

At one point, we probably found ourselves easing into the waters of Christianity. We heard something here and there about God. Then one day we decided to discover what it means to be a Christian. Suddenly, we were seeking the kingdom of God.

As believers, we must be careful to guard against letting that passion fade. God's kingdom is vast, full of wonder and blessing, full of triumph and joy. When we think we have seen the most extraordinary trait of God's nature, He reveals something else to us. To actively seek God and His kingdom takes more than a casual approach. It must turn into our lifelong pursuit.

While our interest in God's kingdom once stirred us to explore Christianity, we should pursue what it means to dwell there. God does not insulate us from pain and suffering, but He does give us the keys to victory in every aspect of our lives. He does not want to see us mired in the sin of the world, but living victoriously above it.

To experience the fullness of what God desires for you, you must pursue Him, for nothing is greater than knowing intimately your heavenly Father—and knowing how much He loves you.

Prayer: Lord, help me to press through all the obstacles that might hinder me from pursuing You today.

Seek first his kingdom and his righteousness, and all these things will be given to you as well (Matthew 6:33).

December 24 — The Daily Way

No Problem Is Too Big or Small

In our pursuit of God's kingdom, distractions attack us from every direction. Doubt, sickness, discouragement, disappointment—they are all tactics the enemy uses to throw us off the trail. However, our ability to press through these obstacles and hindrances will determine how successful we are in our pursuit of God.

God never promises that once we have a relationship with Him all our problems will go away. Instead, He gives us the wisdom and perspective to cope and deal with these issues when they arise in our lives. He also gives us eternal hope for every situation we face.

Yet as believers, keeping our perspective enables us to get through anything. No matter what trouble is facing us today, God will help us get through it. No problem we have is too big for God to handle. And nothing is too small for Him either. He is concerned about every aspect of our lives, even knowing how many hairs we have on our heads.

What gets lost in the fray many times is that we are not in this life alone. We are not ostracized from God. He hears our prayers. He desires to see us transformed into the people He has intended for us to be. When we remember that truth, suddenly life's problems do not present such ominous road blocks.

Regardless of what trials and tribulations stare us in the face, God is bigger than all of them. As we seek Him with all our hearts, we discover how true His Word really is—and we realize how much He loves us and how He will never leave us.

Prayer: Lord, empower me to keep the right perspective as I face each trial in life.

For our struggle is not against flesh and blood, but against the rulers, against the authorities, against the powers of this dark world and against the spiritual forces of evil in the heavenly realms (Ephesians 6:12).

The Daily Way

December 25

The Ultimate City

For now, our minds are earthbound. We do not have the ability to imagine fully what heaven will be like. If we could, we would drastically change the way we live each day.

In heaven, we will not be concerned about the gold beneath our feet, because our hearts and minds will be completely set on the One who has perfectly provided for every need we have. We will be devoted solely to Him and His desires and not our own selfish ambitions.

Whether we know it or not, God is in the process of preparing us to live with Him for eternity. He is getting us ready for the day that we will inhabit His city. The trials and disappointments we face here are being used by Him to shape our character; then we will reflect more of Him and less of ourselves.

The joys and the victories we experience on earth also teach us more about God's faithfulness. When we celebrate His goodness, we are doing what we will do on an even grander scale in heaven.

You may love your city home. Perhaps you live on the socially positioned "right" side of town. Or you may despise where you live, feeling as though the poverty of your area confines and prevents you from reaching your goals and dreams.

God has a word for both situations: "Get ready—I am coming again. I have prepared a place—a city—where you will be with Me for eternity."

You can get ready for His return by being willing to let go of the things that bind your heart with a sense of pride, or ideas that tend to prevent you from seeing His future provision.

Prayer: Lord, right now I can't imagine what it will be like to see You face to face. But I know it will be the greatest blessing—beyond anything this world has seen.

Whom have I in heaven but you? And earth has nothing I desire besides you (Psalm 73:25).

December 26

The Daily Way

Our Temporary Abode

In one of the greatest sections written on the subject, the author of Hebrews writes:

> By faith Abraham, when called to go to a place he would later receive as his inheritance, obeyed and went, even though he did not know where he was going. By faith he made his home in the promised land like a stranger in a foreign country. ... For he was looking forward to the city with foundations, whose architect and builder is God (Hebrews 11:8-10).

An old Norwegian story says, "God our Father called us aside one day in the home palace of heaven and sent us out to this 'island colony' called the earth." Certainly, one of the greatest dangers we will face is the temptation to fall in love with this "island."

Many people live as though they will never leave this earth. They amass a large amount of wealth and material possessions without giving serious thought to how they can contribute to the kingdom work of God on earth. Their minds and hearts are "island-bound" or simply earthbound. They have fallen in love with this temporary abode.

Jesus told His disciples, "Where your treasure is, there your heart will be also" (Matthew 6:21). Abraham was not in love with this world. His heart was set on the city of God and his quest was to live as though he was one step away from seeing it.

Have this world's passions and desires captured your heart? Or are you living as though you are on the brink of experiencing God's holy dwelling place—the city of God?

Prayer: Lord, I want to love only You. Let my heart be Yours, and this earth only my temporary dwelling place.

Store up for yourselves treasures in heaven, where moth and rust do not destroy (Matthew 6:20).

The Daily Way — December 27

A Touch of Heaven

Abraham realized God had a greater plan for His life. Therefore, he shifted his focus from the world around him to the world that was yet to come. The same should be true of us.

The trials we face in this earthly life cannot compare to the glory that one day will be ours. But we can taste heaven on earth now. Once we accept Jesus Christ as our Savior, we are adopted into the family of God. Our names are not only written in the Lamb's Book of Life, they also are recorded in the eternal census records of God's kingdom.

With our citizenship no longer tied to this world, we can live with a sense of eternal hope for the future. Take time to read the entire chapter of Hebrews 11 and you will discover that Abraham is not the only one whose life was changed by devotion to God.

One aspect of Abraham's faith that set him, and other Old Testament believers, apart from the New Testament believers is found in Hebrews 11.

> All these people were still living by faith when they died. They did not receive the things promised; they only saw them and welcomed them from a distance. ... Instead, they were longing for a better country—a heavenly one. Therefore God is not ashamed to be called their God, for he has prepared a city for them (Hebrews 11:13, 16).

He has prepared the same city for you. Because Jesus Christ has saved you from your sins, you can enjoy a touch of heaven on earth as you worship and live your life for Him each day.

Prayer: Lord, thank You for Your gift of salvation. Teach me all I need to know about You and allow me to serve You today.

Our citizenship is in heaven. And we eagerly await a Savior from there, the Lord Jesus Christ (Philippians 3:20).

December 28 — The Daily Way

The Full Armor of God

Many people feel as though we are living in very ungodly times, and they are right. Our world is changing at a very rapid pace. At times, the moral decline of our society seems overwhelming. The lack of true love, respect, and worship for the Lord grows ever stronger.

While these times certainly can seem desperate, they also are some of the most exciting times to be alive. The opportunity to know Christ and to make Him known is greater than any other time in history. Truly, the Lord has provided a broad door for us to travel through as we witness His love at work in our world.

However, with this opened door comes a responsibility—one that demands us to take seriously our call to follow Christ.

Many have drifted in their faith by failing to guard their minds against Satan's evil thoughts, suggestions, and feelings. With little to no thought of the consequences, they have opened their minds to the enemy's temptations and have suffered the consequences of their sin.

Paul sent Titus to the island of Crete for one reason: to establish a plumb line of godly truth and morality. The believers in Crete, like so many New Testament Christians, came from a pagan background. Therefore, the temptation to compromise their walk of faith with Christ was ever increasing.

While the power of temptation was broken on the cross, we must remain keen to the enemy's tactics. Begin each day by putting on the "full armor" of God (Ephesians 6); then you will know how to stand victoriously against the enemy.

Prayer: Father, thank You that I have victory over the enemy, and through Jesus Christ have the power to live with hope for the future!

Teach what is in accord with sound doctrine (Titus 2:1).

The Daily Way — December 29

God's Stamp of Approval

Do you ever find yourself absorbed in the activities of life and wonder how you became so busy? Many people overextend themselves to the point of exhaustion. When asked why they are rushing here and there, they answer that they are just keeping up with the normal details of life.

As amazing as it may seem, it is not unusual to find people doing all kinds of unnecessary "work" in the church. Maybe they are trying to reach a level of acceptance in God's eyes or seeking to please another person.

Striving to gain the approval of others is stressful at best. Trying to gain God's approval is useless. This is because God has already placed His stamp of approval on your life and nothing you do can cause Him to love you more than He does right now. When you accept Jesus Christ as your Savior, you gain everything there is to gain of God's love. Even before you were created in your mother's womb, God loved you fully and completely.

This world has nothing of lasting value to offer us. All of our striving and rushing to gain approval results in only one thing: emptiness of heart and soul. Satan's greatest folly is to tempt us into believing that through our good works or our smart appearance someone will love us more. Nothing could be further from the truth.

Don't allow the enemy to entice you into believing that you can gain the acceptance of others by what you do and how you dress. God accepts you just the way you are. All He longs for you to do is to love Him with a whole heart. You can rest in His peace and know He has an everlasting love for you.

Prayer: Lord, thank You for loving me even when I act unlovable. I surrender my life to You.

I have loved you with an everlasting love; I have drawn you with loving-kindness (Jeremiah 31:3).

December 30 — The Daily Way

Quiet Devotion

In Mark, Jesus makes note of the actions of a simple widow.

> [The Lord] sat down opposite the place where the offerings were put and watched the crowd putting their money into the temple treasury. Many rich people threw in large amounts. But a poor widow came and put in two very small copper coins, worth only a fraction of a penny.
> Calling his disciples to him, Jesus said, "I tell you the truth, this poor widow has put more into the treasury than all the others. They all gave out of their wealth; but she, out of her poverty, put in everything—all she had to live on" (Mark 12:41-44).

While many people came to the temple, hoping to be seen and to make an offering that would bring awe and approval, this humble widow gave all she had to the Lord—seeking only to worship Him and to be found faithful in His eyes. She was not caught up in the trappings of her society. Nor did she wonder what others thought of her. Her only thought was to obey the Lord and to demonstrate her love for Him.

In fact, this woman probably knew that if the temple leaders saw her meager offering, they would scowl, but she knew God would bless her obedience and quiet devotion.

Is the attitude of your heart set on the Savior, or do you compare yourself to others and strive to do what appears right from the world's perspective? God has a different grading scale. It is one of grace and infinite love. When the motivation of your heart is right, you will sense His good pleasure and blessing. All that you do will glorify Him, and He will guard your heart and mind with His mercy and grace.

Prayer: Lord, all that I have I give to You. Make me a blessing to others.

[God] saved us, not because of righteous things we had done, but because of his mercy (Titus 3:5).

The Daily Way — December 31

Are You Ready?

Just like the disciples, most of us would like to know the exact day and time of Christ's return. Jesus, however, said that no one, not even He, knew this information. He did, however, tell us how we should live up until that point of His return. We are to abide in Him and trust Him for the future. We are not to worry or become fretful. God is sovereign and even when it seems as though our world is coming apart, He is still in control.

We can look at the signs of our age and know His return is drawing near.

- The political unrest in the Middle East continues to be front-page news. Each day we hear and read of growing strife in the region.
- The economic future of the modern world is tied up in the Middle East. The unrest there will not end until Jesus returns and until God has established His throne.
- There is an alarming increase of interest in Satanism around the world. Many believers turn a deaf ear to this subject and no longer pray against the enemy's power on earth.
- The entertainment industry is including more and more occult language and anti-God situations in movies and television programs. Our minds are being bombarded with material that is in direct opposition to God's truth and principles.

Are you ready for Christ's return? Most of us would answer yes! But have you taken time to tell someone else about God's saving grace? Jesus told His disciples to take what they had learned from Him and teach it to the entire world. God is preparing a place for us, but He also is continuing to draw men and women to Himself. Your life is a testimony to His eternal love and forgiveness. Let your prayer be to share His love with as many as possible before His return.

Salvation belongs to our God, who sits on the throne, and to the Lamb (Revelation 7:10).

NOTES

NOTES

NOTES

NOTES

NOTES

NOTES

NOTES

NOTES

NOTES

NOTES

NOTES

NOTES

NOTES

NOTES

NOTES

NOTES

NOTES

NOTES

NOTES

NOTES

NOTES

NOTES

NOTES

NOTES

To order ministry resources, call:
877-251-8294
or visit our Web site at:
LTW.org

Or you can write to LEADING THE WAY at:
P.O. Box 20100
Atlanta, GA 30325

In Canada, call:
877-251-8294

In the United Kingdom, call:
0800 432 0419

In Australia, call:
1 300 133 589

LEADING The WAY
with Dr. Michael Youssef